Arafat's War

Also by Efraim Karsh

Fabricating Israeli History: The "New Historians"
Rethinking the Middle East

The Palestine 1948 War

The Iran-Iraq War

Saddam Hussein: A Political Biography (with Inari Karsh)

Empires of the Sand: The Struggle for Mastery in the Middle East

The Gulf Conflict 1990–1991: Diplomacy and War in the New World

Soviet Policy Towards Syria Since 1970

Neutrality and Small States

The Soviet Union and Syria: The Asad Years

The Cautious Bear: Soviet Military Engagement in
Middle East Wars in the Post-1967 Era

Arafat's War

The Man and His Battle for Israeli Conquest

Efraim Karsh

Grove Press
New York

Published simultaneously in Canada
Printed in the United States of America

FIRST EDITION

Library of Congress Cataloging-in-Publication Data
Karsh, Efraim.
    Arafat's war: the man and his battle for Israeli conquest / Efraim Karsh.
        p. cm.
    Includes bibliographical references (p.) and index.
    ISBN 0–8021–1758–9
        1. Arab-Israeli conflict—1993—Peace.   2. Al-Aqsa Intifada, 2000–
    3. Arafat, Yasir,
    1929– I. Title.

DS119.76.K27 2003
956.9405'4—dc2 1

                                                                        2003049079

Grove Press
841 Broadway
New York, NY 10003

03 04 05 06 07   10 9 8 7 6 5 4 3 2 1

For Matan, Ro'i, and Rachel

Contents

Introduction

Our ancestors fought the crusaders for a hundred years, and later
Ottoman imperialism, then British and French imperialism for years
and years. It is our duty to take over the banner of struggle from
them and hand it on untarnished and flying as proudly as ever to
the generations that come after us.

—Yasser Arafat, August 1968

"Struggle, Brother Ceauşescu! Armed struggle and terror are the only
things America respects."

Yasser Arafat finished his speech and gobbled down a dripping bak-
lava that he dunked into a jar of honey. It was the spring of 1978, and he
had just arrived in Bucharest, via Ceauşescu's presidential airplane, for
an urgent meeting with the Romanian dictator. The two had forged an
exceptionally close and warm relationship since they had first met in
the late 1960s, and Ceauşescu was now trying to convince Arafat to feign
moderation so as to allow the Palestine Liberation Organization (PLO)
to join the nascent Egyptian-Israeli peace negotiations.

"How about pretending to break with terrorism?" he suggested. "The
West would love it."

"Just pretending, like your own independence?" Arafat responded,
alluding to the sustained deception campaign conducted by Ceauşescu
since 1972, code-named Operation Horizon, which sought to convince
the West of Romania's political independence from the Soviet Union
and thus extract substantial economic, military, and technological
support.

"Exactly. But pretending over and over. Political influence, like dialectical materialism, is built on the same tenet that quantitative accumulation generates qualitative transformation."

"I'm not the expert on Marxism that you are, Brother Ceauşescu."

"Dialectical materialism works like cocaine, let's say. If you sniff it once or twice, it may not change your life. If you use it day after day, though, it will make you into an addict, a different man. That's the qualitative transformation."

"A snort of a pacifist Arafat day after day . . . ?"

"Exactly, Brother Arafat. The West may even become addicted to you and your PLO."

"That's not easy."

"Do you think it's easy for me to have to sneak off secretly to Moscow, when I used to be received there with fanfares and the trooping of the guard?"

"I don't mind coming here secretly, Brother Ceauşescu. That's for our cause. But we are a revolution, not a government. We were born a revolution, and we should remain an unfettered revolution."

"And you will remain a revolution. The only thing I want to change is the nameplate on your door . . . from the PLO into a Palestinian government-in-exile."

Arafat then launched into a lengthy peroration. He argued that the Palestinians lacked the tradition, unity, and discipline to become a formal state. That a Palestinian state would be a failure from the first day. That it was only something for future generations to consider. That he could not put any laws or other obstacles in the way of the Palestinian struggle against Israel. Ceauşescu's claim that he would be able to sustain his war of terror against Israel behind the respectable facade of a Palestinian government-in-exile failed to impress Arafat. Promising to give the matter serious consideration, he abruptly changed subjects. "I need some more blank passports from you, Brother Ceauşescu. A hundred Israeli, Jordanian, west European. A few American ones, if you can."[1]

One decade later, in November 1988, the Palestinian National Council (PNC), the PLO's semi-parliament, grudgingly accepted General Assembly Resolution 181 of November 29, 1947, calling for the creation of Jewish and Arab states in the territory of Mandatory Palestine, and Security Council Resolution 242, issued in the wake of the Six-Day War of 1967 and recognizing Israel's right to exist. Five years later, on September 13, 1993, Arafat signed the Declaration of Principles on Interim Self-Government Arrangements (known as DOP, or Oslo I) with the Israeli government, in which the PLO renounced the use of violence and committed itself to a peaceful quest of a settlement with Israel.

Yet both these turning points, remarkable as they appeared at the time, were belated attempts in the face of great adversity to act in the manner suggested by Ceauşescu, a desperate bid to transform Arafat's image in Western and Israeli eyes from a hardened terrorist to a man of peace, providing a handy facade behind which he could sustain his dogged quest for Israel's destruction.

In the fifteen years between the meeting in Bucharest and the signing of the DOP, the PLO saw a sharp decline in its fortunes. Its humiliating expulsion from Lebanon in 1982–83—first by Israel, then by Syria—and its consequent move to Tunisia had effectively eliminated the organization's military capabilities and seriously constrained its political maneuverability. Then came the 1990–91 Gulf conflict and the suspension of all financial aid and political backing by the Arab oil states, following Arafat's staunch support for Saddam Hussein's brutal occupation of Kuwait. By the early 1990s, the PLO had become a regional pariah, with Arafat on the brink of political extinction.

These developments were further compounded by the collapse of the Communist bloc in the late 1980s, as well as the 1991 disintegration of the Soviet Union, the PLO's foremost patron. Ceauşescu's overthrow by a spontaneous popular uprising, and his summary execution, were particularly traumatic for Arafat, not only because of the loss of a trusted friend and collaborator but also because it served as a potent reminder of the ultimate penalty for political miscalculation. As a result, when in late 1992 the Israeli government, headed by Yitzhak Rabin, offered Arafat a lifeline in the form of secret peace negotiations in Oslo, it was hardly surprising that the Palestinian leader seized the moment with alacrity.

Arafat thus committed himself to peace with Israel in the DOP and a string of follow-up agreements, but his actual behavior in subsequent years clearly revealed that beneath the rhetoric of compromise lay the commitment to violence and to an ultimate "victory," now fueled by Western indulgence and Israeli accommodation. "It should have been clear from the outset that Arafat does not see Oslo as an instrument of historic reconciliation but as a means of bettering his position,"

the Israeli journalist Ehud Ya'ari wrote in October 1996, shortly after
the Palestinian leader had unleashed his troops on their Israeli peace
partners:

> His "peace of the brave" does not necessarily end in being satisfied with
> a modest portion of the disputed land, but first and foremost, it serves to
> establish a bridgehead. A bridgehead for what? the late Yitzhak Rabin once
> asked me. The only answer that I could give, then and now, is a bridge-
> head for more. Arafat himself is unable to define much more.[2]

There is little doubt that Arafat has known the goal of the "bridgehead"
he established all along. For Arafat and the PLO leadership, the Oslo
process has always been a strategic means not to a two-state solution—
Israel and a Palestinian state in the West Bank and Gaza—but to the
substitution of a Palestinian state for that of Israel.

Reluctant to accept the right of the Jewish people to self-determination in its ancestral homeland, the PLO has viewed Israel as an artificial
alien entity created by Western imperialism and implanted in the midst
of the Arab world in order to divide and weaken it. This belief makes
the Palestine problem something far more profound than an ordinary
territorial dispute between Arabs and Jews: a Manichean struggle over
existence and destiny between the "Arab Nation" and the neo-crusading
"Zionist entity." As long as Palestine remains occupied, the Arab cause
will be imperiled. In Arafat's words:

> Our ancestors fought the crusaders for a hundred years, and later Otto-
> man imperialism, then British and French imperialism for years and years.
> It is our duty to take over the banner of struggle from them and hand it
> on untarnished and flying as proudly as ever to the generations that come
> after us. We shall never commit a crime against them, the crime of per-
> mitting the existence of a racialist state in the heart of the Arab world.[3]

As early as 1968 Arafat defined the PLO's strategic objective as "the
transfer of all resistance bases" into the West Bank and the Gaza Strip,
occupied by Israel during the Six-Day War of 1967, "so that the resistance may be gradually transformed into a popular armed revolution."
This, he reasoned, would allow the PLO to undermine Israel's way of
life by "preventing immigration and encouraging emigration . . . destroy-

ing tourism . . . weakening the Israeli economy and diverting the greater part of it to security requirements. Creating and maintaining an atmosphere of strain and anxiety that will force the Zionists to realize that it is impossible for them to live in Israel."[4]

When this scenario failed to materialize, owing to the low level of national consciousness among the Palestinians and Israel's effective counterinsurgency measures, in June 1974 the PLO adopted the "phased strategy," which was to serve as its guiding principle ever since. This stipulated that the Palestinians take whatever territory surrendered to them by Israel, then use it as a springboard for further territorial gains until achieving the "complete liberation of Palestine."

The Oslo accords complemented this strategy by enabling the PLO to achieve in one fell swoop what it had failed to attain through many years of violence and terrorism. Here was Israel, just over a decade after destroying the PLO's military infrastructure in Lebanon, asking the Palestinian organization, which was still formally committed to its destruction by virtue of its covenant, to establish a firm political and military presence—not in a neighboring Arab country but right on its doorstep. And this wasn't all; it was prepared to arm thousands of (reformed, it was hoped) terrorists who would be incorporated into newly established police and security forces charged with asserting the PLO's authority throughout the territories. This was an offer Arafat couldn't refuse. In the words of prominent PLO leader Faisal Husseini, Israel was willingly introducing into its midst a "Trojan horse" designed to promote the PLO's strategic goal of "Palestine from the [Jordan] river to the [Mediterranean] sea"—that is, a Palestine in place of Israel.[5]

Arafat testified as much as early as September 13, 1993, when he told the Palestinian people, in a prerecorded Arabic-language message broadcast by Jordanian television at about the same time of the peace-treaty signing ceremony on the White House lawn, that the DOP was merely the implementation of the PLO's "phased strategy."[6] During the next seven years, until the launch of his terrorist war in late September 2000, Arafat would play an intricate game of Jekyll and Hyde politics. Whenever addressing Israeli or Western audiences he would habitually extol the "peace of the brave" that he had signed with "my partner Yitzhak Rabin," while at the same time denigrating the peace accords to his Palestinian constituents as a temporary measure to be abandoned at the first available opportunity. This ranged from constant allusions to the "phased strategy," to his insistence on the "right of return," a standard Palestinian euphemism for Israel's destruction through demographic subversion, to Arafat's recurrent use of historical and religious metaphors, most notably the Treaty of Hudaibiya, signed by the Prophet Muhammad with the people of Mecca in 628, only to be reneged on a couple of years later when the situation shifted in Muhammad's favor.

From the moment of his arrival in Gaza, Arafat set out to build up an extensive terrorist infrastructure in flagrant violation of the Oslo accords and in total disregard of the overriding reason he had been brought from Tunisia, namely, to lay the groundwork for Palestinian statehood. Arafat systematically failed to disarm the terrorist groups Hamas and Islamic Jihad as required by the Oslo accords and tacitly approved the murder of hundreds of Israelis by these groups; created a far larger Palestinian army (the so-called police force) than was permitted by the accords; reconstructed the PLO's old terrorist apparatus, mainly under the auspices of Tanzim, the military arm of Fatah, the PLO's largest constituent organization and Arafat's own alma mater; frantically acquired prohibited weapons through the use of large sums of money donated to the Palestinian Authority by the international community for the benefit of the civilian Palestinian population; and, eventually, resorted to outright mass violence, first in September 1996 to publicly discredit the newly elected Israeli prime minister Benjamin Netanyahu, and then in September 2000 with the launch of his war of terror euphemistically titled *al-Aqsa Intifada* after the mosque in Jerusalem, this shortly after being offered by Netanyahu's successor, Ehud Barak, the creation of an independent Palestinian state in 92 percent of the West Bank and 100 percent of the Gaza Strip, with East Jerusalem as its capital.

Yet it was only during their first major counteroffensive during the war, code-named Operation Defensive Shield (April 2002), that the Israelis realized that the magnitude of the terror industry Arafat had established in the territories under his control far exceeded the most chilling assessments of Israel's intelligence services. Every branch of the Palestinian security regime had been directly involved in terrorist activities. Even in the private homes of senior police commanders the

Israeli soldiers found warehouse-quantities of explosives. And there was incontrovertible evidence that Arafat had personally approved payment to many well-known terrorists, and in addition funded the acquisition of illegal weapons. Many such prohibited weapons, together with suicide-bomber belts and chemical substances, indicating that the Palestinian Authority was in the process of developing chemical weapons for use against Israel, were seized in Arafat's presidential compound in Ramallah.[7]

What enabled Arafat to pursue his war preparations with impunity was a combination of international sympathy for his cause and Israeli self-delusion. Fatigued by decades of fighting, and yearning for a normalcy that would allow them at last to enjoy their recently won affluence, many Israelis clung naively to the Oslo process, turning a blind eye to the evolving danger at their doorstep. Even Netanyahu, for all his scathing criticism of Oslo, proved unable to win from Arafat the reciprocity he demanded, and reluctantly he was forced to follow in the footsteps of his two predecessors Yitzhak Rabin and Shimon Peres, albeit at a far slower pace, in surrendering territory to the Palestinian Authority without any tangible return.

In this light, Arafat's rejection of Barak's proposals, followed by the launching of his terrorist war in September of the same year, made perfect sense. Not only did the international community react to the renewed violence by pressuring Israel to moderate its response, and be still more "forthcoming" to Palestinian demands, but the Barak government itself succumbed to Palestinian military pressure. In January 2001, during a summit meeting at the Egyptian resort of Taba, Israel's prime minister ceded 97 percent of the territories to the Palestinians, together with some Israeli territory that would have made the nascent Palestinian state larger than the pre-1967 territory of the West Bank and Gaza, and made breathtaking concessions over Jerusalem and the question of Palestinian refugees.[8]

Had Arafat chosen to pocket these Israeli concessions, a Palestinian state could have been established within months. Instead, and perhaps understandably from Arafat's point of view, he went for broke, insisting with renewed adamancy that no peace would be possible unless Israel guaranteed the right of the Arab refugees of the 1948 war and their descendants to return to their old dwellings in territory that is now part of the state of Israel. Only when faced with the prospect of the destruction of their state through demographic subversion did the Israeli public react decisively, voting Barak out of office within days of the Taba summit. This left Arafat little choice but to intensify his war against Israel in an attempt to coerce the incoming prime minister, Ariel Sharon, into concessions similar to those of his ill-fated predecessor, a strategy that up to that point had worked brilliantly.

That Arafat's war has far less to do with the liberation of the West Bank and Gaza than with the PLO's historic goal of Israel's destruction is demonstrated not only by this objective's constant reassertion by the Palestinian leadership and its tightly controlled media, but also by the conflict's exceptional ferocity, unmatched in scope and intensity since the Arab attempt to abort the creation of a Jewish state in 1948. Since its launch in September 2000, the Palestinian campaign has inflicted many thousands of terrorist attacks on Israeli civilians—homicide bombings, mortar shelling, drive-by shootings, stabbings, lynching, rock throwing—murdering more than eight hundred and wounding some five thousand.

In the entire two decades of Israeli occupation preceding the Oslo accords, some four hundred Israelis were murdered by the PLO and associated terrorist groups; since the conclusion of that peace agreement, three times as many have lost their lives in terrorist attacks. Moreover, many of the worst outrages against Israeli civilians occurred not at moments of breakdown in the Oslo "peace process" but at its high points, when the prospect of Israeli withdrawal appeared brightest and most imminent.

Homicide bombings, for example, were introduced at a time of widespread euphoria only a few months after the historic Rabin-Arafat handshake on the White House lawn: eight people were murdered in April 1994 while riding a bus in the town of Afula. Six months later, twenty-one Israelis were murdered on a bus in Tel Aviv. In the following year, five bombings took the lives of an additional thirty-eight Israelis. During the short-lived government of the dovish Shimon Peres (November 1995–May 1996), following Rabin's assassination on November 4, fifty-eight Israelis were murdered within the span of one week in three suicide bombings in Jerusalem and Tel-Aviv.

In contrast, terrorism was largely *curtailed* following Netanyahu's election in May 1996 and the consequent slowdown in the Oslo process. During Netanyahu's three years in power, some fifty Israelis were murdered in terrorist attacks—a third of the casualty rate during the Rabin government and a sixth of the casualty rate during Peres's term. If the occupation was the cause of terrorism, why was terrorism sparse during the years of actual occupation, why did it increase dramatically with the prospect of the end of the occupation, and why did it escalate into open war upon Israel's most far-reaching concessions ever?

Far from being a manifestation of Palestinian national will, Arafat's war of terror is the culmination of a long-standing schism between two different and, for most part, mutually exclusive visions of the PLO and the population in the West Bank and the Gaza Strip (the "inside," in Palestinian parlance) regarding their preferred future in general and their relationship with Israel in particular. While the PLO, the quintessential representative of the Palestinian diaspora outside the boundaries of Mandatory Palestine (or the "outside"), has been relentlessly committed from its inception to the destruction of the state of Israel, most West Bank and Gaza residents wished by and large to get on with their lives and take advantage of the opportunities afforded by Israeli rule. Hence the paucity of "armed resistance" in the territories during the two and a half decades from their occupation by Israel to the onset of the Oslo process, when most terrorist attacks emanated from the outside—from Jordan in the late 1960s, then from Lebanon. Thus the "inside's" enthusiastic response to the signing of the DOP and its consistent support for the peace process during the 1990s, despite its constant indoctrination with burning hatred for Israelis and Jews by Arafat's Palestinian Authority. This makes Arafat's disingenuous approach to peace, and its culmination in his war of terror, as much a betrayal of the Palestinian people he purports to defend as of his Israeli peace partner.

1

The Man and His World

If Arafat ever once stumbled and told the truth, he would say, "Please forgive me!"
—a close associate of Arafat, October 1996

It is an historical irony that the person who is arguably the world's most famous Palestinian does not conform even to his own definition of what a Palestinian is. According to the Palestinian National Covenant, adopted in 1964 as one of the PLO's two founding documents and revised four years later to remain the organization's foremost article of faith to date, "Palestinians are those Arab residents who, until 1947, lived permanently in Palestine, regardless of whether they were expelled from it or have stayed there."[1]

Born Muhammad Abdel Rahman Abdel Rauf Arafat al-Qudwa al-Husseini in Cairo on August 24, 1929,[2] Arafat was the sixth child of Abdel Rauf al-Qudwa al-Husseini, a small textile merchant of Gazan-Egyptian origin, and of Zawda, a member of the Jerusalmite Abu Saud family. The couple had arrived in Cairo in 1927 and settled in the middle-class Sakakini neighborhood, where the young Arafat spent his youth. Aside from short stays, he never lived in Palestine prior to 1947, or for that matter at any other subsequent time, until his arrival in the Gaza Strip in July 1994 as head of the newly established Palestinian Authority (PA).

Throughout his career, Arafat has gone to great lengths to blur the circumstances of his childhood, especially the fact that his father was half Egyptian. When questioned about his birthplace, Arafat would normally claim to have been born and reared in the Old City of Jerusalem, just a few houses away from the Wailing Wall.[3] Yet he has often contradicted himself. "I was born in Gaza," he told *Playboy* magazine in September 1988. "My mother died when I was four and I was sent to live with my uncle in Jerusalem. I grew up there, in the old city. The house was beside the Wailing Wall. The Israelis blew up the house—demolished it in 1967 when they captured the city."[4] Whenever confronted with these contradictory versions and asked for a definite answer, his winning formula was that "my father was from Gaza and my mother from Jerusalem."[5]

These claims, especially his connection to Jerusalem and the Israelis' demolition of his alleged birth house, create a neat symmetry between Arafat's personal biography and the collective Palestinian experience of loss and dispossession, despite both Arafat's birth certificate and university records naming Cairo as his birthplace, as well as his strong Egyptian accent betraying a childhood spent in Cairo's schools.[6] Indeed, throughout his decades at the helm of the PLO, Arafat has never been able to overcome the widespread displeasure among the organization's rank and file with his strong Egyptian accent. Dialects and accents constitute a central element of collective identity in Arab societies, not least among Palestinians with their persistent sense of loss and the attendant attempt to construct a national consciousness. Every Arab can detect, on the basis of dialect, accent, or intonation, his interlocutor's regional origin, and Arafat's accent leaves little doubt as to his Egyptian, rather than Palestinian, origin. Salah Khalaf (better known by his nom de guerre, Abu Iyad), Arafat's close associate throughout their political careers, recalled his deep dismay at discovering, during their first meeting in Cairo in the 1950s, the heavy Egyptian accent of an aspiring chairman of the Palestinian student union.[7] He wasn't the only one to feel this way. When in the spring of 1966 Arafat was arrested by the Syrian authorities for involvement in the murder of a Palestinian activist, Abu Iyad rushed to Damascus, together with his fellow Fatah leader Farouq Qaddoumi, to secure his release. In a meeting with General Hafez al-Assad, then Syria's defense minister, the two were confronted with a virulent tirade against Arafat. "You're fooled that he is a Palestinian," Assad said. "He isn't. He's an Egyptian agent." This was a devastating charge, especially in light of the acrimonious state of Egyptian-Syrian relations at the time, and one that rested solely on Arafat's Egyptian dialect. Yet for Assad this was a sufficient indictment. "You can go to Mezza [the prison] and take [him] away," he said eventually. "But remember one thing: I do not trust Arafat and I never will."[8] Assad was true to his word until his death on June 10, 2000.

Such is the extent of Arafat's sensitivity to his Egyptian origin that in his meetings with his subjects in the West Bank and Gaza, whom he has come to rule since the mid-1990s as part of the Oslo process, he is regularly accompanied by an aide who whispers in his ear the correct words in Palestinian Arabic whenever the chairman is overtaken by his Egyptian dialect.

Nor did Arafat take any part in the formative experience of Palestinian consciousness—the collapse and dispersion of Palestine's Arab community during the 1948 war—in spite of his extensive mythmaking about this period. "I am a refugee," he argued emotionally in a 1969 interview. "Do you know what it means to be a refugee? I am a poor and helpless man. I have nothing, for I was expelled and dispossessed of my homeland."[9]

As a native and resident of Egypt, Arafat lost no childhood home in Palestine, nor witnessed any of his close relatives expelled and transformed into destitute refugees. As a Palestinian biographer of Arafat observed, "He was not a child of Al Nakba or the disaster, as Palestinians call the 1948 defeat, nor did his father lose the source of his livelihood." Arafat himself complained to a close childhood friend, "My father didn't leave me even two meters of Palestine."[10]

Arafat's bragging about his illustrious war record is equally dubious. One famous story involves the young Arafat stopping an attack by twenty-four Jewish tanks in the area that would come to be known as the Gaza Strip by knocking out the first and the last and trapping the others.[11] Another story tells of Arafat being the "youngest officer" in the militia force of Abdel Qader Husseini, scion of a prominent Jerusalem family, whose death in the battle for the city in early April 1948 instantaneously transformed him from a controversial figure with a mediocre military record into a national hero.[12] "I was in Jerusalem when the Zionists tried to take over the city and make it theirs," Arafat is fond of saying.

> I fought with my father and brother in the streets against the Jewish oppressors, but we were out-manned and had no weapons comparable to what the Jews had. We were finally forced to flee leaving all our possessions

behind . . . My father gathered us—my mother, my brothers and sisters, our grandparents—and we fled. We walked for days across the desert with nothing but a few canteens of water. It was June. We passed through the village of Deir Yasin and saw what the Jews had done there—a horrible massacre. Finally we reached Gaza, where my father's family had some land. We were exhausted and destitute. It was upon our arrival that I vowed to dedicate my life to the recovery of my homeland.[13]

Like other parts of Arafat's biography, this account contains a mix of dramatic ingredients designed to transform his alleged personal experience into the embodiment of Palestinian history: a heroic but hopeless struggle against a brutal and superior enemy, a crushing defeat and the attendant loss and exile. Not only did the Israeli army have no tanks when this alleged incident took place (May 10, 1948), but according to another of Arafat's own accounts he was in Jerusalem at the time and did not take part in the fighting in Gaza. As for Arafat's alleged participation in the battle for Jerusalem, when asked whether he actually engaged in combat operations, he retorted angrily: "You are completely ignorant, I am sorry to say. You have no idea. The British army was still there with all its armaments. The main British forces were in Jerusalem."[14]

With regard to the alleged escape of Arafat's family to freedom, aside from telling two of his biographers that he had arrived in Jerusalem (in late April 1948) on his own, making no mention of other family members,[15] the village of Deir Yasin was captured by Jewish forces in early April 1948, like most of the Tel Aviv–Jerusalem highway, and there was absolutely no way for Palestinian refugees to cross it on their flight. But even if some refugees had passed through the village in June, they would have found no traces of "the horrible massacre" that had taken place two months earlier. Had Arafat and his family really fled Jerusalem via the desert, as he claims, they would have gone in the opposite direction of Deir Yasin. But then the tragedy of Deir Yasin, where some one hundred people were killed in the fighting (the figure given at the time was more than twice as high), has become the defining episode of Palestinian victimization, and as such an obvious choice for appropriation by Arafat.

The truth is that while the Palestinian Arabs were going through the trauma of defeat and dispersal, Arafat "was completing secondary school in Cairo and did not stray far from the Egyptian capital during the great catastrophe."[16] He was of course as mindful as the next man of the unfolding Palestinian tragedy, but it is hard to say whether it affected him on a personal level, as he did not even do what thousands of non-Palestinian Arabs did—Egyptians, Syrians, Iraqis, and the like—and volunteer to fight in Palestine.

It was only natural for Arafat, by way of bridging the glaring gap between his personal biography and the wider Palestinian experience, to create a mythical aura around himself from his first days of political activity in the early 1950s at King Fuad University in Cairo. This was the only way he could compensate for his inherent inferiority vis-à-vis fellow Palestinian students, who really did arrive in Egypt as destitute and dispossessed refugees, and establish his credentials as a quintessential Palestinian, equal to the ambitious task of national leadership he had earmarked for himself. The higher he climbed, the greater was his entanglement in the intricate web of lies and fiction he had woven, steadily blurring the line between his own persona and that of Palestinian collective identity. In the words of two sympathetic biographers: "His own murky identity [is] a metaphor for all the Palestinians. He is the fatherless father, the motherless son, the selfless symbol of a people without identity, the ultimate man without a country."[17]

This carefully contrived world of self-invention, where reality and fiction blend, was to become Arafat's defining characteristic. He claims to have declined a studentship from the University of Texas in the early 1950s, but according to one biographer it is unlikely that he had ever been accepted given his poor command of the English language and the strict requirements at that time that foreign students have both a clean political slate and proof of the means to support themselves. He boasts of cofounding a construction company during his stay in Kuwait during the 1950s and the early 1960s, which made him a millionaire, while in actuality he was an ordinary civil servant who moonlighted in his free time, earning thousands rather than millions of dollars. His boasts of guerrilla exploits in the West Bank and Gaza in the months attending their occupation by Israel in the Six-Day War of 1967, where he was supposedly on the run from the Israeli authorities until early 1968, are dismissed by two of his biographers as being almost certainly an exaggeration.[18]

Arafat's gift for invention extends well beyond his personal biography. Sometime in the mid-1970s, the Yugoslav president Josip Broz Tito, a staunch supporter of the PLO, sent a television crew to film a "model raid" on Israeli targets. Receiving the crew in Damascus, Arafat promised to lead the raid in person, asking the Yugoslavs to wait for him at a certain spot near the Lebanese–Israeli border. They waited there for two full days, only to return to Damascus empty-handed after Arafat failed to show.

Meeting the furious director again in his office, Arafat offered to stage a mock raid on the spot. He instructed the crew to start filming while he sat behind his desk shouting some orders. A number of young fighters dashed into the office and Arafat indicated to them certain areas on a huge map of Palestine, after which the fighters saluted him and left the room. When the filming was over, the director was beside himself with enthusiasm. "You're a good actor, Chairman Arafat." "I used to be, you know," Arafat retorted.[19]

Even among Arafat's admirers and followers he has been viewed as a congenital liar, so much so that in May 1966 he was suspended from his post as Fatah's military commander for, among other things, sending "false reports especially in the military field."[20] "Arafat tells a lie in every sentence" is how a senior Romanian intelligence officer with whom Arafat worked closely described the PLO chairman, while one of Arafat's intimate Palestinian associates has said, "If Arafat ever once stumbled and told the truth, he would say, 'Please forgive me!'"[21]

Terje Larsen, a Norwegian academic who played an important role in the conclusion of the Oslo accords and who later became the United Nations special envoy to the Middle East, recalled an occasion when Arafat was attempting to persuade the Israeli foreign minister Shimon Peres that Peres had made a specific commitment to him:

> Arafat said, "You told me on the phone—" Peres said, "No." Arafat said, "Yes, you said so. Larsen was there in my office. And Mr. Dennis [Ross]" (U.S. peace mediator). "Larsen, you are my international witness. Mr. Peres, I have an international witness!" Everyone else in the room knew that this was untrue.[22]

The American-Arab academic Edward Said had a similar experience some fifteen years earlier when he passed on to Arafat the U.S. administration's

offer to recognize the PLO in return for the latter's implicit acquiescence in Israel's existence.

[I]n March of 1979 I flew to Beirut and went to see Arafat. I said to him,
We need an answer. The first thing he said was, I never received the
message. So for at least ten minutes he began to deny that any message
came. Luckily, Shafiq al-Hout [director of the PLO's Beirut office] was
sitting with us in the room and he said, I delivered the message to you.
Arafat said, I have no recollection of it. Shafiq went into the next room
and brought a copy of it. Arafat looked at it and said, All right, tomorrow
I'll give you my answer.[23]

Others had a less cavalier attitude toward Arafat's inability to tell the
truth. Shortly after the signing ceremony on the White House lawn on
September 13, 1993, Jordan's King Hussein informed the Rabin government that Arafat was certain to violate the peace agreement he had just
signed. "Israel is doing business with the worst possible person," read a
royal message. "Arafat has proved time and again that his word cannot
be trusted." Since the late 1960s, King Hussein had reached numerous
agreements with Arafat only to see each and every one violated by his
partner. "I and the government of the kingdom of Jordan hereby announce that we are unable to coordinate politically with the PLO leadership until such a time as their word becomes their bond, characterized
by commitment, credibility, and constancy," a somber Hussein stated
in an address to the nation on February 19, 1986, shortly after being
duped yet again by Arafat.[24]

President George W. Bush has had a far shorter relationship with Arafat
than the deceased Jordanian monarch. Yet when in early 2002 he was
reassured in writing by the chairman that he had had nothing to do with
a ship carrying some fifty tons of prohibited weapons, purchased by the
Palestinian Authority from Iran, despite conclusive evidence to the contrary, Bush appeared to have joined the list of world leaders profoundly
disillusioned with Arafat's credibility.

For decades Arafat has consistently engaged in a pattern of deceit as
Europeans, Arabs, and even Israelis have been willing to indulge him
despite the blatant transparency of many of his lies. Even the most in-

credible falsehoods, such as accusing Israel of carrying out suicide bombings perpetrated by Palestinian terrorists, assassinating its own minister of tourism in the winter of 2001, and murdering Arab children to get their organs, have failed to dent Arafat's imagined identity.[25]

This pattern of deceit has also allowed Arafat to disguise another major issue of his personal identity. As he rose to public attention in the late 1960s, Arafat's personal life came under increasing scrutiny. Not only had he not married and established a family like most of his fellow terrorists but, since adolescence, he had never been seen publicly with a woman in romantic circumstances, let alone been associated with one on a lasting basis. This has given rise to persistent speculation about his potential homosexuality. According to one of his siblings, Arafat was mercilessly taunted, as early as age three or four, by his peers and by his father for what they viewed as his girlish demeanor.

> At this time in his life Rahman [i.e., Yasser] was fat, soft, ungainly and completely unimpressive. He had a very high voice, and was beginning to suffer from comparisons to girls which were made by the other boys. Even my father started to curse him out in such terms, and he would often shout at my mother for wishing for a daughter before Rahman was born. He blamed my mother for much of what he thought was wrong with Rahman, saying that her dreaming of a girl had caused Rahman to be born more like a girl than a boy.[26]

Arafat was cold and detached toward his father, refusing to attend his funeral in 1954 and abstaining from visiting his grave when he arrived in Gaza forty years later as head of the Palestinian Authority. Death in Muslim and Arab culture is "the great unifier" shared by all human beings, and reverence for the dead supersedes past enmities, feuds, and grudges. Yet for all his religious devotion, and Arafat is a far more committed Muslim than is recognized, his resentment of his father was so deep that he did not even attempt to excuse his absence from his father's funeral.[27]

Arafat's sexual identity was further conflicted by his mother's untimely death when he was four, and by his father's two subsequent remarriages. The family was rife with internecine feuds, with the children violently hostile to their stepmothers. Without a male figure to adjudicate between the parties, as Arafat's father was busy in his work and involved in a prolonged legal battle he was conducting against the authorities over a family property, Arafat was left to be reared by his strict and willful older sister, Inam. "The shouting and the rows, mainly between the females of the household, hurt and scarred Yasser," wrote a biographer. "From that moment on and for nearly twenty years he became, to an extent, anti-woman. Some fifteen years later he was to say to a fellow student at university that he had not so much as shaken the hand of a woman."[28]

Insinuations of Arafat's homosexuality have long been a staple on the Middle East's political grapevine.[29] Leaked intelligence reports told of his alleged liaisons with foreign volunteers who trained in the PLO's camps in Lebanon during the 1970s and early 1980s, while the Syrian minister of defense Mustafa Tlas subtly alluded to Arafat's homosexuality by saying, "One with ugly features does not hope to have women."[30] While such rumors have been dismissed by Arafat's apologists as a defamation campaign by his numerous enemies, no such claim can be made with regard to the revelations by Lieutenant General Ion Mihai Pacepa, head of the Romanian External Intelligence Service (DIE), who defected to the West in 1978.

Since the late 1960s Arafat and the Romanian dictator Nicolae Ceauşescu had developed a close personal relationship, which led to multifaceted cooperation between the Romanian security services and the PLO. (Hani al-Hassan, to mention a prominent example, a leading PLO activist and a close associate of Arafat, was even recruited as a Romanian agent and given, under Ceauşescu's personal direction, the female code name "Annette.") Arafat became a regular visitor to Bucharest where he was received with much pomp and circumstance. Unbeknownst to him, however, the Romanians bugged the guest house in which he and his coterie were staying, thus becoming privy to his personal affairs. "I just called the microphone monitoring center to ask about the 'Fedayee' [i.e., Arafat]," General Constantin Munteanu, the liaison officer to the PLO leadership, told Pacepa during a visit by Arafat to Bucharest in the spring of 1978. "After the meeting with the Comrade, he went directly to the guest house and had dinner. At this very moment, the 'Fedayee' is in his bedroom making love to his bodyguard. The one I knew was his latest lover. He's playing tiger again. The officer monitoring his microphones connected me live with the bedroom, and the squalling almost broke my eardrums. Arafat was roaring like a tiger, and his lover yelping like a hyena."

Pacepa was not surprised. A few years earlier he had read an exhaustive report on Arafat's personal and professional behavior, prepared for him by Munteanu. "The report was indeed an incredible account of fanaticism, of devotion to his cause, of tangled oriental political maneuvers, lies, embezzled PLO funds deposited in Swiss banks, and homosexual relationships, beginning with his teacher when he was a teenager and ending with his current bodyguards," Pacepa wrote in his memoirs. "After reading that report, I felt a compulsion to take a shower whenever I had been kissed by Arafat, or even just shaken his hand."[31]

Such sexual antics could finish off a political career in the most tolerant Western societies, let alone in the Middle East, with its intolerant and macho sociopolitical culture. Homosexuality, however prevalent, is publicly derided and its practitioners persecuted or even imprisoned. (In a highly publicized trial in late 2001, for example, twenty-three Egyptian homosexuals were imprisoned for "debauchery, contempt of religion, falsely interpreting the Koran and exploiting Islam to promote deviant ideas.")[32] Arafat and the PLO have gone out of their way to discredit any such insinuations. Explanations of Arafat's sexual behavior have ranged from shyness with women because of his less than impressive appearance, to religious devotion, to stories of alleged romantic relationships, most notably with Nada Yashruti, a widow of a PLO activist who was killed in the mid-1970s in the Lebanese civil war. But the foremost pretext used to explain Arafat's ostensible prudishness is his "marriage to the Palestinian revolution." "For this reason no girl wanted to marry me," he told *Playboy* magazine. "I work sometimes 24 hours a day. During the battles, I never slept. I usually work 18 hours a day. During the early days I slept an hour or two, sometimes a half hour a day. But I cannot be comfortable, cannot live in a comfortable house . . . while I have this job to do for my people."[33]

What politician would not substitute his own well-being for the general good, especially in Middle Eastern societies where the role of absolute leaders supersedes that of political institutions? Yet for Arafat, whose entire political existence was predicated on a mythical construction that had little to do with reality, the need to keep an unblemished facade is, literally, a matter of life and death. A stark reminder of this was the fate of Ali Naji Adhami, a renowned Palestinian cartoonist who was assassinated on July 22, 1987, on a London street outside the editorial offices of the newspaper he worked for, the Kuwaiti-owned *al-Qabas*. It was later discovered that the attack was planned and executed by members of Arafat's personal guard, code-named Force 17, which at the time maintained an extensive network in Britain.

Why did Arafat order the assassination of a nonpolitical figure that did not even live in the Middle East? In a series of cartoons Adhami had questioned the morality of top PLO brass by implying that Arafat had a relationship with a married woman. Though on the face of it Arafat should have welcomed this insinuation as it helped dispel the rumors about his homosexuality, the austere commander who was "married" to the revolution simply could not afford to be seen to have compromised this devotion by a relationship with another person, man or woman. Even when in the summer of 1990 Arafat married Suha Tawil, a member of a prominent Christian Palestinian family and thirty-four years his junior, it took a year and a half before the marriage was leaked to the world, and no authorized statement by Arafat or his office was ever given. Instead, one of Arafat's closest officials commented sardonically that "she married him but he didn't marry her."[34]

Fifteen years after Adhami's assassination, Arafat would use Force 17 to hide yet another blemish on his moral conduct, this time in financial mismanagement. In the evening hours of January 3, 2002, a group of armed men burst into a hospital in Cairo where Jawad Ghussein, an elderly Palestinian multimillionaire, was recuperating from an operation. They locked family members sitting by his bedside in a neighboring room and removed the hapless patient to Gaza, which had been ruled by Arafat's PA since mid-1994.

Ghussein had known Arafat since the early 1950s and had helped his early efforts to establish a revolutionary organization by introducing him to his cousin Talaat Ghussein, a wealthy businessman in Kuwait who subsequently became one of Fatah's first benefactors.[35] Between 1983 and 1996 Jawad Ghussein served as head of the Palestine National Fund, the PLO's effective finance minister, with billions of dollars from international aid or Palestinians' taxes passing through his account books. From the mid-1990s, he increasingly disagreed with Arafat, charging him and his Palestinian Authority with unbridled abuse of power, as well as pervasive corruption ranging from bribery and the use of government monopolies for personal gain, to siphoning off of public funds into private bank accounts.[36]

This was something Arafat could not afford. For decades he had been carefully cultivating the myth of a selfless leader, one who had donated his personal wealth to the revolution, who possessed no properties or assets of his own, and who maintained an austere way of life. The financial irregularities tied to him in early 1966, which led to his suspension as Fatah's military commander, had been long forgotten.[37] Yet Arafat's total control of the PLO's finances, especially his insistence on having contributions diverted to bank accounts registered in his name, gave rise to persistent rumors of his personal corruption. Particularly scathing criticism of Arafat's irregularities was leveled by the longtime Syrian minister of defense Mustafa Tlas, a sympathizer turned bitter enemy. According to Tlas, during the Israeli siege of Beirut in June 1982 the PLO received ten new Mercedes ambulances as a gift from Kuwait, each worth about $60,000. Rather than use the ambulances to aid casualties, Arafat sold them at half price to the Syrians, then pocketed the difference.[38]

Ghussein was one of the few people intimately familiar with Arafat's financial dealings and thus had to be silenced in response to rising discontent in the West Bank and Gaza over Arafat's financial conduct. To justify its act of kidnapping, the Palestinian Authority claimed that Ghussein had embezzled Palestinian national funds but later changed its story and argued that he had been abducted as a means to force him to repay a $6.5 million loan. Ghussein stood his ground, insisting that he had done nothing wrong and that his unlawful detention had been designed to prevent him from speaking his mind. In mid-August 2002, while being transferred to a Jerusalem hospital for medical treatment, he managed to escape the country with Israeli help and fly to his London home. Once freed, however, he wouldn't elaborate beyond his initial charges. Arafat's mafia-like message had been driven home loud and clear.

Arafat is of course not the first Arab ruler to use violence to silence unwanted criticism. From its creation in the wake of the First World War on the ruins of the Ottoman empire, the contemporary Middle Eastern state system has been plagued by constant violence. Israel (and, to a lesser extent, Turkey) excepted, the Middle East is still a place where the role of the absolute leader supersedes the role of political institutions, and where citizenship is largely synonymous with submission. Power in Arab countries is often concentrated in the hands of small and oppressive minorities (Alawites in Syria, Sunnis in Iraq); religious, ethnic, and tribal conflicts abound; and for sovereigns, the overriding preoccupation is survival. In such circumstances, it is hardly surprising that the primary, if not the sole, instrument of political discourse is physical force.

The scale and the endemic nature of violence in the region are hard to exaggerate. In most Arab countries, political dissent is dealt with by repression, and ethnic and religious differences are settled by internecine strife and murder. (One need mention only Syria's massacres of its Muslim activists in the early 1980s, or the brutal treatment of Iraq's Shiite and Kurdish communities and of the Christian minority in southern Sudan.) As for foreign policy, it too is often pursued by means of crude force, ranging from terrorism and subversion to outright aggression. In the Yemenite, Lebanese, and Algerian civil wars, hundreds of thousands of innocent civilians perished; the Iran-Iraq war claimed nearly a million lives.

The same is true of Arab policy toward Israel. From the very beginning, the Arabs' primary instrument for opposing Jewish national aspirations was violence, and the relative success or failure of that instrument in any given period determined Arab politics and diplomacy. As early as April 1920, Arab nationalists sought to thwart Zionist activity (and to rally support for incorporating Palestine into the short-lived Syrian kingdom headed by King Faisal ibn Hussein) by carrying out a pogrom in Jerusalem in which 5 Jews were killed and 211 wounded. The following year, Arab riots claimed a far higher toll—some ninety dead and hundreds wounded. In the summer of 1929, another wave of violence resulted in the death of 133 Jews and the wounding of hundreds more.

Arab violence intensified in 1936–39, when a general Palestinian uprising claimed hundreds of Jewish lives, reaching its peak in November 1947. Then, in the face of the imminent expiration of the British mandate, the UN General Assembly voted to partition Palestine. Rejecting this solution, the Arab nations resolved instead to destroy the state of Israel at its inception and gain the whole for themselves.

This was the political scene into which Arafat entered in the late 1950s when, together with a number of fellow activists, he established the Movement for the Liberation of Palestine (Harakat Tahrir Filastin), its Arabic acronym reversed from Hataf (death) to Fatah to match the Koranic word for "conquest." He did not draw up the rules of the game in the cruel system of inter-Arab politics, though he has undoubtedly been one of its most devious and savage players. While for most Arab leaders, with the partial exception of the deposed Iraqi dictator Saddam Hussein, violence is a necessary evil, something to be unflinchingly used for political survival or national expansion, for Arafat it has been an integral part of his personal being. When Jordan's King Hussein killed thousands of Palestinians in the single month of September 1970, or when President Assad of Syria slaughtered many thousands of his subjects in the city of Hama in February 1982, they were fighting for their political and physical survival. They did not glorify the violence they unleashed, or for that matter any ideology of violence. But for Arafat and his Fatah cofounders, violence has assumed from the outset mythic proportions.

Arafat's love affair with violence, however, goes well beyond the issue of practicality. His domineering nature and strong streak of cruelty apart, violence has constituted a useful tool to surmount his intractable problems of identity and self-denial. It has allowed a physically unassuming young man—short (5 feet 4 inches tall), chubby, soft, with bulging eyes and protruding lower lip—to prove his manliness, and the Egyptian outsider to establish his patriotic Palestinian credentials. Like other twentieth-century outsiders who came to reign over their supposed nations—the Austrian Adolf Hitler and the Georgian Joseph Stalin being the best known examples—only to take them to monstrous heights of violence and brutality, from the onset of his political career Arafat has pursued a zero-sum approach of all or nothing vis-à-vis Israel, regardless of the true interests and wishes of the Palestinians, with the "armed struggle"—the standard euphemism for terrorism—as its foremost instrument.

Arafat killed his first victim sometime in 1949 or 1950. Those were the immediate postwar days, the full scope of the Arab defeat was just sinking in, and Hajj Amin al-Husseini, the former mufti of Jerusalem, who had led the Palestinian attempt to abort the creation of the state of Israel with devastating consequences for his own people, was trying to reassert his authority in the Gaza Strip, then occupied by Egypt. The young Arafat was part of a group of Husseini thugs whose task was to intimidate supporters of the less militant Nashashibi clan, the mufti's erstwhile rivals. One night, as the squad was about to set fire to an orchard, they were ambushed by a group of Nashashibi laborers armed with knives and clubs. "We regrouped back in the city, in a shed behind the cemetery," recalled one of the squad members.

> It was just dawn. We were all bruised and bloody, all but Hamid [a member of the group]. He looked very sheepish. We had several pistols stored in the shed. Yasser kept looking accusingly at Hamid. I guess we all did. We were all thinking to ourselves that he was the one who had forewarned the Nashashibis of our mission. Finally, in a very soft voice, Yasser spoke what we were thinking. Hamid vehemently denied it. Yasser stood up and we all noticed that he had a pistol behind his back. He walked over to Hamid, who was by now in tears over the accusations, and shot him in the head.

"We discovered later that it hadn't been Hamid who betrayed us," the eyewitness continued. "It was one of Hajj Amin's own men, and it was done deliberately in the hope that we would be killed and the killings would turn the whole of Gaza against the Nashashibis. When Yasser learned this, it did not bother him in the least that he had killed Hamid. I remember him saying that Hamid had been the first person he had ever personally killed, and for that reason Hamid had served a valuable Ikhwan [Muslim Brotherhood] purpose." Another member of the squad corroborated the story, describing the twenty-year-old Arafat: "He was almost what you called a dual personality, very diffident at times, very hyped up at others."[39]

Arafat's ruthlessness and his indifferent attitude to human life were to become the hallmarks of his political career. "This is my brother Hani Hassan," Arafat introduced his longtime associate to the Romanian president Nicolae Ceauşescu in October 1972. "He is the one who, just a few months ago, prepared our answer to the Olympic Committee's decision not to allow a team of Palestinian athletes to participate in the Munich games. He is the brain who put our organization's name on the front page of every single newspaper."[40]

Arafat was referring to the September 5, 1972, massacre of eleven Israeli athletes by a team of PLO terrorists during the Munich Olympic

Games. While the crime was universally condemned, for Arafat it was a public relations coup that brought the PLO and its leader worldwide attention. So did the murder of the U.S. ambassador to the Sudan, Cleo A. Noel, and his chargé d'affaires, George Curtis Moore, the following year. The two were taken hostage, together with several other foreign diplomats, on the evening of March 1, 1973, when a group of PLO terrorists stormed the Saudi embassy in Khartoum during a farewell party for Moore. In exchange for their hostages, the terrorists demanded the release of a group of international outlaws, including Sirhan Sirhan, Robert Kennedy's assassin, the Palestinian archterrorist Abu Daoud, then imprisoned in Jordan, and several members of the notorious Baader-Meinhof gang, serving long prison sentences in West Germany. As the United States, Jordan, and West Germany all refused to negotiate, the terrorists remained in close and constant contact with Fatah leadership in Beirut throughout the affair and looked to their headquarters for instructions. Shortly after 8 P.M. on Friday, March 2, 1973, twenty-five hours after storming the embassy, the terrorists received the order to kill the hostages. "Remember Nahr al-Bard," Abu Iyad told the commander of the operation. "The people's blood in the Nahr al-Bard cries out for vengeance. These are our final orders. We and the rest of the world are watching you." Nahr al-Bard (cold river) was a refugee camp and terrorist training facility in northern Lebanon, raided by the Israelis shortly before the Khartoum operation was launched. It was also the code word for the execution of the Western diplomats. The diplomats— one of whom was the highest-ranking African American in the foreign service—were thus taken to the embassy basement, tortured, and killed in cold blood. The torture they suffered was so barbarous that later "authorities couldn't tell which was black and which was white." To prolong the agony of their victims, the terrorists fired from the floor upward, striking them first in the feet and legs, before administering the coup de grâce.[41]

Two months later, during a private dinner with Ceauşescu, Arafat excitedly bragged about his Khartoum operation. "Be careful," Ion Gheorghe Maurer, a Western-educated lawyer who had just retired as Romanian prime minister, told him. "No matter how high-up you are, you can still be convicted for killing and stealing." "Who, me? I never had anything to do with that operation," Arafat said, winking mischievously.[42] Shortly before the attack, American intelligence intercepted a phone conversation between Arafat and Khalil al-Wazir (aka Abu Jihad), the PLO's chief of operations, discussing an operation about to occur in Khartoum. In addition to the logistics, the intercepts revealed the code name for the operation—Nahr al-Bard—but owing to some mix-up between the National Security Agency and the State Department the warning reached Khartoum only on March 2, by which time the diplomats were already dead.[43]

Arafat was directly implicated in ordering the killing of the diplomats. Unaware of their execution, he personally contacted the terrorists' commander to ascertain that they understood the Nahr al-Bard code word, only to be told that the murders had already been committed. In a subsequent radio transmission from Arafat to his henchmen in the Saudi embassy in Khartoum, intercepted by the American embassy in Beirut, he told them that their mission was over: "Release [the] Saudi and Jordanian diplomats. Submit in courage to [the] Sudanese authorities to explain your just cause to [the] great Sudanese Arab masses and international opinion. We are with you on the same road. Glory and immortality to [the] martyrs of the Nahr al-Bard."[44]

Israelis and Americans are not the only ones to suffer from Arafat's callous disregard for human life. In the summer of 1976, when the Palestinian refugee camp of Tel Zaatar in Beirut was being besieged by Christian militias, backed by the Syrian army, Arafat ordered the camp's inhabitants not to surrender, knowing full well that they would be defeated and many of them slaughtered. The survivors themselves later accused Arafat of sacrificing them because he needed martyrs to attract world attention to their plight, and there were plenty of them. During the fifty-five-day siege and the massacres that came in its immediate wake, some thirty-five hundred Palestinians, mostly civilians, were killed. When Arafat came to visit the camp's refugees, temporarily accommodated in the nearby town of Damour, destroyed by the PLO a few months earlier and its Christian population slaughtered and expelled, several women stood by their hovels and shouted "traitor" at him, while others threw rotten vegetables at him.[45]

This unscrupulous sacrifice of his own people pales in comparison with Arafat's wider predilection to wreak havoc on some of the Arab states and societies that have hosted the Palestinians since 1948 and have facilitated their anti-Israel activities. Whenever the PLO has managed to gain a firm foothold in an Arab state, it's only a matter of time before Arafat's calling cards of violence, destruction, and death follow.

Jordan was the first to learn this lesson, when after the Six-Day War of 1967 it allowed the Palestinian organizations to use its territory as their foremost springboard for anti-Israel attacks. For King Hussein this was a means to pressure the Israelis to return the West Bank of his kingdom, which they occupied during the war. Arafat, however, had no intention of confining himself to the limited role ascribed to him by the Jordanian monarch. Instead, he sought to transform Jordan, with its large Palestinian population and its long border with Israel, into an Arab North Vietnam, the platform from which the Palestinian resistance would pursue its struggle against Israel until the eventual destruction of the Jewish state. Before long these two mutually exclusive visions put Arafat and Hussein on a collision course, as the king realized that, far from rewarding his hospitality, his Palestinian guests were progressively undermining the stability and well-being of his kingdom.

Palestinian defiance of Jordanian authority began from the moment of their arrival in Jordan, becoming increasingly brazen after the Karameh battle of March 1968, in which Palestinian guerrillas, with Jordanian army reinforcements, managed to hold out for some time against an Israeli raiding force. Though Palestinian casualties were far higher than on the Israeli side, and their qualified battlefield success owed as much to Jordanian help as to their own fighting ability, and while Arafat himself fled the battle at an early stage, he quickly turned Karameh into an historic watershed in Palestinian military annals and a major sales pitch for mass recruitment. Prior to the battle, Fatah had some two thousand men under arms. By August 1970 it had swelled to ten thousand fighters.[46]

As their power grew, the guerrillas established their own "state within a state" in Jordan, setting up autonomous governmental institutions in all spheres—military, political, and social. They ran their own police forces and courts, arresting and punishing people in total disregard of the law of the land. They set up roadblocks, where they levied illegal taxes, and roamed the streets of Amman at will, often attacking soldiers and policemen. Entire areas became inaccessible to Jordanian authorities. The Wahadat refugee camp near Amman was dubbed the Republic of Palestine, with the Palestinian flag flying at its entrance.

Between mid-1968 and the end of 1969 there were no fewer than five hundred violent clashes between the Palestinian guerrillas and the Jordanian army and security forces. The Palestinians kidnapped Arab diplomats and unfriendly Jordanian journalists, attacked government buildings, and publicly insulted the Jordanian flag in front of Jordanian subjects. Incidents of thuggery and crime abounded, including sexual molestation and rape and acts of vandalism against bakeries that left some of the population without bread. Recalling a particularly chilling incident, Zeid Rifai, chief of the Jordanian royal court, graphically described how "the *fedayeen* killed a soldier, beheaded him, and played soccer with his head in the area where he used to live."[47]

Arafat relished his newly gained prowess. Behaving like a feudal warlord, he spent his time touring guerrilla bases throughout Jordan, loosely overseeing the anarchy spread by his forces without making the slightest attempt to rein anyone in. Hussein's desperate attempts to pacify the situation were fruitless, as Arafat unflinchingly violated the numerous agreements he had signed with the king. Repeated clashes between February and June 1970, which claimed nearly a thousand lives, failed to convince Arafat to clamp down on the guerrillas. In the following months, Hussein narrowly escaped a number of attempts on his life, with Arafat himself implicated in at least one coup d'état, which he had plotted together with Jordanian officers. In August he even convened the Palestine National Council for a special meeting in Amman, which openly debated the issue of replacing the king. Infuriated by this gratuitous act of thanklessness and fearing for the survival of his kingdom in the face of growing anarchy, Hussein in September 1970 exploited the hijacking and subsequent blowing up of four Western airliners by PLO terrorists to move against the Palestinian organizations and, in a bloody war that resulted in horrendous atrocities on both sides and claimed thousands of lives, drove them out of Jordan. "The blame for the Jordanian mess which led to the Black September rests with Yasser Arafat, the one person who was capable of defusing the situation," a Palestinian biographer of Arafat commented.[48]

With his Jordanian base in ruins, Arafat quickly reestablished himself in Lebanon, which he occasionally had been using since the mid-1960s for terrorist attacks against Israeli civilian targets. As with Jordan, it did not take long before he helped turn his host country into an inferno, this time by playing a key role in triggering one of the bloodiest civil wars in modern Middle Eastern history, which raged for more than a decade and claimed hundreds of thousands of lives.

Lebanese-Palestinian relations had been strained from the moment Palestinian refugees began pouring into the country during the 1948 Palestine War. Viewing the new arrivals as cowards who had shamefully deserted their homeland expecting others to fight on their behalf, many Lebanese demanded the return of the refugees to Palestine, or at the very least the expulsion of young men of fighting age, many of whom had arrived under the pretext of volunteering for the pan-Arab forces that were being organized for intervention in Palestine. Camille Chamoun, then minister of the interior and the future president of Lebanon, publicly asserted in May 1948 that "at this decisive stage of the fighting the [Palestinians] have not remained so dignified in their stand; they lack organization and omitted to arm themselves as well as their enemy did. Many of them did not assist their brothers from nearby Arab countries who hastened to help them."[49]

In the following decades a fragile modus vivendi evolved between the Lebanese population and its Palestinian guests, whose stay turned out to be far more permanent than initially envisaged. While most Palestinians were denied Lebanese citizenship, thus being condemned to an inferior existence in squalid refugee camps with little hope of social mobility, Beirut was perhaps the one city where the Palestinians were most successfully integrated. Many of them, mainly Christians who managed to acquire Lebanese nationality, became bankers, businessmen, doctors, and academics.[50]

The mass arrival of the guerrillas in the early 1970s undermined this delicate coexistence as many Palestinians, especially in the refugee camps, turned on their Lebanese hosts. "Until the early 1970s, all Palestinian residents in our country feverishly professed to their being Lebanese," lamented a Lebanese Muslim intellectual. "Once the PLO established itself in the country, they suddenly reclaimed a Palestinian identity and began to look down on us."[51]

In a repeat of their Jordanian lawlessness, Palestinian guerrillas quickly turned the vibrant and thriving Lebanese state, whose capital Beirut was internationally acclaimed as the "Paris of the Middle East," into a hotbed of violence and anarchy. Several districts of Beirut and the refugee camps came under exclusive Palestinian control, so much so that they became generally known as the Fakhani Republic, after the Beirut district in which Arafat had set up his headquarters. So did substantial parts of southern Lebanon, or "Fatahland." In a flagrant violation of Lebanese sovereignty, the guerrillas set up roadblocks, took over buildings and drove out local residents, operated extortion rackets, protected criminals fleeing from Lebanese justice, requisitioned cars, opened unlicensed shops, bars, and nightclubs, and issued their own passes and permits. In short, "they behaved like urban gangsters or armed Mexican *banditos*."[52]

To make things worse, Arafat not only failed to restrain his forces but also became actively involved in internal Lebanese politics, which for more than a century had been plagued by a bitter feud between the country's Christian and Muslim communities. When on April 13, 1975, Christian militiamen ambushed a Palestinian bus and killed its twenty-eight passengers, in revenge for the killing of four Christians earlier that day, mortar and machine-gun battles between Palestinian guerrillas and Christian forces erupted all over Beirut, accompanied by wholesale acts of violence against hapless civilians. It was a familiar pattern, which would dominate Lebanon over the following eighteen months. Adding to the conflagration, Arafat supported a demand by the Lebanese leftist alliance to remove the Phalanges Christian party from government for its apparent involvement in the April 13 massacre, a decision that put the Palestinians squarely on one side of the historic Lebanese divide. "I remember literally screaming at him in my own house," the Palestinian academic Walid Khalidi, then based in Beirut, recalled, along with his desperate attempts to dissuade Arafat from taking sides. "I was really very angry because it just didn't make sense for him to say that. I told him that we as Palestinians had no business calling for the ostracism of the Phalangists, and that it would drive them all the way into the hands of the Israelis."[53]

By June 1976, the Lebanese government had exhausted its ability to contain the conflict and asked for Syrian intervention. In the following years, Lebanon would gradually come under Syrian sway without the abating of the civil war. Syria prevented a clear-cut military outcome by supporting the weaker force then turning against it once it had gained the upper hand, all in an effort to strengthen its say in Lebanese affairs. The Christians sought to counterbalance Syria's heavy-handed presence by seeking Israeli help, and in June 1982 Israel invaded Lebanon in force, further escalating the conflict. Within three months Israel had destroyed the PLO's military infrastructure up to Beirut and expelled Arafat and many of his terrorists from Lebanon. A year later, Arafat attempted to return but was yet again driven out, this time by the Syrians, who had also engineered a revolt against him within his own organization, the Fatah.

Yet this long and painful record of mayhem and destruction seems to have left little impact on Arafat. He has never publicly acknowledged any responsibility for the Black September tragedy, let alone the Lebanese civil war, and in fact looks back on his Lebanese days with fondness. "You see what happened after we departed from Lebanon, these dirty groups . . ." he told a pair of biographers in 1989 in a diatribe against the Shi'ite militant organization Hizbullah. "While I was there, I could keep these dirty groups under control!"[54] He bragged similarly four years later in an attempt to reassure Israelis of his ability to enforce law and order in the territories that were to be placed under his control as part of the Oslo accords. "I controlled the whole of Lebanon," he said. "Do you think I cannot control Palestine?"[55]

For the many Israelis and Arabs who remembered the PLO's excesses in Lebanon, these words offered anything but comfort. "Arafat wronged Jordan and King Hussein expelled him," Mustafa Tlas, the Syrian minister of defense, observed. "He wronged Syria and Hafez al-Assad kicked him out . . . And in Tunis, the Tunisians will expel him as well. He causes destruction wherever he goes."[56]

Tlas was wrong in one important respect. Rather than being expelled by the Tunisians, Arafat was saved by the Israeli government headed by Yitzhak Rabin, which offered him the Oslo peace deal. As a man who had made a political career out of war, the promise of peace came to Arafat when he needed it most.

2

The Road to Oslo

Palestine was lost in blood and iron, and it can only be recovered by blood and iron; and blood and iron have nothing to do with philosophies and theories.

—Yasser Arafat, August 2, 1968

On November 29, 1947, the UN General Assembly passed a resolution calling for the partition of Palestine into two independent states—one Jewish, the other Arab—linked in an economic union. The city of Jerusalem was to be placed under an international regime, with its residents given the right to citizenship in either the Jewish or the Arab states. Thirty-three UN members supported the resolution, thirteen voted against, and ten abstained, including Great Britain, which had ruled Palestine since the early 1920s under a League of Nations mandate.

For Jews all over the world this was the fulfillment of a millenarian yearning for national rebirth in the ancestral homeland. For Arabs it was an unmitigated disaster, an act of betrayal by the international community that surrendered an integral part of the Arab world to foreign invaders. In Tel Aviv, crowds danced in the streets. In the Arab capitals there were violent demonstrations. "We would rather die than accept minority rights in a prospective Jewish state," said Hajj Amin Husseini, head of the Arab Higher Committee (AHC), the effective government of the Palestinian Arabs, as the General Assembly was about to cast its vote. His deputy, Jamal Husseini, wrote to UN Secretary-General Trygve Lie that "The Arabs of Palestine . . . will never submit or yield to any Power going to Palestine to enforce partition. The only way to establish partition is first to wipe them out—man, woman, and child."[1]

The 1948 Palestine War was probably the most important Middle Eastern armed confrontation since the destruction of the Ottoman empire and the creation of a new regional order in the wake of the First World War. By the time fighting ended in the summer of 1949 Israel, albeit at the exorbitant human cost of 1 percent of its population, had survived Arab attempts to destroy it at birth and asserted its control over wider territories than those assigned to it by the UN Partition Resolution.

The Palestinian Arab community was profoundly shattered. Even before the outbreak of hostilities, many of its members had already fled their homes and still larger numbers left before war reached their front door. By April 1948, a month before Israel's declaration of independence, and at a time when the Arabs appeared to be winning the war, some 100,000 Palestinians, mostly from the main urban centers of Jaffa, Haifa, and Jerusalem and from villages in the coastal plain, had left. Within another month those numbers had nearly doubled, and by early June, according to an internal Israeli report, some 390,000 Palestinians had fled. By the time the fighting was over, the number of refugees had risen to between 550,000 and 600,000, nearly half of Palestine's Arab population.[2] Muhammad Nimr al-Khatib, a prominent Palestinian leader during the 1948 war, summed up his nation's dispersion: "The Palestinians had neighboring Arab states which opened their borders and doors to the refugees, while the Jews had no alternative but to triumph or to die."[3]

From the moment of the refugees' arrival, tension between the Palestinians and the host societies ran high. The Palestinians considered the Arab world derelict for having issued wild promises of military support on which they never made good. Meanwhile, many Arab host states regarded the Palestinians as having shamefully deserted their homeland while expecting others to fight for them.[4]

In a letter to the Syrian representative at the UN, Jamal Husseini argued that "The regular [Arab] armies did not enable the inhabitants of the country to defend themselves, but merely facilitated their escape from Palestine." The prominent Palestinian leader Emile Ghoury was even more forthright. In an interview with the London *Telegraph* in August 1948, Ghoury blamed the Arab states for the creation of the refugee problem; so did the organizers of protest demonstrations that took place in many West Bank towns on the first anniversary of Israel's establishment.[5] During a fact-finding mission to Gaza in June 1949, Sir John Troutbeck, head of the British Middle East office in Cairo and no friend to Israel or the Jews, was surprised to discover that while the refugees

> express no bitterness against the Jews (or for that matter against the Americans or ourselves) they speak with the utmost bitterness of the Egyptians and other Arab states. "We know who our enemies are," they will say, and they are referring to their Arab brothers who, they declare, persuaded them unnecessarily to leave their homes.[6]

The prevailing conviction among Palestinians that they had been, and remained, the victims of their fellow Arabs rather than of Israeli aggression was grounded not only in experience but in the larger facts of inter-Arab politics. Indeed, had the Jewish state lost the war, its territory would not have fallen to the Palestinians but would have been divided among the invading Arab forces.

As occupiers after 1948 of, respectively, the Gaza Strip and the West Bank, neither Egypt nor Jordan ever allowed Palestinian self-determination. Their purposes were better served by forcing the Palestinian refugees to remain in squalid, harshly supervised camps, where they could serve as a rallying point for anti-Israel sentiment. "The Palestinians are useful to the Arab states as they are," Egyptian president Gamal Abdel Nasser candidly responded to an inquiring Western reporter in 1956. "We will always see that they do not become too powerful. Can you imagine yet another nation on the shores of the eastern Mediterranean!"[7]

Against this backdrop, it was almost a foregone conclusion for the young generation of politically aware Palestinians to attempt to take its fate into its own hands rather than entrust it to the Arab states. Numerous secret political groups and societies flowered throughout the Middle East during the 1950s and early '60s to discuss the various courses of action for national deliverance. Most of them left no lasting impact, yet two groups quickly emerged to play a crucial role in the development of Palestinian nationalism: the Arab Nationalists Movement (ANM), parent to the Popular Front for the Liberation of Palestine (PFLP) and the

Popular Democratic Front for the Liberation of Palestine (PDFLP), and the Movement for the Liberation of Palestine, better known by its Arabic name Fatah. The ANM was established in 1951 by a group of students at the American University of Beirut, headed by medical student George Habash, son of a Greek Orthodox merchant from Lydda, and Hani al-Hindi, scion of a respected Damascene family. Fatah was formed in Kuwait seven years later by five young professionals—Yasser Arafat, Khalil al-Wazir (aka Abu Jihad), Salah Khalaf (Abu Iyad), Farouq Qaddoumi, and Khaled al-Hassan—of whom Arafat quickly established himself as primus inter pares due to his unrivaled energy and utter ruthlessness.

Both groups considered the Arab states the main culprits of the 1948 disaster and were driven by a relentless yearning for revenge and redemption of lost honor. They also shared an unwavering belief in the preeminence of "armed struggle" for national deliverance. Mesmerized by the writings of the African thinker Franz Fanon on the Algerian war of independence, especially the concept of "sacred violence" as a means to national self-purification, Fatah founders viewed the armed struggle not only as the sole means for fighting Israel but also as the vehicle for Palestinian national revival. "We, the people of Palestine, are in need of a revolutionary upheaval in our daily lives after having been afflicted by the Catastrophe [of 1948] with the worst diseases of dependency, division, and defeatism," read a Fatah memorandum. "This upheaval in [our] lives will not occur except through our practice of the armed struggle." The organization's hymn put the idea in equally unmistakable terms:

> Farewell, tears and sorrow,
> Farewell, sighs and grief,
> Our people has come to loathe you;
> Welcome, blood and heroic death.[8]

There was, however, a fundamental difference between the strategic outlook of the two nascent organizations. Viewing pan-Arab unity as a prerequisite for the "liberation" of Palestine, the ANM tied its colors to Nasser's tireless drive to unify the Arab world under his leadership, concentrating its efforts on confronting the conservative and pro-Western regimes rather than on fighting Israel. Fatah maintained that Palestine's liberation would pave the road to Arab unification rather than the other way around, bracing itself for the initiation of armed attacks on Israeli targets to the exasperation of Egypt's President Nasser, who feared being dragged into a new confrontation with Israel not on his own terms.

In January 1964, the first all-Arab summit convened in Cairo at Nasser's initiative and instructed Ahmad Shuqeiri, a Lebanon-born politician of mixed Egyptian, Hijazi, and Turkish descent who since October 1963 had served as Palestine's representative in the Arab League, to "lay the proper foundations for organizing the Palestinian people and enabling it to fulfill its role in the liberation of its homeland and its self-determination." Four months later, a gathering of 422 Palestinian activists in East Jerusalem, then under Jordanian rule, established the Palestine Liberation Organization, approved its two founding documents—the organization's Basic Constitution and the Palestinian National Covenant—and reconstituted itself as the Palestine National Council (PNC). This semi-parliamentary body would be the PLO's supreme decision-making body, with wide legislative and policy making powers.[9]

While the ANM welcomed the creation of the PLO as "the beginning of a long and hard road to united Palestinian action" that should be encouraged and supported, Fatah viewed this development with considerable alarm, if not outright hostility. To Arafat and his fellow activists, Shuqeiri epitomized the older generation of Arab politicians responsible for the catastrophe befalling the Palestinian people, whereas Fatah saw themselves as the "revenge generation," destined to redeem lost honor and restore usurped rights. As an Arab League appointee with no Palestinian constituency of his own, Shuqeiri, and by implication the PLO, were bound to be subservient to the interests of the Arab regimes, and more specifically to Nasser's political agenda. It was precisely this subordination of the Palestine cause to inter-Arab politics that, in Fatah's view, had constituted the root cause of the Nakba. As a caption accompanying a picture of a derelict Palestinian village in its official bulletin, *Our Palestine,* pointedly noted: "Houses demolished as a result of the designs of the Arab League in 1948."[10]

Fatah leaders also feared that the PLO, and especially its envisaged military arm the Palestine Liberation Army (PLA), would deprive their fledgling organization of vital political, financial, and material resources, as well as potential recruits. In early 1964 Fatah held a series of meetings with Shuqeiri in an attempt to convince him to establish tacit coordination between the PLO and Fatah similar to that between the pre-1948 Jewish Agency and its clandestine military arm, the *Hagana*. When the proposal was dismissed out of hand, Fatah remained at arm's length with regard to the PLO. It sent delegates to the Jerusalem congress, in an attempt to exploit this unique gathering as a platform for winning new supporters, yet refused to participate in the PLO's permanent institutions.

In an attempt to overshadow the PLO and project itself as the true champion of the Palestinian cause, Fatah in early 1965 launched its "armed struggle" against Israel. The beginning was unimpressive, if not embarrassing. The first attack, pompously announced by a Fatah statement on January 1, 1965, never took place, as a Lebanese patrol detained the raiding parties before they could cross the border into Israel. The following night, another team managed to sneak into Israel and laid an explosive charge in a water canal near the Lake of the Galilee, but this failed to detonate. Fatah, however, steadily intensified its attacks, followed later by the ANM and a number of smaller militant groups. By the outbreak of the Six-Day War of June 1967, according to Israeli sources, the various Palestinian groups had mounted 113 sabotage and terrorist attacks against Israeli targets (though Fatah alone claimed 300).[11] This campaign gained considerable momentum in the wake of the war, as the guerrilla organizations, Fatah in particular, transformed Jordan into a springboard for terrorist attacks against Israel.

Initially frowned upon by the PLO and its foremost patron, President Nasser, who feared an undesirable regional conflagration, Fatah's militancy brought it handsome dividends. The stated objective of Fatah and its new sponsor in Damascus, the radical faction of the Ba'th Party, which seized power in February 1966, believed in "a popular war as the only means of liberating Palestine." Yet as this terrorist campaign failed to spark a major escalation (killing merely eleven Israelis and wounding sixty-seven between January 1965 and June 1967), while simultaneously enhancing the prestige of its perpetrators and exposing the PLO's pathetic passivity, Cairo's overtones became more approving in nature.

In a desperate bid to arrest the decline in the PLO's fortunes, in the spring of 1967 Shuqeiri changed tack and tried to lure Fatah into the

PLO through generous promises of political coordination as well as financial and material aid. It was now Fatah's turn to distance itself. Certain that Shuqeiri's days at the helm were numbered, Arafat and his associates were not interested in a partnership but rather in a takeover of the PLO and decided to wait things out. It was a good strategy. On December 24, 1967, Shuqeiri was forced to resign his posts as PLO chairman and Palestine's representative to the Arab League, and he was replaced by Yahaya Hammuda, a left-wing member of the executive committee and clearly a transitional appointment. Hammuda was not a figure of national stature and had no power base of his own. More important, Nasser seemed increasingly disposed to embracing Fatah as the frontrunner of the Palestinian national struggle.[12] The group had unequivocally established itself as the largest and most broadly based of the Palestinian guerrilla organizations, boasting at least two thousand men under arms as well as a rapidly expanding network of nonmilitary institutions responsible for many aspects of Palestinian daily life.

For his part, Arafat was pining for an official pan-Arab recognition of Fatah that would institutionalize its growing preeminence, and while Nasser lost much of his prewar aura following his defeat in the Six-Day War, he nevertheless remained the main power broker in the Arab world by a wide margin. This convergence of interests culminated in an historic meeting between Arafat and Nasser in April 1968.

Arriving at the president's residence wearing his ubiquitous pistol, Arafat was asked by security to remove it for the duration of the meeting. He refused, and Nasser was promptly consulted about what should happen next. The Egyptian security services had long been concerned by the association between Arafat and other Fatah leaders, notably Abu Iyad and Abu Jihad, and the militant religious organization the Muslim Brethren, which for decades had been seeking to undermine the Egyptian regime. In 1948 the Brethren assassinated the Egyptian prime minister Nuqrashi Pasha, and they did not shun attempts on Nasser's life. The Egyptian president was thus warned that Fatah could be plotting to murder him and under no circumstances should he receive an armed Arafat.

Nasser decided to allow Arafat keep his gun during the meeting. "My intelligence people are telling me that you insist on bringing your gun because you intend to kill me," he told Arafat as he entered his office. "At this very moment that is what they are saying."

The ever theatrical Arafat did not fail to rise to the occasion. Slowly and deliberately he unbuckled his gun belt. Then with both hands he offered Nasser the belt and the pistol. "Mr. President," he said, "your intelligence people are wrong. I offer you my freedom fighter's gun as proof of that fact."

A broad smile crept onto Nasser's face. "No. You keep it. You need it, and more," he replied. "I would be more than glad if you could represent the Palestinian people and the Palestinian will to resist, politically by your presence and militarily by your actions," he added, advising his guest to preserve Fatah's independence from the Arab regimes and to draw up a political program that would clarify the organization's objectives. Revolutionaries had the right to dream, he argued, but they also had to live in the real world. And if they were truly to serve the interests of their people, they had to be practical and draw a clear distinction between what they desired and what they could actually attain, at least pro forma.[13]

By way of rewarding Nasser's generosity and facilitating his efforts on their behalf, in June 1968 Arafat and his Fatah stalwarts found the winning formula that would allow them to feign moderation while renouncing none of their fundamental articles of faith. In contrast to Shuqeiri's spurious bombast, notably his repeated pledge to "drive Israel into the sea," Fatah asserted that the liberation of Palestine did not mean the expulsion of the country's entire Jewish population but rather the destruction of Israel as a political entity and the establishment of a democratic multidenominational entity on its ruins.[14] "Muslims and Christians live side by side in the Arab countries," Arafat told *Der Spiegel* magazine. "I believe that the same option will be open to the Jews. The Jews have lived in Arab Palestine in the past in peace without experiencing racial or religious discrimination. The situation continued until the emergence of Zionism. We want to build up our country regardless of racial or religious discrimination." Eight months later, in February 1969, the idea was officially endorsed by the PNC, which defined the objective of the Palestinian people as the creation of "a free and democratic society in Palestine, for all Palestinians, including Muslims, Christians, and Jews, and [the liberation of] Palestine and its people from the domination of international Zionism."[15]

Nasser fully reciprocated this display of pragmatism. Immediately after his meeting with Arafat, he publicly took Fatah under his wing, announcing his readiness to support and arm the "resistance movement," and then had the name of the Voice of Palestine radio broadcasts from Cairo changed to Sawt al-Asifa (Voice of the Storm, Fatah's military arm), giving Fatah full control over these broadcasts. He also attached Arafat to his entourage during his visit to Moscow in July 1968, and arranged Arafat's first ever meeting with the Soviet leadership. Later that month, with Nasser's blessing, Fatah and the other guerrilla organizations joined the PNC for the first time and, in a few months, Fatah had gained complete control over its apparatus. On February 3, 1969, in the presence of President Nasser, the PNC convened in Cairo for its fifth annual session and duly elected Arafat chairman of the PLO's executive committee.

Pragmatism, however, must not be mistaken for moderation. While turning its vision of "a free and democratic society in Palestine for all Palestinians, including Muslims, Christians, and Jews" into an effective propaganda device, especially in its dealings with unsuspecting international audiences who failed to grasp its true meaning, Fatah and the PLO had never hidden from their own constituents the idea that their political slogan was little more than a euphemism for the destruction of Israel.

The new "free and democratic society" was perceived not as a true partnership between equal groups sharing sovereignty over a specific territory, but rather as an Arab-Muslim state in which Jews would be reduced to a permanent minority status, a modern-day version of the *ahl al-dhimma* system of "protected non-Muslim minorities" that had existed since Islam's early days. In the words of the Arab-American academic Edward Said: "I don't find the idea of a Jewish state terribly interesting . . . the Jews are a minority everywhere. They are a minority in America. They can certainly be a minority in Israel."[16]

The PLO's pretence that those Jewish citizens of the defunct state of Israel who would like to become citizens of the new Arab Palestine would be allowed to do so was patently false. Its founding document, the Palestinian National Covenant, revised in July 1968 to reflect the more militant line of Fatah and the guerrilla organizations, states explicitly that only those Jews "who were normally resident in Palestine up to the beginning of the Zionist invasion are Palestinians."[17] Since most of Israel's citizens are an integral part of this very "Zionist invasion," the practical meaning of this declaration is that the prospective Palestinian state would be virtually *Judenrein*.

Arafat's idyllic picture of peaceful Arab-Jewish coexistence in Palestine prior to the "Zionist invasion" is likewise at odds with the historical record. Persecution of Jews in the Islamic world would never reach the scale of Christian Europe, but that did not spare the "Jews of Islam" (to borrow historian Bernard Lewis's phraseology) from centuries of legally institutionalized inferiority, humiliating social restrictions, and the sporadic rapacity of local officials and the Muslim population at large. In pre-Zionist Palestine, Arab peasants revolting in the 1830s against a military conscription imposed by Egyptian authorities took the occasion to ravage the Jewish communities of Safed and Jerusalem. When Arab forces arrived from Egypt to quell the insurrection, the Jews of Hebron were slaughtered. Jews could not even perform their religious observance in peace without paying bribes to their Muslim neighbors, while their religious sites and places of worship were regularly desecrated. The Wailing Wall, remnant of King Solomon's Temple and Judaism's holiest shrine, "drew the spite and malice of the resident Arabs, who took every opportunity to harass the hapless worshippers, scattering broken glass through the alleys leading to the Wall, dumping their garbage and sewage against it, fouling it with urine and feces."[18]

For all their protestations to the contrary, Arabs have never really distinguished between Zionists, Israelis, and Jews, and often use these terms interchangeably. Indeed, the fact that Arab anti-Zionism has invariably reflected a hatred well beyond the "normal" level of hostility to be expected of a prolonged and bitter conflict would seem to suggest that, rather than being a response to Zionist activity, it is a manifestation of long-standing prejudice that has been brought out into the open by the vicissitudes of the Arab-Israel conflict. As Lutfi Abdel Azim, the editor of a prestigious Egyptian weekly, wrote in 1982, three years *after* the conclusion of an Egyptian-Israeli peace treaty:

A Jew is a Jew, and hasn't changed for thousands of years. He is base, contemptible, scorns all moral values, gnaws on live flesh and sucks blood for a pittance. The Jewish Merchant of Venice is no different from the arch-executioners of Deir Yasin and those at the [Palestinian] refugee camps. Both are similar models of inhuman depravity.[19]

This uncompromising commitment to Israel's destruction and the expulsion of most of its Jewish population, so profoundly enshrined in many of the Palestinian Covenant's articles, was matched only by the extremity of the means used to achieve these ends. "Armed struggle is the only way to liberate Palestine, and is thus strategic, not tactical," states the Covenant's Article 9, again reflecting Fatah's obsession with violence. "The Palestinian Arab people hereby affirm their unwavering determination to carry on the armed struggle and to press on towards popular revolution for the liberation of and return to their homeland."[20]

It was soon obvious that "armed struggle" was essentially a handy euphemism for outright terrorism. Only a small fraction of the armed attacks by Fatah and the other Palestinian organizations, both prior to the Six-Day War and in its aftermath, was directed against military targets, with most attacks aimed at innocent civilians. Palestinian terrorists planted bombs in public places, fired at civilian vehicles, and raided villages and towns, taking hostages and murdering at will. In the summer of 1968, the Palestinian organizations widened the geographical scope of their terrorist campaign beyond Israel by hijacking an El Al airliner en route from Rome to Tel Aviv. As Israel tightened security measures on its airplanes, the PLO began targeting Western airlines, and in February 1970 blew up a Swiss airliner in midair, killing all forty-seven people on board. It also launched a sustained terrorist campaign against Israeli and Jewish targets throughout Europe, most notably the attack on the Israeli team during the 1972 Munich Olympics, which resulted in the killing of eleven athletes.

In May 1972, terrorists massacred twenty-seven passengers and wounded eighty in Israel's Lod international airport. Exactly two years later, PLO terrorists held ninety children hostage at a school in the small town of Maalot in northern Israel. When negotiations broke down and Israeli troops stormed the building, the terrorists machine-gunned the children, killing twenty-seven and wounding many others.

Nor was the Covenant's talk about a "popular revolution" any less euphemistic. Arafat's tireless efforts to entice the residents of the West Bank and Gaza into a popular struggle against Israel in the immediate wake of the Six-Day War failed to make any real headway. Here Israel's counterinsurgency measures must be given credit along with the low level of national consciousness among the Palestinians and the sheer rapidity and scope of the improvements in their standard of living under Israeli rule. "The war that Arafat was waging against Israel was not true guerrilla warfare," wrote Palestinian author Said Aburish. "Unlike the then recent examples of the Algerians and the Vietnamese, and the resistance against the Japanese in China and the Germans in Yugoslavia during the Second World War, Arafat was operating not on home ground but from safe bases outside Israel."[21]

In an effort to cover up this embarrassing contradiction, Fatah adopted the slogan that "there is no difference between inside and outside." But there was a difference, and a rather fundamental one. The collapse and dispersion of Palestinian society following the 1948 defeat had shattered an already fragile communal fabric, and the subsequent physical separation of the various parts of the Palestinian diaspora prevented the crystallization of a national identity. Arab host regimes actively colluded in discouraging any such sense of national identity from arising. Upon occupying the West Bank during the 1948 war, King Abdallah moved quickly to erase all traces of corporate Palestinian identity. On April 4, 1950, the territory was formally annexed by Jordan, its residents becoming Jordanian citizens who were increasingly integrated into the kingdom's economic, political, and social structures.

For its part, the Egyptian government showed no desire to annex the Gaza Strip but had instead ruled the newly acquired area as an occupied military zone. This did not imply support of Palestinian nationalism, however, or foster any sort of collective political awareness among the Palestinians. The local population was kept under tight control, was denied Egyptian citizenship, and was subjected to severe restrictions on travel.

The deep divide between the "inside" and the "outside" was substantially widened by the astounding social and economic progress made by the Palestinian population of the West Bank and the Gaza Strip under Israeli occupation. At its inception, conditions in the territories were bleak. Life expectancy was low, malnutrition, infectious diseases, and child mortality were rife, and the level of education was very poor. Prior to the 1967 war, fewer than 60 percent of all male adults had been employed, with unemployment among refugees running as high as 83 percent. Within a brief period after the war, Israeli occupation led to dramatic improvements in their quality of life, placing the population of the territories ahead of most of their Arab neighbors.

In the economic sphere, most of this progress was the result of access to the far larger and more advanced Israeli economy. The number of Palestinians working in Israel rose from zero in 1967 to 66,000 in 1975 and 109,000 by 1986, accounting for 35 percent of the employed population of the West Bank and 45 percent in Gaza. Close to two thousand industrial plants, employing almost half of the workforce, were established in the territories under Israeli rule.

During the 1970s, the West Bank and Gaza constituted the fourth fastest growing economy in the world—ahead of such "wonders" as Singapore, Hong Kong, and Korea, and substantially ahead of Israel itself. Although GNP per capita grew somewhat more slowly, the rate was still high by international standards, with per capita GNP expanding tenfold between 1968 and 1991 from $165 to $1,715 (compared with Jordan's $1,050, Egypt's $600, Turkey's $1,630, and Tunisia's $1,440).

Under Israeli rule, the Palestinians also made vast progress in social welfare. Perhaps most significantly, mortality rates in the West Bank and Gaza fell by more than two-thirds between 1970 and 1990, while life expectancy rose from forty-eight years in 1967 to seventy-two in 2000 (compared to an average of sixty-eight years for all the countries of the Middle East and North Africa). Israeli medical programs reduced the infant-mortality rate of 60 per 1,000 live births in 1968 to 15 per 1,000 in 2000 (in Iraq the rate is 64, in Egypt 40, in Jordan 23, in Syria 22). In addition, under a systematic program of inoculation, childhood diseases like polio, whooping cough, tetanus, and measles were eradicated.

No less remarkable were advances in the Palestinians' standard of living. By 1986, 92.8 percent of the population in the West Bank and Gaza had electricity around the clock, as compared with 20.5 percent in 1967; 85 percent had running water in dwellings, as compared to 16 percent in 1967; 84 percent had electric or gas ranges for cooking, as compared to 4 percent in 1967; and so on for refrigerators, televisions, and cars.

Finally, and perhaps most important, during the two decades preceding the intifada of the late 1980s, the number of schoolchildren in the territories grew by 102 percent, and the number of classes by 99 percent, though the population itself had grown by only 28 percent. Even more dramatic was the progress in higher education. At the onset of the Israeli occupation of Gaza and the West Bank, not a single university existed in these territories. By the early 1990s, there were seven such institutions, boasting some 16,500 students, as compared with six in Israel or seven in the Irish Republic. Illiteracy rates dropped to 14 percent of adults over age fifteen, compared with 69 percent in Morocco, 61 percent in Egypt, 45 percent in Tunisia, and 44 percent in Syria.[22]

All this means that while the PLO's constituency consisted of Diaspora refugees who had predominantly originated from northern Israel and who wanted to return to their dwellings in territory that was now part of the state of Israel, the current residents of the West Bank and the Gaza Strip wanted to get on with their lives and take advantage of the opportunities afforded by Israeli rule. Had the West Bank eventually been returned to Jordan, its residents, all of whom had been Jordanian citizens before 1967, might well have reverted to that status. Alternatively, had Israel prevented the spread of the PLO's influence in the territories, something that was perfectly within its capacity, a local leadership better attuned to the interests and desires of the people and more amenable to peaceful coexistence with Israel might have emerged.

Yet even as the PLO proclaimed its ongoing commitment to the destruction of the Jewish state, the Israelis did surprisingly little to limit its political influence in the territories. The publication of pro-PLO editorials was permitted in the local press, and anti-Israel activities by PLO supporters were tolerated as long as they did not involve overt incitements to violence. Israel also allowed the free flow of PLO-controlled funds, a deluded policy justified by Minister of Defense Ezer Weizmann in 1978: "It does not matter that they get money from the PLO, as long as they don't build arms factories with it."[23]

Nor, with very few exceptions, did Israel encourage the formation of Palestinian political institutions that might serve as a counterweight to the PLO. As a result, the PLO gradually established itself as the predominant force in the territories, relegating the pragmatic traditional leadership to the fringes of the political system. By the mid-1970s, the

PLO had made itself into the "sole representative of the Palestinian people," and in short order Jordan and Egypt washed their hands of the West Bank and Gaza. Whatever the desires of the people living in the territories was irrelevant, as the PLO had vowed from the moment of its inception 1964—well before the Six-Day War—to pursue its "revolution until victory," that is, until the destruction of the Jewish state. "In the name of the Palestinian revolution I hereby declare that we shall oppose the establishment of this state to the last member of the Palestinian people," Arafat reprimanded a group of West Bank leaders, who had pleaded with him shortly after the Black September calamity that the PLO content itself with a state in the West Bank and the Gaza Strip. "For if ever such a state is established it will spell the end of the whole Palestinian cause."[24]

It is true that in its twelfth session, in June 1974, the PNC adopted a political program that called for the creation of an "independent combatant national authority for the people over every part of Palestinian territory that is liberated." Yet this had nothing to do with acceptance of a two-state solution—of Israel and a Palestinian state in the West Bank and Gaza, as suggested by PLO apologists. With Israeli society failing to crumble under the weight of the terrorist campaign, and its army successfully defeating a surprise Egyptian-Syrian attack in the Yom Kippur War of October 1973, Arafat and his associates begrudgingly concluded that the destruction of the Jewish state could not be achieved all at once but would rather have to be accomplished through a graduated or "phased" strategy. They were further pushed in this direction by Egypt's President Anwar Sadat, who sought to translate the momentum created by the 1973 war into concrete political gains, by their growing alarm over Jordan's energetic attempts to regain its influence in the West Bank, and by the more outspoken readiness of "inside" politicians to accept a "two-state solution." Yet for all these pressures, the PLO leadership never lost sight of its ultimate goal. In the words of Abu Iyad, Fatah's principal ideologue: "Until we achieve the strategic aim we need a safe base, whose fate should not be similar to the one in Jordan . . . Gaining even twenty-three percent of Palestine is an interim achievement."[25]

Indeed, nearly every article of the "phased plan" resonates rejection of Israel's legitimacy and commitment to its destruction. Its preamble equates regional peace with the creation of a Palestinian state on Israel's ruins as stipulated by the Palestinian National Covenant: "It is impossible for a permanent and just peace to be established in the area unless our Palestinian people recover all their national rights, and, first and foremost, their rights to return and to self-determination on the whole of the soil of their homeland."[26]

This would make the various UN proposals for Middle East peace, passed in the wake of the Six-Day War, null and void. The main proposal, Resolution 242, passed by the Security Council in November 1967, recognized Israel's right to secure existence and established the principle of "land for peace" as the cornerstone of future Arab-Israeli peace negotiations. Israel, for its part, was asked to withdraw "from territories occupied in the recent conflict"—the Sinai Peninsula, the Golan Heights, the West Bank, and the Gaza Strip. (The absence of the definite article "the" before "territories," which, had it been included, would have required a *complete* Israeli withdrawal, was no accident; the resolution, issued a mere six months after Israel's astounding triumph over the concerted Arab attempt to obliterate the Jewish state, reflected an awareness of the existential threat posed by its pre-1967 boundaries.) The UN Security Council expected negotiations between Israel and the Arabs to produce a more defensible frontier, one consistent with, in the resolution's other key formulation, the right of every state in the region "to live in peace with secure and recognized boundaries."

Not surprisingly the PLO quickly denounced the resolution as a "Zionist plot" aimed at obliterating Palestinian national existence. "We have had enough of United Nations resolutions and recommendations," protested Arafat. "This is why our people have taken up arms and have come to realize that a revolutionary war of liberation is the only way to achieve their aims."[27] An official PLO statement was even more forthright:

This resolution was concocted in the corridors of the United Nations to accord [with] the Zionist racist colonial illegal occupation in Palestine. . . . Acceptance of the provisions embodied in this resolution is a treasonable act not only against the Palestinian people but against the whole Arab nation.[28]

The "phased plan" was somewhat more tempered in its language yet no less categorical in its disavowal of the resolution. "Resolution 242 . . . obliterates the national right of our people and deals with the cause of our people as a problem of refugees," read its first article. "The Council therefore refuses to have anything to do with this resolution at any level, Arab or international, including the Geneva Conference." Article 3 asserts more specifically that "the PLO will struggle against any scheme for the establishment of a Palestinian entity the price of which is recognition, conciliation, secure borders, [and] renunciation of the national right."

Having dismissed out of hand the notion of reconciliation with Israel, the phased plan outlined in some detail its ultimate goal: "Any liberation step that is achieved represents a step for continuing [the efforts] to achieve the PLO strategy for the establishment of the Palestinian democratic state stipulated in the resolutions of the previous national councils." Dispelling any remaining doubts about the PLO's real agenda, Article 8 detailed the strategy to be adopted for the "complete liberation" of Palestine:

> The Palestinian national authority, after its establishment, will struggle for the unity of the confrontation states for the sake of completing the liberation of all Palestinian soil and as a step on the road toward total Arab unity.

Interestingly, Israel was not the only state whose destruction was envisaged by the phased plan. The Hashemite kingdom of Jordan was also destined to be subverted by a joint "Jordanian-Palestinian national front" and replaced by "a democratic national authority in close contact with the Palestinian entity that is established through the struggle."[29] And yet rather than reprimand this intended obliteration of a fellow Arab state, four months after the adoption of the phased strategy, on October 28, 1974, an Arab League summit in Rabat, the Moroccan capital, designated the PLO as the "sole legitimate representative" of the Palestinian people, promising to finance it to the tune of $50 million a year. Two weeks later, on November 14, Arafat scored a spectacular propaganda coup when he became the first nonstate leader to address the UN General Assembly. Soon afterward, the United Nations granted observer status to the PLO.

What made this achievement all the more extraordinary was that it involved no quid pro quo from the Palestinians. The PLO had been required to neither renounce its commitment to the destruction of two member states of the United Nations (Israel and Jordan) nor even eschew terrorism. Quite the contrary, not only did the phased plan specifically designate the so-called armed struggle, or rather terrorism, as the PLO's foremost means of political communication, but within ten days of Arafat's speech—on the very day the General Assembly voted to grant official status to the PLO—Palestinian terrorists hijacked a British airliner in Dubai, eventually flying it to Tunisia where a passenger was killed. Two months later, in January 1975, PLO terrorists mounted two additional attacks on Israeli airliners at Paris's Orly Airport.

During the following decade, Palestinian terrorists launched numerous attacks on Israeli and Western targets. These ranged from the hijacking of a plane to the Ugandan town of Entebbe (where Israeli commandos rescued all but three passengers), to an attack on a passenger terminal in Istanbul, to the hijacking of an Israeli bus and the murder of twenty-six civilians, to a grenade attack on Jewish children in Antwerp and the shooting of civilians in Brussels. While all these atrocities were taking place, the United Nations declared its first International Day of Solidarity with the Palestinian people and passed a resolution equating Zionism with racism. Meanwhile Arafat met with Austrian chancellor Bruno Kreisky, former West German chancellor Willy Brandt, the prime minister of Spain, and the president of Portugal.[30]

In these circumstances where terrorism "was proving itself more effective than any form of diplomacy,"[31] Arafat felt no need to abandon his outright recalcitrance despite repeated attempts by anxious third parties to drive him to moderation. In the late 1970s the U.S. administration informed Arafat of its readiness to inaugurate Israeli-Palestinian peace negotiations should he accept Resolution 242, with a reservation to be added by the PLO (accepted by the United States) that stipulated an insistence on the national rights of the Palestinian people, as well as Palestinian self-determination. Arafat categorically turned down the offer, as he'd done with all similar offers. "Edward, I want you to tell [Secretary of State Cyrus] Vance that we're not interested," he told Edward Said, who had passed him the administration's offer.

We don't want the Americans. The Americans have stabbed us in the back.
This is a lousy deal. We want Palestine. We're not interested in bits of Palestine. We don't want to negotiate with the Israelis. We're going to fight.[32]

It was only in November 1988, more than two decades after the resolution's passage, that an extraordinary session of the Palestine National
Congress, convened in Algiers, declared the establishment of an independent Palestinian state and accepted Resolution 242. Remarkable as
this decision appeared at the time, it was actually a tactical response to
a string of adverse political and military developments, foremost among
these the PLO's expulsion from Lebanon in 1982–83 first by Israel, and
then by Syria, and the destruction of its military infrastructure there.
The PLO's terrorist capacity was incapacitated further by the substitution of Tunis for Lebanon as its operational base. Tunisia's physical re-
moteness from Israel and political detachment from the Middle East
conflict denied the PLO a territorial base for attacks on the Jewish state
and narrowed its ability to maneuver so as not to expose Tunis to Israeli
retaliation.

Equally important as an impetus was the PLO's growing dependence
on Egypt, which was eager to embrace the Palestinian cause as a means
to redeem its 1979 peace treaty with Israel, and the dramatic policy shift
in Moscow, the PLO's foremost international patron, following Mikhail
Gorbachev's rise to power (in 1985) and his unwavering conviction that
"reliance on military force in settling the Arab-Israeli conflict has completely lost its credibility."[33]

The Palestinian uprising, or the intifada, which broke in the West
Bank and the Gaza Strip in December 1987, provided the final catalyst.
Doing more to redeem Palestinian dignity and self-esteem than decades
of PLO terrorism, it pushed the Palestinian problem to the forefront of
the Arab-Israeli conflict and boxed Arafat into a corner. Were he to fail
to seize the moment, the PLO's claim to championship of the armed
struggle, let alone to exclusive representation of the Palestinian people,
might be largely discredited, with the gap between the "inside" and the
"outside" becoming increasingly unbridgeable.

The intifada was as much an act of protest against the PLO's failure
as it was a revolt against the Israeli occupation. A young and dynamic
leadership was rapidly developing in the West Bank and Gaza, and new

political groups were making significant inroads into Palestinian society, notably the Islamic Religious Movement, better known by its Arabic acronym, Hamas. Arafat feared that any indecision on his part would result in the loss of the influence the PLO had built in the territories during the 1970s and '80s. He therefore moved quickly to assert control over the unexpected uprising, while at the same time strove to achieve a political and diplomatic breakthrough that would convince those inside that their sacrifices had not been in vain.

Yet while the Algiers decision seemed to have achieved a measure of success by opening a dialogue with the U.S. administration, Palestinian leaders went out of their way to reassure their Arab constituents that this was merely a tactical ploy aimed at enhancing the PLO's international standing and, as a consequence, its ability to achieve the ultimate objective of Israel's destruction. "We in the PLO make a clear distinction between covenants and political programs, whereby the former determine the permanent strategic line while the latter are tactical by nature," argued Ahmad Sidqi Dajani, a senior PLO member. "We would like some of our brothers to take note of this difference, that is, of our continued adherence to the Palestinian National Covenant."[34]

Abu Iyad, by now Arafat's second in command, was even more forthright. "We vowed to liberate Palestine before 1967," he declared shortly after the Algiers session. "We will restore Palestine step by step and not in one fell swoop, just as the Jews had done. We are learning from them and there is nothing wrong in this." He added, "The borders of our state noted [by the PNC Algiers declaration] represent only a part of our national aspirations. "We will strive to expand them so as to realize our ambition for the entire territory of Palestine." A few days later he reiterated this pledge: "The establishment of a Palestinian state on any part of Palestine is but a step toward the [liberation of the] whole of Palestine."[35]

"It's obvious that as soon as I'm attacked I'll attack Israel," Saddam Hussein told Arafat and Abu Iyad when they came to see him in Baghdad. "Israeli involvement in the conflict will change everyone's attitude in the Arab world, and the aggression against Iraq will be seen as an American-Zionist plot," Saddam promised his enthusiastic guests.[36]

The Iraqi occupation of Kuwait in the summer of 1990 offered the PLO leadership a golden opportunity to shed its feigned moderation and align itself with Saddam, who sought to gain Arab acquiescence in his predatory move by presenting it as the first step toward "the liberation of Jerusalem." Arafat had been striving for decades to entangle the Arab states in a war with Israel on the Palestinians' behalf. Now the most powerful Arab state was apparently prepared to place its massive war machine in the service of the Palestinian cause. The reward was too great for Arafat to refuse, even if the price was the sacrifice of the ruling Kuwaiti family, or the potential elimination of Kuwait as an independent state.

Addressing a popular rally in Baghdad a week before the outbreak of hostilities, Arafat dramatically declared that, should war break out, the Palestinians would be "in the same trench with the Iraqi people to confront the U.S.–Zionist–Atlantic buildup of invading forces, which are desecrating Arab lands." Abu Iyad resorted to even more fiery rhetoric. "The Palestinian and Jordanian people will stand by fraternal Iraq in any aggression against it," he announced at a public rally in Amman, pledging "to liberate Palestine inch by inch from the [Mediterranean] sea to the [Jordan] river."[37]

As the primary financiers of the Palestinian cause the Gulf monarchies felt betrayed by their beneficiaries; as hosts to a large population of Palestinian workers they felt threatened. "You Palestinians seem to be completely unaware of everything the Kuwaitis have done for you," King Fahd of Saudi Arabia blustered to Arafat and Abu Iyad, shortly after the Iraqi invasion. "You've never done anything in return for the trust and the help they've given you."[38] Syrian Minister of Defense Mustafa Tlas was no less scathing. "The entire world knows that Saudi Arabia and the Gulf states are those which helped the Palestinian resistance and provided it with money and weapons," he told a Saudi newspaper shortly after the 1991 Gulf war. "We helped them too, and in the end Arafat turned his back on Syria, Egypt, and Saudi Arabia, and spoke only on the help given [to the Palestinians] by Saddam. Arafat also turned his back on Kuwait and the ruling al-Sabah family, where the Fatah movement was born, nurtured, and financed. But Arafat coveted another $2 billion so as to add them to the billions he holds overseas."[39]

If this was indeed one of Arafat's objectives, he had seriously miscalculated the situation. Not only did the PLO fail to make any financial gain as a result of the Iraqi misadventure, but it also lost the $133 million in annual contributions as the Gulf states suspended their financial support to the Palestinian organization. Following the liberation of Kuwait, most of the 400,000 Palestinians who had been living and working in the emirate were expelled, creating an epic-scale humanitarian problem and denying the PLO the substantial income regularly received from the earnings of every worker. Added to the loss of funds and investments in Kuwaiti banks, the total amount forfeited to the PLO as a direct result of the Gulf crisis was in excess of $10 billion, bringing the organization to the verge of bankruptcy. Arafat was forced to reduce the PLO's financial support for the West Bank and Gaza from an estimated $120 million a year to some $45 million, to slash staff and salaries worldwide, to sell off the organization's valuable real estate holdings, and to close down its newspapers.[40]

Starved of financial resources, ostracized by its Arab peers, and increasingly overpowered in the West Bank and Gaza by the militant Islamic movement Hamas, the PLO was desperate for political rehabilitation—and Arafat for a personal comeback. Particularly alarming for the PLO leader was the insistence of the leadership in the West Bank and the Gaza Strip to participate in the peace process, which was launched with the Madrid Conference in October 1991 and continued in Washington in the form of bilateral talks between Israel and its Arab neighbors.

As early as the 1991 Gulf war, West Bank politicians were telling their Israeli counterparts of their hope that Arafat's weakening international standing would improve their maneuverability vis-à-vis the PLO. U.S. Secretary of State James Baker explicitly told inside leaders of Arab leaders' adamant refusal to have anything to do with Arafat (in an Arab League summit in mid-1991, the PLO was not even allowed to raise the Palestinian issue). The East Jerusalem Arabic press began voicing criticism of the PLO's blunder during the Gulf crisis with articles that articulated the heretical idea of introducing "some new blood into the Palestinian leadership."

Arafat quickly engaged in damage control. At the PNC's twentieth session, convened in Algiers in late September 1991, he prevailed over the more conservative elements in the PLO to endorse the participation of an inside delegation in the peace process with Israel's right-wing Likud government. Yet Arafat also demonstrated who was pulling the strings behind the process, providing minimal funding to the delegation's headquarters in Jerusalem and to the various projects of self-governing bodies in the territories. In August 1992, he even blocked a meeting between the delegation's highly articulate spokeswoman, Hanan Ashrawi, and the French foreign minister, Roland Dumas, apparently for fear that she would overshadow the PLO's "foreign minister," Farouq Qaddoumi, who was scheduled to meet with Dumas the following day. Similarly, Arafat forbade members of the delegation from accepting an Israeli offer to meet with the newly elected prime minister, Yitzhak Rabin, and his foreign minister, Shimon Peres.

These measures could hardly disguise the growing fissure between the inside delegation and the PLO as its nominal master. Faisal Husseini, scion of a prominent Jerusalem family and Fatah's most prominent inside leader, blamed the PLO for the deepening economic plight in the territories and demanded that the organization apologize to Saudi Arabia for its misbehavior during the Kuwait crisis. Ashrawi, for her part, was increasingly exasperated with the PLO's intransigence and its aversion even to the appearance of progress on technical issues. Haidar Abdel Shafi, the grand old man of Gazan politics and head of the delegation, went as far as accusing the PLO of undemocratic practices and demanding that participation in the negotiations be determined by popular referendum rather than by the Tunis leadership. So deep was the distrust between the PLO and the Washington delegation that when Ashrawi responded to the crashing of Arafat's private plane in the Libyan desert in April 1992 by expressing hope for his safety, while asserting that the Palestinian cause would survive regardless of the outcome, the PLO headquarters in Tunis accused her of treason and demanded a retraction.[41]

Fortunately for Arafat, a lifeline was suddenly offered from the least expected source. As in the 1970s, when Israel's hands-off policy in the political and administrative spheres allowed the PLO to establish control over West Bank and Gaza politics, so the Rabin government salvaged the PLO at one of the darkest moments in its history and allowed it to regain its grip over the inside at a time when it seemed to be rapidly slipping. Brought to power in July 1992 for the second time in twenty years on a straightforward peace platform, the seventy-one-year-old Rabin, who had masterminded Israel's 1967 victory, was well aware that this was his last chance to go down in history as Israel's greatest peace-maker and was prepared to secure his legacy regardless of the costs, even if this meant breaking the taboo to which Israeli governments had long subscribed—negotiating directly with the PLO.

Upon his election, Rabin had promised to try to reach an agreement with the Palestinians within nine months. As the negotiations in Washington dragged on, Rabin became increasingly exasperated, especially after realizing that the Syrians, with whom he also had hoped to reach a quick agreement, were not prepared to make their peace with Israel. So when in February 1993 Foreign Minister Peres informed Rabin of secret talks in the Norwegian capital of Oslo between a couple of Israeli academics, sent by Peres's deputy and longtime protégé Yossi Beilin, and Ahmad Qurei (alias Abu Ala), director of Samed, the PLO's financial arm and Arafat's confidant, Rabin gave his cautious approval. Peres recalled, "I said, 'Why should we keep [Arafat] in Tunisia, making trouble from there? Let him be on the spot in Gaza.' Rabin was shocked. It was like bringing your enemy as a guest to a party."[42]

By late May 1993, negotiations had made sufficient progress for Rabin to agree that Uri Savir, the newly appointed director general of the Foreign Ministry, should go to Oslo to negotiate with Abu Ala. Three months later, on August 20, the two had signed a draft peace agreement at the Norwegian government's guest house. On September 13, 1993, a festive ceremony on the White house lawn was televised throughout the world, in which Shimon Peres and Mahmoud Abbas (alias Abu Mazen), Arafat's second in command since Abu Iyad's assassination in 1991, signed the Declaration of Principles on Interim Self-Government Arrangement. The DOP provided for Palestinian self-rule in the entire West Bank and the Gaza Strip for a transitional period not to exceed five years, during which Israel and the Palestinians would negotiate a permanent peace settlement. During this interim period the territories would be administered by a Palestinian Council, to be freely and democratically elected after the withdrawal of Israeli military forces both from the Gaza Strip and from the populated areas of the West Bank.[43]

In his speech at the signing ceremony, the taciturn and private Rabin, who had rarely betrayed his inner feelings in public, was swept with emotion. "We are destined to live together on the same soil in the same land," he said. "We who have fought against you, the Palestinians, we say to you today in a loud and a clear voice: Enough of blood and tears. Enough! The time for peace has come."

Arafat, reveling in his reemergence into the center of world attention from one of the lowest ebbs in his career, was somewhat more restrained. "Let me assure the people of Israel that the difficult decision we have reached together was one that required great and exceptional courage," he said. "Our two peoples are awaiting today this historic hope, and they want to give peace a real chance."

This statement was well short of the Israeli expectations. On the eve of the signing ceremony, Arafat had promised the Norwegian foreign minister Johan Jorgen Holst that in his speech he would specifically call on his people to abandon the road of violence and terrorism.[44] Yet for a person who had avowedly devoted his life to the destruction of the Jewish state, these were remarkable words that ran contrary to everything he had been saying and doing for decades. Was this a genuine transformation or rather the greatest and most devious deception of his political career?

3

A Trojan Horse

I have no use for Jews. They are and remain Jews. We now need all the help we can get from you in our battle for a united Palestine under Arab rule.
—Yasser Arafat to Arab diplomats in Stockholm, January 1996

On January 30, 1996, Arafat held a closed meeting with some forty Arab diplomats in the sumptuous Spiegel Salon at the Grand Hotel in Stockholm. The PLO leader was in the Swedish capital to receive a peace prize, shared by Fatah youth and the Israeli peace movement Peace Now, and he was in a euphoric mood. Earlier that month, Israeli forces had been withdrawn from the West Bank's populated areas with the exception of Hebron, thus relinquishing control over most of the area's 1.4 million residents (withdrawal from the Gaza Strip had already been completed by May 1994). On January 20, 1996, elections to the Palestinian Council were held, and shortly afterward both the Israeli civil administration and military government were dissolved. Arafat himself was elected president of the Palestinian Authority with an overwhelming majority of 81.1 percent, although his candidacy had been virtually uncontested (he ran against a seventy-two-year-old woman, Samiha Khalil—a political nonentity). Arriving at the meeting from a welcome party thrown on his behalf by the Swedish foreign minister, Arafat treated his Arab guests to an unexpected surprise. Rather than give an informal briefing on the development of the Oslo process, as he was scheduled to do, he unveiled a highly sinister vision of "peace." "We plan to eliminate the state of Israel and establish a purely Palestinian state," he said.

We will make life unbearable for Jews by psychological warfare and population explosion. Jews will not want to live among Arabs . . . They will give up their dwelling and leave for the U.S. We Palestinians will take over everything, including all of Jerusalem. [Prime Minister Shimon] Peres and [Minister Yossi] Beilin have already promised us half of Jerusalem. The Golan Heights, too, have already been given away, subject to just a few details. And when they are returned, at least half a million rich Jews will leave Israel.

Arafat expected civil war to erupt in Israel, in which Russian immigrants, "half of whom are Christian or Muslims," will fight for "a united Palestinian state." Further outlining his strategy for the final stage of the "peace process," he said:

The PLO will now concentrate on splitting Israel psychologically into two camps. Within five years we will have six to seven million Arabs living on the West Bank and Jerusalem. All Palestinian Arabs will be welcomed by us. If the Jews can import all kinds of Ethiopians, Russians, Uzbekians, and Ukrainians as Jews, we can import all kinds of Arabs.

"I have no use for Jews. They are and remain Jews," he concluded. "We now need all the help we can get from you in our battle for a united Palestine under Arab rule."[1]

This was not the first time that Arafat had told an Arab audience that the string of peace agreements he had signed with Israel since September 1993 were nothing but a strategic deception aimed at bringing about the Jewish state's eventual demise. He had been saying this ever since news of the Oslo agreement broke to the world. Yet never before had he spelt out his vision of "peace" with such brutal clarity. Ordinarily, Arafat resorted to a panoply of catchphrases and metaphors, both secular and religious, whose meaning was clear and unmistakable to Arabs and Muslims but incomprehensible to Western audiences. Two of Arafat's most commonly used euphemisms have been the "regaining of full Palestinian rights" and a "just and comprehensive peace." To Western ears, there is seemingly no loftier ideal than peace based on justice or restoration of usurped rights. Yet in Arab and Palestinian parlance, such "justice" has always meant the "return of the whole of Palestine to its rightful owners," that is, the establishment of a Palestinian state on Israel's ruins, as has the constant pledge to "fly the Palestinian flag over the walls of Jerusalem." Used extensively by Arafat well before the signing of the Oslo accords, these are euphemisms rooted in Islamic and Arab history for the liberation of the whole of Palestine from "foreign occupiers." In the words given during a Palestinian Authority television broadcast: "Jerusalem is Palestine's eternal capital. Occupied by the sword of Caliph Omar [Prophet Muhammad's comrade in arms and the second in line in his succession] and freed [from the crusaders] by Saladin. And now Your Excellency [i.e., Arafat], if you are not going to liberate it, who will?"[2]

A no less prominent indicator of Arafat's instrumental perception of the Oslo process has been his repeated evocation of the 1974 "phased strategy," which stipulated the creation of an "independent combatant national authority for the people over every part of Palestinian territory that is liberated" as a stepping-stone toward the ultimate goal of Palestinian "self-determination on the whole of the soil of their homeland." In September 1993 alone, Arafat evoked the phased strategy more than a dozen times in media appearances throughout the Arab world,[3] most notably in a personal message to the Palestinian people, broadcast in Arabic by Jordanian television at about the same time of the signing ceremony on the White House lawn. "O my beloved ones," Arafat told his prospective subjects.

> Do not forget that our Palestine National Council accepted the decision in 1974. It called for the establishment of a national authority on any part of Palestinian land that is liberated or from which the Israelis withdrew. This is the fruit of your struggle, your sacrifices, and your jihad . . . This is the moment of return, the moment of gaining a foothold on the first liberated Palestinian land . . . Long live Palestine, liberated and Arab.[4]

Needless to say, this vision of a "liberated and Arab Palestine," that is, a Palestine in which Israel does not exist, was not mentioned in any of Arafat's interviews with the Israeli and Western media at the time, where Arafat invariably lauded the "peace of the brave" he had just signed. Only once, in an interview with the Israeli weekly *Ha'olam Ha'ze*, on September 8, 1993, Arafat temporarily dropped his guard. "I may not live to see it," he told the Israeli journalist who came to see him in his Tunis headquarters, "but I promise you that in the future, Israel and

Palestine will be one united state in which Israelis and Palestinians will live together."

"But Abu Ammar, this is precisely what we offered in 1969," interjected Um Jihad, widow of Abu Jihad, one of Fatah's founding fathers, assassinated in 1988 by Israeli commandos.

"Not in 1969 but rather in 1968," Arafat corrected. "In any event, I am certain that the future will bring a unified state in which we and you will live in peace."

The interviewer could hardly believe his ears. It had long been common knowledge among Arabs and Israelis alike that the PLO's advocacy of a "democratic state in the whole of Palestine" was a euphemism for the destruction of the state of Israel, and here was Arafat, days from the signing of a historic peace agreement with Israel, reiterating this old commitment. "You Israelis are still full of inhibitions," he argued. "You have a psychological block with regard to Palestinians. However, once peace comes, I have no doubt that the relations between Palestinians and Israelis will improve beyond recognition."[5]

At a closed meeting with South African Muslim leaders on May 10, 1994, Arafat claimed that the Oslo agreements fell into the same category as the Treaty of Hudaibiya that was signed by the Prophet Muhammad with the people of Mecca in 628, only to be reneged on a couple of years later when the situation tilted in Muhammad's favor. Unknown to him, his words were recorded by a member of the Jewish community who managed to infiltrate the meeting disguised as a Muslim.[6]

The Israelis were stunned. A week earlier they had signed the Gaza-Jericho Agreement (also known as the Cairo Agreement) on the establishment of a Palestinian Authority in these territories as a preliminary stage in the DOP's implementation, and here was their cosignatory presenting these agreements as a tactical ploy that could be discarded at the first available opportunity. Rabin angrily demanded that Arafat "reaffirm his commitment to his agreement with us." So did the left-wing minister of the environment, Yossi Sarid, one of the most dovish members of the Israeli government. "Arafat has to announce that his grave words at the Johannesburg mosque are null and void," he said. "He should pronounce his complete adherence to the agreement with Israel and prove this abidance through an open and determined struggle against terrorism. Should he fail to do this, the crisis of confidence will persist and Arafat will be able to choose between being a mayor of Jericho or the ruler of Gaza. In such circumstances, Gaza and Jericho will be the end of the process."[7]

Arafat remained unperturbed. Three weeks later, on May 30, he repeated the same analogy, only this time in public. "What we achieved was not all that we wanted but the best we could get at the worst possible time," he told a group of Palestinian contractors visiting him in Tunis. "Prophet Muhammad reached [a similar] agreement with the infidels in Hudaibiya and it was torn down two years later."[8]

Arafat's choice for comparison was deliberate. A deeply religious person thoroughly steeped in Islamic themes and metaphors, he received his initial religious training as a young child by his great-uncle Yusuf Akbar, a rabid anti-Semite who spent hours telling his young great-nephew about the supposed treachery and corruptness of Judaism and Jews.[9] Arafat also had a longtime association with the militant Egyptian organization the Muslim Brethren. Little wonder then that the Hudaibiya analogy, the religious equivalent of the "phased strategy," became a regular feature of Arafat's public rhetoric throughout the 1990s. "Those of you who have ten reservations regarding the Oslo agreement should know I have one thousand reservations," he told students at al-Azhar University in Gaza on August 21, 1995, a couple of weeks before signing the Interim Agreement on Israel's gradual withdrawal from the West Bank.

> But let's take an example from the Prophet . . . When the Prophet signed the Hudaibiya Agreement, [Caliph] Omar ibn Khattab derided it as a treaty of humiliation and asked the Prophet: "How can we accept this humiliation to our religion?" . . .
> Did the Prophet, Allah's Messenger, the Last of the Prophets, really accept a humiliation? No, and no again. He did not accept a humiliation. But every situation has its own circumstances.[10]

At a meeting with representatives of the Egyptian press a couple of days later, Arafat was asked his opinion of the scathing criticism of the Oslo process by Palestinian religious groups. "I would like to remind them," he said, "that when Omar ibn Khattab derided the Hudaibiya agreement between the Prophet and the Jews [*sic*] as a 'despicable treaty' and expressed his opposition to this peace, he was reprimanded by Prophet Muhammad who told him to keep quiet."[11]

Time has done little to temper this ideology. In an address to the Palestinian Legislative Council on May 15, 2002, at the height of his terrorist war against Israel, Arafat reminded his listeners of the instrumental nature of this agreement as a means of buying a vital respite in the struggle against the infidels until the reversal of the balance of forces.[12]

Viewing the peace process as a grand deception aimed at bringing about Israel's eventual destruction was fully embraced by the Palestinian leadership. In *The Historic Danger and the Boundaries of National Identity,* a book published several months after the signing of the DOP, Sakhr Habash, a member of Fatah's central committee and head of its ideological department, explained the PLO's decision to enter the Oslo process as grounded in the PNC's phased strategy. In accordance with Article 10 of this plan, which allowed "the leadership of the revolution [to] determine the tactics, which will serve and make possible the realization of the objectives," the PLO decided to exploit the growing disillusionment among Israelis with the dream of "Greater Israel" in order to gain a firm foothold on Palestinian soil with the goal being its ultimate liberation. The first stage of this process involved an interim agreement that would lead to complete Palestinian control over the West Bank and the Gaza Strip. Once this objective had been achieved, the Palestinians would proceed to the "final solution," namely the establishment of a "democratic state" on the whole of Palestine and the return of the 1948 refugees to their homes.[13]

Another prominent Fatah ideologue, Othman Abu Gharbiya, the PA's director of political indoctrination and editor of its weekly *al-Ra'i,* was no less explicit in his vision of "peace." "Every Palestinian must clearly understand that the independent Palestinian state, with Jerusalem as its capital, is not the end of the process but rather a stage on the road to a democratic state in the whole of Palestine," he said in November 1999. "This will be followed by a third phase, namely Palestine's complete amalgamation in the Arab and Islamic cultural, national, historic, and geographic environment. This is the permanent status solution."[14] In a lengthy book on Fatah's history and ideology published in the same year, Abu Gharbiya further stated that "the basic goal of the PLO movement will remain the establishment of a democratic Palestinian state on all national land, in which there will be equal rights and obligations between all citizens regardless of religion, race, sex, or color. All PLO activity is connected to this goal, flows from it, and strives for it."[15]

Other Palestinian leaders were more blunt. As early as November 1992, when Israeli-Palestinian peace negotiations were being held in Washington, Faisal Husseini, son of Abdel Qader Husseini of the 1948 war fame and one of the most moderate of Palestinian leaders, publicly spelled out his vision of peace. "In the life of all nations there are two strategies: the historical and the political," he told a public gathering in Amman.

> While we have not conceded, and will never surrender, any of the obligations to which we have been committed for more than seventy years . . . our slogan at the current phase is not "from the [Mediterranean] Sea to the [Jordan] River" . . . We have within our Palestinian Arab society the ability to deal with the divided Israeli society, which is torn by internal conflicts . . . Sooner or later, we will force Israeli society to be incorporated into . . . our Arab society, and eventually to dissolve the "Zionist entity."[16]

The Oslo accords did little to change Husseini's equation of peace with Israel's phased destruction. "All Palestinians agree that the just boundaries of Palestine are the Jordan River and the Mediterranean [that is, Palestine in place of Israel]," he told Syrian television on September 9, 1996. "Realistically, whatever can be obtained now should be accepted [in the hope that] subsequent events, perhaps in the next fifteen or twenty years, would present us with an opportunity to realize the just boundaries of Palestine."[17]

Husseini remained committed to this vision to his final days. "One must draw a distinction between the strategic aspirations of the Palestinian people, who would not surrender one grain of Palestinian soil, and their political striving, based on the balance of power and the nature of the current international system," he said in March 2001. "Our eyes will continue to be focused on the strategic goal—a Palestine from the [Jordan] River to the [Mediterranean] Sea—and nothing that we take today can make us forget this supreme truth."[18]

By this time Arafat had already launched his war of terror against Israel, and Husseini could have reassured his Israeli peace partners that the goals of this latest confrontation were limited to the attainment of Palestinian statehood in the West Bank and Gaza. He did not, instead choosing to underscore Israel's demise as the ultimate Palestinian objective. In June 2001, shortly before his death from a heart attack, Husseini candidly told an Egyptian newspaper, "When we ask all Palestinian forces and factions to regard the Oslo Accord and other arrangements as temporary measures, or phased goals, this means that we are baiting the Israelis or duping them." He explained:

> We distinguish the strategic, long-term goals from the political phased goals, which we are forced to temporarily accept owing to international pressure . . . Though agreeing to declare our state over what is now only 22 percent of Palestine, namely the West Bank and Gaza, our ultimate goal remains the liberation of all historical Palestine from the river to the sea, even if this means the continuation of the conflict for another thousand years or for many generations.

Had the Israelis and the Americans realized that the Oslo accords were merely a "Trojan horse" designed to promote the higher goal of Palestine's complete liberation, he argued, "they would never have opened their fortified gates and let it inside their walls." As they had been duped into this strategic blunder, the Palestinians, like the ancient Greeks, were bound to triumph: "The people of Troy . . . cheered and celebrated thinking that the Greek troops were routed, and while retreating, they left a harmless wooden horse as spoils of war. So they opened the gates of the city and brought in the wooden horse. We all know what happened next."[19]

Other Palestinian leaders were equally explicit. Yasser Abd Rabbo, the minister of information and culture at the Palestinian Authority, was quoted in July 1994 as vowing that the Palestinians would regain "all of Palestine,"[20] while Sheik Hamad Bitawi, a PA-appointed preacher at al-Aqsa Mosque, told a 300,000-strong audience in February 1996 that "religion will liberate Palestine . . . from the sea to the river."[21] That very month, speaking at the ceremony of Arafat's swearing in as president of the Palestinian Authority, Salim Zaanun, the PNC's acting speaker, stated, "We are living this day for our Arab and Islamic nation, the triumph of Saladin."[22]

In Arab and Muslim parlance, the "triumph of Saladin," the legendary warrior who defeated the crusaders and destroyed their kingdom, was coded language for the destruction of Israel, widely viewed by Arabs as a neocrusading state. The foremost champions of the pan-Arab and anti-Israel struggle—from Syria's Hafez Assad to Iraq's Saddam Hussein, himself a native of Saladin's hometown of Tikrit—had styled themselves as present-day Saladins, as did Arafat. From the moment he arrived in Gaza in July 1994, Arafat had been vying with Jordan for control of al-Haram al-Sharif, as Muslims call the Temple Mount, and other Islamic institutions in Jerusalem. He named his own mufti in the city, forcing the Jordanian-appointed mufti into retirement, appointed a minister for religious affairs, and had King Hussein's portraits, which had hung on the walls in the offices of the Waqf religious endowment authority, replaced with his own portraits.

This struggle came to a head in October 2002 over the pulpit in the al-Aqsa mosque. Named after Saladin, the pulpit was damaged by fire in 1969 when a deranged Australian attempted to burn down the mosque. It was taken to Jordan, where the late King Hussein sold a private home in London to finance the renovation of the pulpit and mosque. Now that the Jordanians asked the Israeli authorities for permission to reinstate the pulpit in a high-profile ceremony Arafat was greatly alarmed. Not only would such a move have emphasized that the Hashemite royal family had never relinquished its claim to Jerusalem's Islamic sites, but it would have also undermined his tireless efforts to fashion himself as the new Saladin. For years Arafat had shown great interest in the state of the pulpit, which, according to one of his close associates, he envisaged bringing with him to al-Aqsa upon his triumphal entry to Jerusalem, and he was not going to allow King Hussein stand in the way of this dream.[23]

Now that Zaanun had bestowed him with this great honor, in full view of the Palestinian population in the West Bank and Gaza, Arafat did not demur. When asked whether he wished to make a speech, he said that he had nothing to add to Zaanun's words. Yet his face could barely disguise the satisfaction of his equation with the legendary Saladin.

Arafat was under greater pressure to respond when Farouq Qaddoumi, head of the PLO's political department, called for Israel's destruction in as direct a statement as possible. "There is a state that was established through historical force and it must be destroyed," Qaddoumi argued. "This is the Palestinian way."[24] At a joint press conference with Rabin, a day after Qaddoumi had made his statement, Arafat skillfully ducked requests for clarification. "This is his point of view, not that of the PLO," he said. But wasn't Qaddoumi a senior PLO official, an astonished journalist asked. "He is our foreign minister!"[25]

In mid-September 1995, as he was about to sign the Interim Agreement on Israel's withdrawal from the West Bank, Arafat was similarly coy when pressed by Israeli journalists on his vision of an independent Palestinian state. Would the territory of this state be confined to the West Bank and the Gaza Strip, or would it comprise the whole of Palestine? "Don't pressure me with the wrong questions," he said semi-jokingly. Yet, on November 11, with the start of the handover of responsibility for the West Bank's populated areas, Arafat was not deterred from claiming that "the campaign will not be over until all of Palestine is liberated."[26] The fact that Prime Minister Rabin, his alleged partner to the "peace of the brave," had been assassinated a few days earlier did little to curb Arafat's militant zeal. As late as June 25, 2000, a couple of weeks before the convocation of the Camp David summit to discuss the final-status agreement between Israelis and Palestinians, an ecstatic Arafat shouted in a public rally: "Palestine is ours, ours, ours."[27]

Even the foremost moderates in the Palestinian leadership, and architects of the Oslo process—Abu Mazen and Abu Ala—were not deterred from implying their hope for Israel's eventual destruction. In an interview with the Israeli daily *Maariv*, on January 19, 1996, Abu Mazen gently reiterated the PLO's old formula of a democratic state comprising the whole of Palestine. "I hope that in the future we will reach a state of complete mixture [among Israelis and Palestinians], though it may take some time to overcome past enmities," he said. "And then [Palestinians] will be able to run for the Knesset while [Israelis] will be able to run for the Palestinian Parliament, and perhaps a confederation will emerge. For dreams can at times be realized."

Abu Ala was more direct. "We did not sign a peace treaty with Israel, but interim agreements that had been imposed on us," he said in June 1996.

> When we accepted the Oslo agreement, we obtained territory but not all the Palestinian territory. We obtained rights, but not all of our rights. We did not and will not relinquish one inch of this territory or the right of any Palestinian to live on it with dignity.

A year later, in public rally in Ramallah, Abu Ala demonstratively stepped over the remains of an Israeli flag that had been set on fire in front of his eyes. At another demonstration he told a cheering crowd that, "With Allah's will, the return is coming soon."[28]

Abu Ala's pledge touched one of the most emotive and intractable manifestations of Palestinian rejection of Israel: the "right of return." In Arab and Palestinian discourse—though not when addressing Western audiences—the demand for the return of the 1948 refugees and their descendants to territory that is now part of the state of Israel, and their financial compensation for their losses and suffering, is yet another prong of Arafat's phased strategy, in this case the destruction of Israel through demographic subversion.

At the end of the 1948 war, the Israeli government set the number of Palestinian refugees at between 550,000 and 600,000; the British Foreign Office leaned toward the higher end of this estimate. Within a year, as large masses of people sought to benefit from the unprecedented influx of international funds to the area, some 914,000 alleged refugees had been registered with the UN Relief and Works Agency (UNRWA).

More than a half century later, these exaggerated initial numbers have swollen further. As of June 2000, according to UNRWA, the approximate total had climbed to three- and three-quarters of a million refugees. While UNRWA admits that the statistics are inflated, since they "are based on information voluntarily supplied by refugees primarily for the purpose of obtaining access to Agency services," the PLO has set a still higher figure of five million refugees, claiming that many have never registered with UNRWA.

For its part, Israel has challenged UNRWA's figures as well as those of the PLO. Its own unofficial estimates are closer to two million. Even if the more restrictive Israeli figures were accepted, there is little doubt the influx of these refugees into the Jewish state would irrevocably transform its demographic composition. At the moment, Jews constitute about 80 percent of Israel's population of six and a half million, a figure that would rapidly dwindle to under 60 percent. Given the Palestinians' far higher birthrate, the implementation of a right of return, even by the most conservative estimates, would be tantamount to Israel's transformation into an "ordinary" Arab state.

Not that this stark scenario should surprise anyone. As early as October 1949, the Egyptian politician Muhammad Salah al-Din, soon to become his country's foreign minister, wrote in the influential Egyptian daily *al-Misri* that "In demanding the restoration of the refugees to Palestine, the Arabs intend that they shall return as the masters of the homeland and not as slaves. More specifically, they intend to annihilate the state of Israel."[29]

In subsequent years, this concept of the right of return was reiterated by all Arab leaders, from Gamal Abdel Nasser, to Hafez Assad, to Yasser Arafat. As Faisal Husseini offered, in a speech he made on Arafat's behalf in the summer of 2001:

> The [Israeli] options are far more difficult than our options. At the moment there are nearly four million Palestinians between the river and the sea, compared with four million non-Palestinians. By 2010 the number of Palestinians and non-Palestinians will have been equalized. By the year 2045 Palestinians will constitute 75 percent of all residents in Palestine.[30]

Despite its formal commitment to peace with Israel, the PLO quickly reassured its constituents of its unwavering commitment to the implementation of the right of return. Arafat himself underscored this point in a string of interviews in September 1993,[31] while a report by the PLO's Information Department, titled "Palestinian Refugees and the Right of Return," was leaked to a Lebanese newspaper a week after the historic handshake on the White House lawn by "a source close to Arafat." Reissued a couple of years later by the PA's Ministry of Information, this booklet mirrors the Palestinian Covenant, which rejects Israel's very right to exist, and the abolition of which constitutes one of the most fundamental conditions on which the Oslo process is predicated. Comparing the Palestinian refugees to Jewish Holocaust survivors, the report demands that the international community ensure their compensation and repatriation, just as it had forced postwar Germany to compensate its Jewish victims and allowed them to immigrate to Palestine. "The right of return is an inalienable right that cannot be measured by money," read the document. "No compensation, however substantial, will be of any value so long as the refugees do not have an independent state on their own land."[32]

Numerous statements, articles, and studies after the signing of the DOP point again and again to the Palestinian conception of the right of return as an integral part of the Oslo process.[33] As early as September 9, 1993, Nabil Shaath, Arafat's political adviser, and the prominent West Bank politician Hanan Ashrawi told Israeli journalists that "the Palestinian leadership believes that the Israeli-Palestinian negotiations imply Israel's recognition of the right of return of Palestinian refugees," while Farouq Qaddoumi argued that "the refugee problem is a basic one. Unless it is made completely clear that the refugees' case will be tackled according to international legitimacy, it will be impossible for us to come to an agreement." Several months later, in July 1994, Ashrawi described Arafat's arrival in Gaza as "the first step toward the great Palestinian return."[34]

The idea of the right of return occupied a place of pride among the guiding principles of the Palestinian Authority, published shortly after its establishment in mid-May 1994. Drawing a direct historical line between Palestinian rejection of Jewish statehood in 1948 and the Oslo accords, and making extensive use of the language and vocabulary of the phased plan, these guidelines committed the PA "to work for the achievement of the legitimate Palestinian goals: independence, freedom, equality, and the return, through a graduated process."

This graduated process was not confined to the "liberation" of the West Bank and Gaza. The document makes repeated allusions to "international legitimacy," especially Resolution 194, passed by the UN General Assembly on December 11, 1948, and widely interpreted by Arabs as ensuring the Palestinian "right of return." In fact, far from recommending the return of the Palestinian refugees as the only viable solution, the resolution advocated that "the refugees wishing to return to their homes and live at peace with their neighbors should be permitted to do so at the earliest practicable date," but also that efforts should be made to facilitate the "resettlement and economic and social rehabilitation of the refugees."

It was these very clauses in Resolution 194 that made it anathema to the Arabs, who opposed it vehemently and voted unanimously *against* it. Equating return and resettlement as possible solutions to the refugee problem, linking resolution of this issue to the achievement of a comprehensive Arab-Israeli peace, placing on the Arab states some of the burden for resolving the refugee problem, and above all establishing no absolute right of return, the measure was seen as harmful to Arab concerns. Only in the late 1960s, and with the connivance of their Soviet and third world supporters, did the Arabs begin to transform Resolution 194 into the cornerstone of an utterly spurious legal claim to a so-called right of return, thus turning it into one of their foremost euphemisms for the destruction of Israel.

Moreover, the PA's guidelines underscored both the "Arabness of Palestine and its being a part of the Arab nation," as well as "the Palestinian and Arab identity of our people in the Galilee, the Triangle, and the Negev" (i.e., within Israel proper).[35] Borrowed directly from the Palestinian Covenant, these phrases effectively reject Israel's very legitimacy by presenting it as a usurper of Palestinian-Arab land and oppressor of the Palestinian nation.

Indeed, while for most Western observers the term "occupation" describes Israel's control of the Gaza Strip and the West Bank, areas that it conquered during the Six-Day War of June 1967, for Palestinians and Arabs the Israeli presence in these territories represents only the latest chapter in an uninterrupted story of "occupations," dating back to the very creation of Israel on "stolen" land. Hence the "right of return" is meant to reverse the effects of the "1948 occupation"—i.e., the establishment of the state of Israel itself.

Palestinian intellectuals and politicians routinely blur any distinction between Israel's post- and pre-1967 "occupations." "I come to you today with a heavy heart," Ashrawi told the now infamous World Conference Against Racism in Durban in summer 2001, "leaving behind a nation in captivity held hostage to an ongoing *nakba* [catastrophe.]"

> In 1948, we became subject to a grave historical injustice manifested in
> a dual victimization: on the one hand, the injustice of dispossession, dis-

persion, and exile forcibly enacted on the population. . . . On the other hand, those who remained were subjected to the systematic oppression and brutality of an inhuman occupation that robbed them of all their rights and liberties.[36]

Ashrawi's allusion to the creation and existence of the state of Israel as the original "occupation" was not an accident. The above-noted PLO report on the "Palestinian Refugees and the Right of Return," published twenty-six years after the 1967 war, speaks about "more than four decades of occupation," that is, dating to Israel's creation in 1948. More significantly, in a message to the leaders of Israel's Arab community, on the first anniversary of his terrorist war, Arafat was similarly reluctant to recognize Israel's right to exist. Putting the 1948 and 1967 "occupations" on par with each other, he praised the Israeli Arabs as the "natural depth and fortified wall of our Palestinian people and its just cause," which for more than half a century had resisted "the worst of occupiers ever known in history . . . the robbers of the twentieth century, the creators of international terrorism, the killers of children, women, and the elderly, plunderers of land and livelihood, who destroy and burn the soil, the seeds, and the rocks."

Now that the war had consolidated "the ties that connect the sons of Jerusalem, the West Bank, and the Gaza Strip with those of the cities occupied since 1948," the Palestinian people "will draw up with blood the map of the one homeland and the one people," namely, by destroying the state of Israel.[37]

While freely spelling out in inter-Arab forums the dire consequences of the right of return, PLO spokesmen have taken great care to hide the essence of this "right" from their Israeli interlocutors, not to speak of Western audiences, skillfully evading all requests for clarification. When asked by an Israeli interviewer on the day of the signing of the DOP whether the right of return applied to Israel's pre-1967 territory in addition to the West Bank and Gaza, Arafat replied obliquely that the issue of the 1948 refugees had been deferred to the permanent status phase. On another occasion he totally ignored the question, delving instead into a lengthy monologue on the 1967 rather than the 1948 refugees.[38] This technique had the desired effect, as most Israelis chose to think of the "right of return" as a bargaining chip, to be reserved for talks on a final-status settlement and then somehow disposed of symbolically or through some token concessions.

In these circumstances, it was hardly surprising that the reintroduction of this issue at the Camp David and Taba summits of July 2000 and January 2001, at a time when Israel had effectively agreed to withdraw to its pre-1967 lines, shook the Israeli peace camp to its core. All of a sudden, it realized that the Arab states and the Palestinians really meant what they had been saying for so long—namely, that peace was not a matter of adjusting borders and territory but was rather a euphemism for eliminating the Jewish state altogether, in this case through demographic subversion. "Implementing the 'right of return' means eradicating Israel," lamented Amos Oz, the renowned author and peace advocate. "It will make the Jewish people a minor ethnic group at the mercy of Muslims, a 'protected minority,' just as fundamentalist Islam would have it."

Oz's plaintive cry struck no responsive chord with his Palestinian counterparts. "We as Palestinians do not view our job to safeguard Zionism. It is our job to safeguard our rights," stated Ashrawi, vowing to uphold their right of return even at the cost of undermining Israel's demographic bal ance. "The fact that the Zionist project requires a Jewish majority," she stated, "does not justify conceding the legitimate right [of the refugees] to return and to receive compensation."[39] Sakhr Habash offered a more brutal assessment. "Once the Palestinian Authority is transformed into a full-fledged state, it will become a host country [for the refugees], just like Jordan," he said on July 16, 2000, at the height of the Camp David summit talks. "Every refugee must return home and receive compensation." Will this return be confined to the newly established Palestinian state or will it be applied to Israeli territory as well? Habash was convinced. "As a returnee, the moment I am given the right of return I will go back to my village of Beit Dajan as an Israeli citizen," he said. "Because it is my dream that the territory called Palestine, between the river and the sea, will revert to its old self-democratic Palestine."[40]

4

A License to Hate

Israel must not demand that the PLO alter its covenant, just as
the PLO does not demand that the Jewish nation cancel the Bible.
—Ziad Abu Ziad, October 1993

No document clarifies the PLO's total rejection of Israel's right to exist
more bluntly, or more comprehensively, than the Palestinian National
Covenant. Adopted in June 1964 as one of the PLO's two founding documents (the other being its constitution), and amended four years later
to reflect the organization's growing militancy following its takeover by
Fatah and the smaller guerrilla groups, well over half of the covenant's
thirty-three articles revolve around the illegitimacy of the Jewish state
and the need for its destruction. The covenant is as much a denial of
the "other" as it is an act of national self-assertion, a demeaning and
dehumanizing document that accords one's adversary no rights whatsoever, not even recognition of its collective existence. The late Israeli
academic Yehoshafat Harkabi, who brought the covenant to the attention of the non-Arab world, commented:

> The Palestinian movement claims absoluteness and "totality"—there is
> absolute justice in the Palestinian stand in contrast to the absolute injus-
> tice of Israel; an unqualified Manichean division of good and evil; right is
> on the Palestinian side only; only they are worthy of self-determination;
> the Israelis are barely human creatures who at most may be tolerated in
> the Palestinian state as individuals or as a religious community, with their
> numbers reduced to 5 percent of their present level (Article 6 in the 1968
> version) and then assimilated in the Arab environment.[1]

Viewing Palestine, as it existed during the British Mandate—between
the Jordan River and the Mediterranean—as "an indivisible territorial

unit . . . [and] an inseparable part of the greater Arab homeland," the covenant rejects altogether "the partition of Palestine, which took place in 1947, and the establishment of Israel," or for that matter any Jewish right to national self-determination. "Claims of historical or religious ties of Jews with Palestine are incompatible with the facts of history and the true conception of what constitutes statehood," it argues. "Judaism, being a religion, is not an independent nationality. Nor do Jews constitute a single nation with an identity of its own; they are citizens of the states to which they belong."

This means that Zionism is not the national liberation movement it claims to be but rather "a fanatical and racist" political movement, which is "organically associated with world imperialism" and which employs Nazi methods in its attempt to stunt "all liberation movements or movements for progress in the world." Israel is little more than a "cat's paw for the Zionist movement, a geographic and manpower base for world imperialism and a springboard for its thrust into the Arab homeland to frustrate the aspirations of the Arab nation to liberation, unity, and progress." Since Israel not only constitutes a lethal impediment to Palestinian national self-determination but also poses "a constant threat to peace in the Middle East and the whole world," its destruction is presented as an act of nearly cosmic proportions that will "establish in the Holy Land an atmosphere of peace and tranquillity" and will make a substantial contribution to world peace.

> The demands of peace and security and the exigencies of right and justice require that all nations should regard Zionism as an illegitimate movement and outlaw it and its activities, out of considerations for the ties of friendship between peoples and for the loyalty of citizens to their homelands.[2]

This utter rejection of Zionism remained intact since its institutionalization in 1968, surviving the PLO's various attempts to project a moderate image. When in November 1988 an Austrian interviewer questioned the sincerity of the PLO's pretence of peace at a time when its covenant advocated the destruction of Israel, Arafat exploded. "If you like to speak of our charter, we have to speak of their flag," he shouted. "You know the meaning of their flag? Two blue lines—this means the Euphrates and the Nile Rivers—and in between the Star of David. They have repeatedly stated in their slogans and political documents that the land of Israel goes from the Euphrates to the Nile."[3]

Arafat's response is not difficult to understand. The covenant is the PLO's most cherished article of faith, the embodiment of its very essence, an absolute commitment to the "liberation of the whole of Palestine" and the destruction of the state of Israel. Any attempt at revision, therefore, means far more than a policy shift or even a philosophical change. It amounts to a subversion of the most profound precepts of the PLO ethos that will effectively herald the organization's demise and its transformation, in Harkabi's words, from the PLO to the PPLO (Part of Palestine Liberation Organization).[4]

From the onset of the Oslo negotiations, the Israelis made amending the covenant a precondition to any peace agreement, only to find their Palestinian interlocutors loathe to make the necessary leap of faith. "The Covenant hasn't been operative for years, and it certainly isn't in effect," argued Abu Ala. "We decided to recognize Israel's existence back in 1988." Arafat made the same argument to the Norwegian foreign minister Johan Jorgen Holst, who visited him in his Tunis headquarters in July 1993, asking that he convince Israel to accept the reiteration of his assurance, from four years earlier, that the covenant was no longer operative. The Israelis remained unimpressed, so the Palestinians came up with an ingenious pretext, arguing that they could not find an English version of the covenant. Having anticipated this ploy, the Israelis quickly showed them the problematic clauses in the text that they had brought along from Jerusalem.

Things came to a head on September 9, 1993, as Rabin would not sign the DOP without an unequivocal commitment to revoke the covenant's clauses calling for Israel's destruction. With Arafat procrastinating for days, under the pretext of having to consult his colleagues in the PLO leadership, the anxious Holst decided to call him on the phone. "Abu Ammar, you must decide," he said. "You cannot convene your colleagues now." Arafat promised to consult his advisers and call back shortly. Later that night the PLO Executive Committee approved the requested Israeli demand, and Arafat put this in writing in a personal letter to Rabin. "The PLO affirms that those articles of the Palestinian Covenant which deny Israel's right to exist, and the provisions of the Covenant which are inconsistent with the commitments of this letter, are now inoperative and no longer valid," he wrote. "Consequently, the PLO undertakes to submit to the Palestinian National Council for formal approval the necessary changes in regard to the Palestinian Covenant."[5] In a follow-up letter to Rabin on May 4, 1994, accompanying the newly signed Gaza-Jericho Agreement on the implementation of the first stage of the DOP, Arafat went a step further by committing the PLO "to submit *to the next meeting of the Palestinian National Council* for formal approval the necessary changes in regard to the Palestinian Covenant, as undertaken in the letter dated September 9, 1993, signed by the Chairman of the PLO and addressed to the Prime Minister of Israel."[6]

Arafat had no intention whatsoever of abiding by his pledge, instead embarking on a protracted cat-and-mouse game with the Israelis over this issue. As early as October 1993, the prominent West Bank politician Ziad Abu Ziad, widely regarded as a moderate, told a visiting delegation of American Jewish leaders that "Israel must not demand that the PLO alter its covenant, just as the PLO does not demand that the Jewish nation cancel the Bible."[7]

At a meeting with Rabin and Peres on July 7, 1994, a few days after his triumphant arrival in Gaza, Arafat promised to convene the Palestine National Council in the "very near future." Rabin agreed to wait "a reasonable time," only to learn a couple of days later from Arafat's political adviser that "there will be no convention [of the PNC] without all the members getting invitations and coming in legally." Anxious to deny the PLO any pretext for further procrastination, Rabin announced that all PNC members would be allowed to attend its meeting in Gaza, including those hitherto banned by the Israeli government as terrorists. Arafat, however, would not budge. Speaking at a press conference in Gaza later that month, after meeting Peres and the Norwegian foreign minister, he again accused Israel of preventing many PNC members from entering Gaza and Jericho. Peres's emphatic denial fell on deaf ears, while Arafat insisted that he could not guarantee the PNC's revocation of the clauses in the covenant calling for Israel's destruction as promised in his letter of September 9, 1993. "I haven't the right to [promise] this," he argued. "You have to respect our democracy. This is the business of the members of the PNC."

Farouq Qaddoumi argued that "Rabin cannot ask the Palestinians to change or amend their charter until an Israeli withdrawal is completed from all Arab territories." Faisal Husseini concurred. "If we convene the PNC, we want something positive," he said. "We need more than [a] two-thirds [majority] and therefore I must have something in my hand to convince people who are not yet convinced."[8]

The following month, Israel's demand for amending the covenant took another step backward when at least 73 of the PNC's 468 members were among 171 Palestinian notables who signed a declaration rejecting any change of the covenant under Israeli pressure. A meeting of Fatah's Central Committee in Tunis, chaired by Arafat, decided to put off the convocation of the PNC for an indefinite period of time. According to Sakhr Habash, a committee member and Fatah's foremost ideologue, the meeting decided, "There should be no meeting of the Palestinian National Council before the Palestinian Authority takes full control over all occupied territories." Sheik Abdel Hamid Sayah, the PNC's outgoing speaker, presented the decision in much bleaker terms. "If Israel does not recognize the establishment of a Palestinian state with East Jerusalem as [its] capital," he said, "there would not be any decision to cancel the clauses of the charter calling for the liberation of Palestine." His designated successor, Salim Zaanun, had a similarly onerous list of demands. "I do not deny that there is a Palestinian commitment to amend the covenant," he said.

> But the appropriate time for this would be when the following four conditions will have been met: that the [Palestinian] Authority takes control over the entire territory of the West Bank and the [Gaza] Strip; that the PNC members would enter the territories as citizens and not as visitors; that the detainees would be released; and that the representatives of the "inside," whose participation Israel used to reject, should be elected.[9]

The ever-optimistic Peres tried to put a positive spin on these statements. "We did not sign an agreement with the PNC's speaker," he said. "We signed it with the PLO's leadership and it is incumbent upon them to ensure its implementation. We always knew that there would be majority and minority views and I hope that a wise and responsible majority will be found." Rabin, in contrast, was becoming increasingly exasperated with Arafat's evasive tactics. As long as the PLO failed to amend those covenant clauses calling for Israel's destruction, he announced, the Israeli government would not allow Palestinian elections to take place—a prerequisite for further Israeli withdrawal and the establishment of a Palestinian Council.[10]

Neither this threat nor the suggestion by U.S. Secretary of State Warren Christopher that the covenant's amendment would assist administration efforts to secure congressional authorization for dealing with the PA made any impact on Arafat. All he was prepared to concede was the inclusion of a clause in his party's electoral platform indicating a readiness to amend the covenant at some future point—a far cry from his September 9 pledge.[11] Rabin was thus forced to accept the postponement of the covenant's revision until after the Palestinian elections. Yet he managed to insert into the Interim Agreement on the West Bank and the Gaza Strip (also known as Oslo II) a clear-cut commitment from the PLO that "within two months of the date of the inauguration of the Council, the Palestinian National Council will convene and formally approve the necessary changes in regard to the Palestinian Covenant."[12]

Arafat had since adopted the position that the covenant did not need amending because the PNC had already renounced terrorism and recognized Israel's right to exist. "It was amended in 1974, after the glorious October war, when it was announced that a Palestinian state would be established on any liberated part of the land," he told the Egyptian news agency in January 1996. "In 1991 it was amended when we accepted former U.S. President George Bush's initiative on the basis of land for peace, Security Council resolutions 242 and 338, and participated in the Madrid conference." He reiterated the same claim at a meeting with a group of American Peace Now activists later that month, telling them that the covenant had effectively lost its validity because of the agreements that had been signed with Israel. "You do not change the constitution, you only add amendments," he added, comparing the Palestinian Covenant to the U.S. Constitution.[13]

Precisely because the covenant was a founding document of the PLO, and the most authoritative statement of its aspirations and objectives, it could be amended only by the PNC, at a special meeting called for this purpose, and with the privileged majority of *two-thirds of its total members*—which is exactly what Arafat had promised to do in his September 9 letter to Rabin. That more than two years after making this pledge, and four months after accepting a strict timetable for the amendment of the covenant, Arafat and other PLO leaders were doing their utmost to shun this ultimate act of reconciliation offered yet more proof of their refusal to accept the Oslo process as the beginning of a real and lasting peace.

On November 4, 1995, Rabin was assassinated by a Jewish zealot. His successor, Shimon Peres, confronted with a sharp drop in public support for the peace process following a wave of Palestinian suicide bombings in early 1996, was determined to salvage the process by ensuring the amendment of the Palestinian Covenant as required by the 1995 Interim Agreement. Peres was supported in his efforts by the Clinton administration, which feared that Peres's loss of power to Benjamin Netanyahu, head of the right-wing Likud party and openly skeptical of the Oslo process, would grind talks to a halt. (Warren Christopher reportedly promised Arafat economic assistance of $400 million over three months in exchange for amending the covenant before the Israeli elections, scheduled for late May 1996.) Yet despite their obvious reluctance to see a Likud victory, the PLO leaders could not bring themselves to fix a date for the convocation of the PNC. Acting speaker Zaanun claimed that there was nothing sacred about the scheduled date for amending the covenant since Israel had not kept its side of the bargain, and that the two parties should set a new date for discussing the matter. Meanwhile a meeting of the PLO Executive Committee convened in the Egyptian town of al-Arish in early February 1996 adjourned without agreeing a date for the PNC's convocation, having decided that, rather than repeal the covenant's clauses implying the destruction of Israel, the PNC would formulate a new document that would serve as the charter of the prospective Palestinian state. "If Israel is adamant that the covenant be amended, which is above all an internal Palestinian affair stemming from Israel's inception in 1948 and the ensuing expulsion and migration of Palestinians," the east Jerusalem newspaper *al-Quds* noted, "it is logical that . . . such a step be accompanied by an Israeli commitment to respect the Palestinian people's aspiration in establishing their independent state."[14]

This was unacceptable to an Israeli government adamant that there could be no substitute for an outright, unequivocal repeal of the offensive covenant clauses, especially since Israel had rewarded the PLO for this (promised) move in advance by recognizing it as the sole representative of the Palestinian people. Yet when it became clear that Arafat would try to extract Israel's agreement to the establishment of a Palestinian state in return for the covenant's amendment, in effect selling the same goods twice, Peres relented yet again. Successive public opinion polls in Israel showed him running neck and neck with Netanyahu, and it was evident that going to the elections without the covenant's amendment would cause the Labor Party irreparable damage, as PLO leaders kept piling on additional demands for such a move.

Given these circumstances, it was hardly surprising that Peres was overjoyed when on May 4 he received an official letter from Arafat informing him that at its twenty-first session, held in Gaza between April 22 and 25, 1996, the PNC amended its covenant.[15] "This is the most important event in the Middle East in a hundred years," Peres exclaimed, while the effusive U.S. administration invited Arafat for his first official meeting with President Clinton, in what was to become a lengthy friendship between the two. By the end of the Clinton presidency in January 2001, Arafat had paid more visits to the Oval Office than any other world leader.

It was soon discovered that Arafat had once again managed to dupe the Israelis and the Americans and that the Palestinian National Covenant had been anything but amended. Arafat's letter to Peres misleadingly mistranslated the PNC decision. The original Arabic version, as announced by the Palestinian Authority's official radio, stated that a decision had been made "to amend (ta'adil) the covenant" at some future point, and the English translation by the American consulate general in Jerusalem sent to the administration in Washington rendered it correctly. Arafat, however, misrepresented this general statement by asserting, "The Covenant is hereby amended."[16]

This was not a mere technicality. The PNC abstained from naming the specific clauses that were supposedly abolished, choosing instead the sweeping formula of "canceling the articles that are contrary to the letters exchanged between the PLO and the Government of Israel on

9–10 September 1993," and assigning its legal committee "with the task of redrafting the Palestinian National Charter in order to present it to the first session of the Palestine Central Council."

This deliberate ambiguity left numerous participants in the PNC session uncertain as to the nature of the changes they had ostensibly introduced, including which particular articles had been amended or canceled, how they had been changed, or when the supposed changes were to go into effect. Some members said that only one article (Article 19, declaring the establishment of Israel null and void) was canceled, while others mentioned six. Salim Zaanun, promoted during the PNC's twenty-first session from acting speaker to speaker, maintained that no specific articles had been canceled at all; Nabil Shaath said his "feeling" was that seven articles were abolished; while Sufian Abu Zaida, head of the PA's Israel desk, argued that all thirty-three of the covenant's articles had been canceled. For his part, Faisal Hamdi Husseini, head of the PNC's legal committee, charged with redrafting the covenant, stated on May 5 that he would submit a new covenant within three months in which twenty-one articles would be changed or canceled, implying that none had actually been amended to this point.[17]

This was also the opinion of PLO spokesman Marwan Kanfani, who told reporters immediately after the vote, "This is not an amendment. This is a license to start a new charter." Sakhr Habash concurred with this assessment. "The text of the covenant remains as it is since it has not been amended yet. Therefore, it is frozen, not canceled," he argued, adding, "Israel's adherence to previous and subsequent commitments will be taken into consideration when the new covenant is drafted."[18] An internal report by Fatah, published shortly after the PNC session, echoed the same sentiment. "The text of the Palestinian National Covenant remains as it was and no changes whatsoever were made to it," the report stated. "This has caused it to be frozen, but not annulled. The drafting of the new National Covenant will take into account the extent of Israeli fulfillment of its previous and coming obligations, and the extent of the commitment of the new Israeli Prime Minister who will be elected at the end of May."

Dismissing Israel's demand for the amendment of the covenant as a devious plot to undermine Palestinian national identity, the report went on to explain why the covenant had not actually been amended.

The rulers of Israel demanded that the summons of the PNC would be specifically made for amending the Charter and for the cancellation of those articles which deny Israel's right to exist. However, these are the same articles that proclaim the goal of liberating Palestine. Consequently, the cancellation thereof means the cancellation of the goal for which the PLO had been established. The Israeli and the Zionist demand from the PNC was a self-issued death certificate amounting to a suicidal act by the PLO.[19]

The PNC itself failed to make any mention of the supposed amendment of the covenant in its closing statement. This included nineteen specific resolutions and decisions on a variety of subjects, ranging from Jerusalem to settlement activity to the refugee problem. Israel was condemned for having subjected the Palestinians to "the ugliest injustice in history," for having destroyed the economic infrastructure of the West Bank and the Gaza Strip, and for attempting to subvert the Oslo accords on the pretext of security. Yet no reference whatsoever was made to a decision to amend the covenant and the far-reaching consequences these changes implied. Reverting to its old militant jargon, the closing statement upheld the Palestinian right to "establish an independent state, and enjoy full sovereignty on the soil of their homeland"—the by now standard euphemism for the creation of a Palestinian state on Israel's ruins.[20]

In a filmed segment of the voting session, made by Palestinian TV and subsequently purchased by an Israeli research center and shown on Israeli television (unlike the PNC's other meetings, which were open to the public, the voting session was held behind closed doors), PNC speaker Zaanun is seen explaining to the assembled delegates that they could either amend the covenant as demanded by Israel or delay the process by at least six months by deciding to draft a new proposal. The PNC, he said,

> must fulfill the commitment demanded at the lowest possible price. Therefore, it was said that if we amend those articles whose amendments is demanded, it will mean that we have paid a very high price, and if we prepare a new proposal, it will be less damaging . . . The version that was drafted is the least damaging that we could submit. It gives us an extension of six months until the central committee convenes. And then the central committee will discuss it. And it is within its rights to say: "I leave it for the National Council."[21]

The PNC's resolution did not change the covenant but rather began a long and arduous march in this direction by assigning to another group responsibility for amending it in unspecified ways without any clear schedule. At some undetermined point, this revised version was to go to yet another group, which would then act upon it, and there was no certainty that even the new document would be officially and legally approved.[22] The new covenant was still awaiting approval at the outbreak of Arafat's war in September 2000.

Arafat himself never acted as if the covenant had been amended in letter, let alone in spirit. In a series of interviews and public appearances on the eve of the PNC's convocation he sidestepped alluding to the amendment instead elaborated on his vision of peace, including the creation of "a democratic state in which Muslims, Christians, and Jews can coexist"—well understood as a euphemism for Israel's destruction. In his welcome address at the PNC opening session, Arafat went to great lengths to frame the entire peace process within the "phased plan," leaving little doubt in the minds of his listeners as to the PLO's ultimate objectives. "One foothold on the land of Palestine is more dear to me, and much more important than all words on paper, now that the miracle has been achieved, that the Palestinian entity was established, and that we started the 1,000–mile journey," he declared. "Yes, the Palestinian national entity and the Palestinian national authority, which the PNC endorsed in 1974. The PNC then endorsed the establishment of a national authority on any part of Palestinian territory which is liberated, or from which the Israelis withdraw."[23]

At a meeting with the Libyan dictator Muammar Qaddafi shortly after the PNC session, Arafat claimed that the covenant had not been amended. When asked at the National Press Club in Washington, during his first official visit to the United States in May 1996, whether the Palestinians had "changed their dream of taking control of all of Palestine," he became "suddenly angry," saying, "I, I not answer this . . . this is unfair question." When asked a follow-up question about Hamas's murderous campaign of suicide bombings, he repeated his favorite conspiracy theory that "an Israeli fanatic group" collaborated with Hamas and Islamic Jihad in "killing Palestinians and Jews."[24]

Arafat's comments should have cast serious doubts about the sincerity of his commitment to peace. The Peres government ignored him, expressing satisfaction that the sections of the covenant calling for Israel's destruction were indeed "null and void in all points." Uri Savir, director general of the foreign office and the chief Oslo negotiator, said he had been reassured by Abu Mazen, Arafat's second in command and an architect of the Oslo accords, that a new charter, which "will not contradict the commitment of the Palestinian Authority" to the peace agreement, would be drafted within six months.[25]

The Palestinians had deliberately deceived their Israeli interlocutors on this particular issue. Shortly before the PNC session, Yoel Singer, legal adviser to the Israeli foreign ministry and an Oslo negotiator, prepared with Abu Mazen a draft resolution that abolished the Palestinian Covenant in its entirety and provided for the drafting and approval of a new charter within six months. The draft resolution was approved by Peres and Arafat, but a couple of days before the voting session Abu Mazen suddenly informed Singer that he would not be submitting it to the PNC for approval. Feverish consultations between the two parties ensued, at the end of which the prime minister agreed to a different wording for the PNC resolution. The new version no longer canceled the entire covenant but rather amended it by abolishing, *with immediate effect*, those clauses that conflicted with the 1993 letters of mutual recognition. Without consulting the Israelis, the PNC adopted a resolution implying its readiness in principle to amend the covenant rather than its actual revision.[26]

Semantics took a backseat when Netanyahu came to power in June 1996. Unlike his Labor predecessors who had tied their fortunes to the Oslo process while losing sight of its major shortcomings, Netanyahu was a relentless critic of the process from the outset and was therefore unperturbed by its possible demise. Yet as he was bound by his predecessors' international commitments, he tried to make the best of what he considered a catastrophic situation by conditioning Israel's behavior on Palestinian compliance with written obligations.

This brought the covenant to the fore of Israeli-Palestinian relations. As the six-month deadline for the drafting of a new Palestinian covenant elapsed without any evidence that the legal committee had moved to complete a new text, the Netanyahu government, which considered the

PNC's 1996 vote a sham, insisted on a renewed and more definite Palestinian commitment to amend the covenant. The Note for the Record accompanying the January 1997 Hebron Protocol on Israel's redeployment in the city was the PLO's reaffirmed commitment to "complete the process of revising the Palestinian National Charter" and to do so "immediately and in parallel" with other remaining commitments.[27]

No sooner had the ink dried on the Hebron Protocol than Arafat reneged on his latest written commitment. "We have already canceled the articles that were in contradiction to the Oslo agreements," he told the French dailies *Le Monde* and *Liberation*. "We have fulfilled our commitments. The rest of it concerns us only. The Israelis want us to adopt a new charter. As far as I know, the Israelis do not have a constitution. When they will have one, we will do the same."[28]

Given that the redrafting of a new charter was a Palestinian rather than an Israeli idea, and intended to circumvent the covenant's actual amendment, Arafat's refusal to complete the process he himself had initiated gave Netanyahu additional support to refuse authorizing further Israeli redeployments before the amendment of the covenant. On January 22, 1998, Arafat gave President Clinton a letter specifying the provisions of the covenant that allegedly had been annulled. "From time to time, questions have been raised about the effect of the Palestine National Council's action, particularly concerning which of the 33 articles of the Palestinian Covenant have been changed," he wrote. "We would like to put to rest these concerns. The PNC's resolution in accordance with Article 33 of the covenant is a comprehensive amendment of the covenant."

"All of the provisions of the covenant which are inconsistent with the PLO commitment to recognize Israel are no longer in effect," continued the letter.

> As a result, Articles 6 through 10, 15, 19 through 23, and 30, have been nullified. And the parts of Articles 1 through 5, 11 through 14, 16 through 18, 25 through 27, and 29, which are inconsistent with the above-mentioned commitments have also been nullified. These changes will be reflected in any official publication of the charter.[29]

Arafat's letter was doubtless a step forward. For the first time in the nearly two years since the PNC vote, an official Palestinian source gave a detailed interpretation and listing of the articles that were "in contradiction to the Oslo Agreement." Yet his retroactive attempt to define what delegates had in mind when they cast their votes was still riddled with inconsistencies. The number of covenant clauses mentioned in Arafat's letter contradicted numerous statements made by Palestinian officials, most notably Faisal Hamdi Husseini, who was charged with redrawing the covenant. The letter also remained conspicuously ambiguous about the new wording of the articles that allegedly had been revised through the cancellation of parts "which are inconsistent with the [Oslo] commitments." Article 2, for example, asserts that "Palestine, with the boundaries it had during the British Mandate, is an indivisible territorial unit." It is difficult to see how this article, deliberately drafted to preclude the possibility of a two-state solution, can be changed short of complete revision or revocation. That Arafat refrained from doing this, as he did with regard to a string of similarly phrased articles, indicated his determination to leave the largest possible number of clauses virtually intact.

Above all, no Palestinian leader or body, apart from the PNC, could amend the covenant, let alone retroactively. In the 1997 Note for the Record the PLO committed itself to completing the required formal process of amendment, which would have required a reconvened PNC to revise, in a clear and unequivocal fashion, all articles denying Israel's right to exist and advocating the use of violence and terror. This was precisely what Arafat's latest ploy sought to avoid. "As far as we are concerned, this issue has been put to rest," he told reporters following an hour-long meeting at the White House, during which he presented his letter to Clinton, adding that he was "encouraged" by what he had heard from the American president.

Arafat's optimism proved premature. While the administration was prepared to draw the covenant issue to a close, the Israeli government remained unmoved. "A letter won't do," said David Bar-Illan, Netanyahu's communications adviser. "Only the reconvening of the Palestinian National Council and going through all the procedures dictated by the covenant itself" can lead to a genuine revision, he said, adding, "We don't want any fake cancellations."[30]

At the Wye River summit of October 1998 Arafat tried yet again to evade the amendment of the covenant. "I already convened the PNC in 1996, in coordination with the Israelis and the Americans and in front of the entire world," he argued. "I cannot reconvene it again. I will be accused of having cheated them all." His position was supported by the Clinton administration, which sought to convince Netanyahu to drop the demand for the covenant's revision. The administration believed it would be advisable to let the PNC wither away as a remnant of the past, rather than sustain its central role in Palestinian national life. In the end, a compromise formula was devised in the Wye River Memorandum, which outlined a series of Israeli and Palestinian steps to facilitate the implementation of the 1995 Interim Agreement. This obliged the PLO's Executive and Central committees to reaffirm Arafat's 1998 letter to Clinton. Following this, the PNC members, as well as members of the Legislative Council and the PA's heads of ministries, would be officially invited to "a meeting to be addressed by President Clinton to reaffirm their support for the peace process and the aforementioned decisions of the Executive Committee and the Central Committee."[31]

As the two committees approved Arafat's letter to Clinton, on December 14, 1998, hundreds of PNC and Legislative Council delegates convened in the Rashad Shawaa Cultural Center in Gaza and by a show of hands, but not a formal vote, supported Arafat's changes to the covenant. Visibly touched by this mass display of unity made on his behalf, Clinton hailed the vote as a momentous move, promising to request congressional support of "several hundred million dollars" for the Palestinians. "I thank you for your rejection—fully, finally, and forever—of the passages in the Palestinian charter calling for the destruction of Israel," he told the audience. "By turning this page on the past, you are taking the lead in writing a new story for the future. And you have issued a challenge to the government of Israel to walk down the path with you. I thank you for doing that."[32]

While there is no doubting the historic symbolism of this ceremony, the fact that more than five years of intense pressure were required to overcome an endless series of evasive maneuvers underscores the PLO's extreme reluctance to disown its legacy of hate and rejection. Yet even at this "final" moment of truth, the PLO could not bring itself to follow the necessary procedure, required by its own covenant to this end, opting instead for a substitute, however spectacular, that left a substantial number of offensive clauses virtually unchanged. This allowed the PLO to ostensibly abide by its commitment to the extent that was required for a substantial Israeli quid pro quo, while at the same time signaling to its constituency that its historic slogan "Struggle until Victory" was still the ultimate goal.

When one views the unwillingness of the Palestinian leadership to amend the covenant in these terms, it also becomes apparent why it was so vehemently opposed to the possible dissolving of the PLO itself after the establishment of an independent Palestinian state in the West Bank and the Gaza Strip. A body created with the goal of "liberating the whole of Palestine" (i.e., destroying Israel) still serves a vital function in a post-Oslo world where the original goals of the covenant remain the same. As Salim Zaanun believes,

> The PLO will not disband under any circumstances after the establish-
> ment of a Palestinian state [in the West Bank and Gaza]. The PLO is a
> national and historic accomplishment of the Palestinian people and be-
> longs to them. It was founded to fight for liberation and independence
> and will continue its struggle until all the Palestinian rights are attained,
> particularly the right of return of Palestinian refugees.[33]

5

Hate Thy Neighbor

The noble soul has two goals: death and the desire for it.
—*Our Beautiful Language*, textbook for the sixth
grade, Palestinian Authority

Peace, according to the great seventeenth-century philosopher Baruch Spinoza, is not merely the absence of war but rather a state of mind: a disposition to benevolence, confidence, and justice. From the birth of the Zionist movement, that disposition has remained conspicuously absent from the mind of Arab and Palestinian leaders. Reluctant to accept the right of the Jewish people to national self-determination in its ancestral homeland, they have invariably viewed the establishment of Israel as an imperialist plot to divide and weaken the "Arab nation" by implanting an artificial entity in its midst. Since the road to the cherished ideal of Arab unity runs through the "elimination of the traces of imperialism," the struggle over Palestine involves nothing less than Arab national existence.

It has thus been Israel's technological edge, the commitment and resilience of its society, and, above all, the performance of its armed forces in its decisive military victories that have gradually driven the Arabs toward the path of politics and a grudging acceptance of its existence with every Arab defeat or military setback. It would be wrong, however, to construe this as a fundamental acceptance of Israel's legitimacy, as demonstrated by the Egyptian-Israeli peace treaty of March 1979, the first to be signed between the Jewish state and its Arab neighbors. While one can only speculate about Anwar Sadat's own ultimate intentions—he was assassinated in October 1981 for having gone as far toward peace with Israel as he did—there is little doubt that his

successor, Muhammad Hosni Mubarak, has never had any desire to transform the formal Egyptian peace with Israel into a genuine reconciliation. Over the decades, Mubarak has reduced interaction with Israel to
a minimum, while simultaneously transforming the Egyptian army into
a formidable fighting force. He has also fostered a culture of virulent anti-
Semitism in Egypt. All in all, contractual peace with Israel has represented, for Arab parties, not a recognition of legitimacy but a tacit
admission that, at least for the time being, the Arabs have been unable
to defeat Israel by force of arms.

Living under these circumstances it was only natural for Israel to go to
great lengths to ensure that its peace agreements with the PLO would
provide for the widest possible cooperation at the grassroots level: educational, economic, scientific-technological, and people-to-people programs.
No less important, by way of overcoming the long and painful legacy of
hostility and distrust between the two peoples, the agreements included
a number of concrete confidence-building measures, starting with the
stipulation, in the Gaza and Jericho Agreement of May 1994, that

> Israel and the Palestinian Authority shall seek to foster mutual understand-
> ing and tolerance and shall accordingly abstain from incitement, includ-
> ing hostile propaganda, against each other and, without derogating from
> the principle of freedom of expression, shall take legal measures to pre-
> vent such incitement by any organizations, groups or individuals within
> their jurisdiction.

This commitment was reiterated the following year in the Interim Agreement on the West Bank and the Gaza Strip (Oslo II), with the added
provision that "Israel and the [Palestinian] Council will ensure that their
respective educational systems contribute to the peace between the
Israeli and Palestinian peoples and to peace in the entire region, and
will refrain from the introduction of any motifs that could adversely af-
fect the process of reconciliation."

The Wye River Memorandum of October 1998 took these commitments a step further by obliging the Palestinians to issue "a decree
prohibiting all forms of incitement to violence or terror, and establishing mechanisms for acting systematically against all expressions or
threats of violence or terror. This decree will be comparable to the
existing Israeli legislation which deals with the same subject." In ad-

dition, a trilateral American-Palestinian-Israeli committee was to meet on a regular basis "to monitor cases of possible incitement to violence or terror and to make recommendations and reports on how to prevent such incitement."[1]

Arafat and his Palestinian Authority have never abided by these commitments. Not only have they done little to build trust between Israelis and Palestinians but, flagrantly violating their obligations under Oslo, they have indoctrinated their people, particularly their young people, to an ineradicable enmity toward both the state of Israel and Jews and Judaism. There has been no Palestinian peace education, only preparation for violence and war.

Arafat set the tone before the signing of the DOP when he defined Israel as the enemy rather than a peace partner. "Judea and Samaria no longer exist," he said in a radio interview on September 1, 1993. "There is occupied Palestinian territory from which the enemy, the Israelis, will gradually withdraw."[2] The following month he asserted that there would be no normalization with Israel before its complete withdrawal from the territories, the restoration of full Palestinian rights, and comprehensive peace with the Arab world. In a visit to Senegal shortly after the signing of the DOP, Arafat called on the African states not to recognize Israel until the creation of a Palestinian state, while his deputy Abu Mazen made the same plea to the Arab states.[3]

"Israel is still our enemy," Hanan Ashrawi told a group of Arab-American political activists shortly after the signing of the DOP. "The agreement does not change the situation in the territories into a rose garden."[4] Freih Abu Medein, the PA's minister of justice, told students in Gaza (in April 1995) that "Israel is the foremost enemy of the Palestinian people, now and forever." The following month, reading a speech on Arafat's behalf at a Gaza cultural event, Medein reiterated, "Israel will continue to be the enemy of the Palestinian people, not only in the present time but also in the future."[5] Medein also declared, "The death penalty will be imposed on anyone who is convicted of selling one inch [of land] to Israel. Even middlemen involved in such deals will face the same penalty." The declaration received Arafat's full support. "They are isolated traitors, and we will act against them according to the law."[6]

Seizing a symbolic opportunity to indicate to his Palestinian constituents that the Oslo process was not his own choice but rather a constraint forced upon the PLO by a unique combination of adverse regional and international circumstances, Arafat broke all protocol and custom at the signing ceremony of the Gaza and Jericho Agreement in Cairo by refusing to sign the maps attached to the accord. Hectic attempts at persuasion ensued to the astonished disbelief of hundreds of millions of viewers throughout the world who watched the ceremony live on television. Rabin's protest that they had shaken hands on the deal the previous night had no impact on the Palestinian leader.[7] It took the forceful prodding of the host, President Mubarak, to end the bizarre episode. "Sign immediately, you dog," he snapped behind clenched teeth. Arafat begrudgingly complied, but not before demonstratively failing to sit down to sign the deal, instead stooping over casually to attach his signature to the documents.[8]

During Arafat's triumphant arrival in the territories two months later, rather than promoting the agreement that had enabled this momentous development he used the occasion to discredit the deal and to smear his new peace partner. "I know that many of you are unhappy with the agreement I have signed," he told a group of young militants at a Gaza refugee camp. "I am not happy with it either." In an address in Jericho, Arafat went a significant step further. To the audience's ecstatic chants of "With our lives and our blood we will redeem Palestine," he unleashed a lengthy diatribe against Israel, which, he claimed, had always sought, and was still seeking, to destroy the Palestinian people. Parroting the Arab version of the notorious anti-Semitic tract "Protocols of the Elders of Zion," he told his audience of the alleged Zionist grand design to take over Palestine step by step:

> Since 1897 the Zionists have been claiming that Palestine is "a land without a people for a people without a land," thus denying altogether the existence of the Palestinian people. In 1907 the whole of Europe accepted this assertion. In 1917 the Balfour Declaration was pronounced, in 1947 the Partition Resolution was passed, and in 1967 the whole of Palestine was occupied.

"We must understand that all of this has been designed to wipe the Palestinian people off the map and that the conspiracy to obliterate the Palestinian people persists to this very day," Arafat continued, as if Israel was not a peace partner but a mortal enemy. "But I keep on telling them that no one can destroy or humiliate the Palestinian people. The children of the stones have proved to the world that this people is irrepressible . . . It is a nation of giants. Yes, my brothers, efforts are being made to divide our ranks," he added, visibly exhilarated by the chants for Palestine's violent "liberation." "They think that they can sow divisions within the Palestinian people and are acting in this vein. Which is why I am telling you, my beloved brothers: Unity, unity, unity . . . until we establish our independent state with holy Jerusalem as its capital."[9] Arafat's speech in Gaza a couple of days earlier, though substantially toned down in advance by President Mubarak so as to avert a direct confrontation with Israel, went even further, ending with a pledge to "liberate" Israel's Arab citizens—not the residents of the West Bank and Gaza—from their alleged subjugation. "I am saying it clearly and loudly to all our brothers, from the Negev to the Galilee," he said, "and let me quote Allah's words: 'We desired to be gracious to those that were abased in the land, and to make them leaders, and to make them the inheritors, and to establish them in the land.'"[10]

A common charge leveled by Arafat against Israel from the onset of the peace process has stemmed from its alleged destruction of the West Bank's and Gaza's infrastructure during its control of these territories after the Six-Day War of June 1967. "All our infrastructure has been destroyed. We are facing starvation in Gaza," Arafat told the BBC a day after the signing of the DOP. A week later he told French television that "the occupation destroyed [Palestinian] infrastructure and we have to start from point zero, or even below that." In an interview with Egyptian journalists in August 1995, on the eve of the signing of the Interim Agreement, Arafat was far more scathing. "You can't imagine the poor shape in which we received Gaza," he said. "The infrastructure was totally ruined. The Israelis took everything before their departure: doors, windows, lightbulbs, and taps. The Palestinian administration had to operate for nine months from carton shackles. There is no ill from which Gaza does not suffer."[11]

Far from plunging into a steep decline under Israeli rule, the West Bank and Gaza experienced astounding social and economic progress that placed them well ahead of most Arab states in terms of per capita income and standard of living. Yet Arafat was not a person bothered by the facts. As his Authority took control over the Palestinian population of the territories Israelis, and Jews more generally, were invariably portrayed as the source of all evil and responsible for every problem, real or imaginary, in the territories, a synonym for evil, corruption, and decadence. Palestinians have been told of the most outlandish Israeli plots to corrupt and ruin them, yet are wholly congruent with the medieval myths of Jews as secret destroyers and poisoners of wells. Thus, Arafat has charged Israel with killing Palestinian children to get their organs, while the PA's minister of health, Riad Zaanun, has accused Israeli doctors of using "Palestinian patients for experimental medicines." The Palestinian representative to the Human Rights Commission in Geneva charged Israel with injecting Palestinian children with the AIDS virus, while the director of medical guidance in the PA's anti-drug directorate accused Israel of distributing drugs in the Palestinian territories in order to destroy Palestinian society and create crime and social problems among youth. The PA minister of ecology, Yusuf Abu Safiyyah, indicted Israel for "dumping liquid waste . . . in Palestinian areas in the West Bank and Gaza," a charge famously amplified by Suha Arafat when, in the presence of Hillary Clinton, she told an attentive audience in Gaza in November 1999 that "our people have been subjected to the daily and extensive use of poisonous gas by the Israeli forces, which has led to an increase in cancer cases among women and children."[12]

Perhaps the most successful anti-Semitic import in the Muslim-Arab world is the theory of an organized Jewish conspiracy to achieve world domination, as spelled out in the notorious "Protocols of the Elders of Zion." This virulent anti-Semitic tract, fabricated by the Russian secret police at the turn of the twentieth century, made its appearance in western Europe during and immediately after World War I. Translated into Arabic in the mid-1920s, the work has remained enormously popular to this day, published in numerous editions and in several translations, including one by the brother of Egyptian president Gamal Abdel Nasser. (Nasser himself would recommend the pamphlet as a useful guide to the "Jewish mind," as would his successor Anwar Sadat, King Faisal of Saudi Arabia, and Muammar Qaddafi of Libya, among many others.)

The Palestinian Authority has repeatedly referred to the "Protocols" and its tightly controlled media has been rife with numerous stories about Jewish "plots" and "conspiracies." Arafat borrowed from the "Protocols" in his welcome speech in Jericho in July 1994, and in late 1997, when a dispute ensued about the scope of Israel's military redeployment in the West Bank, the PA's largest daily, *al-Hayat al-Jadida,* derided the maps presented by the Israeli government as the latest manifestation of the alleged Zionist grand design, expressed in the "Protocols of the Elders of Zion" to expand from the Nile to the Euphrates. Subsequent articles went even further, elaborating on the devious plots devised in the "Protocols" for manipulating world public opinion on behalf of Zionism. According to this account, already in its first general congress in Basle (1897) the Zion-ist movement recognized that unless it gained complete and unassailable control over the world media, the press in particular, its cherished goal of establishing a Jewish state would never come to fruition. After some initial setbacks, this goal had been achieved by the mid-twentieth century:

> A glance at the number of news agencies, newspapers, magazines, and TV networks under Jewish control demonstrates their overwhelming influence over the mass media. They control several French and British newspapers, including the *Times,* through its owner, the Australian-based Jew Rupert Murdoch [in fact Murdoch is not Jewish], who also owns three magazines that specialize in spreading prostitution. Jews have managed to monopolize the British chattering classes. In addition to the *Times,* they have taken over the *Daily Express, Daily Mail* and the *Observer,* among numerous other journals. In the United States, [the Jews control] the *New York Times, New York Post, Washington Post,* the *New Yorker* magazine, *Business Week,* and so forth and so on. In France, [they own] *Nouveaux Cahiers, L'Express, Le Figaro, Le Cotidiene de Paris* and *France Soir.* In other Western countries, like Australia, they also own a fair share of the media, including the world's leading TV networks. ABC, NBC, CBS, and many more are all controlled by Jews.
>
> It is evident that Jewish control over the mass media has been exploited for putting a fine lining on the vile image of Jews, while at the same time vilifying Arabs, so as to persuade world public opinion that Arabs are the historic enemies of Christian culture . . . Furthermore, Jews spread prostitution as a means of plunging the world into decadence, abomination, and corruption.

"Corruption is a Jewish trait worldwide, to the extent that one can hardly find corruption that is not associated with Jews," argued yet another article in *al-Hayat al-Jadida:*

Their intense love of money and its accumulation is common knowledge, and they have no scruples about how to get it. To the contrary, they use the most degrading means to realize their aims, as long as the persons involved are not Jewish . . . They have concentrated all their efforts on devising evil schemes since they believe that the secret of their survival lies in controlling the economies of the countries that have opened their doors to them and have sheltered them from persecution . . . They have also concocted scandals implicating [non-Jewish] leaders so as to allow Jews to gain influence over them and sway them in the direction of their interests . . . [One of these] has been Bill Clinton, President of the most powerful nation on earth. Zionists began to implicate him already when he was governor. Since then he has been complying with the dictates of World Zionism, fearing that his scandals would be exposed.[13]

This pervasive denigration of Jews has been accompanied by a systematic denial of the Jewish state's legitimacy by both the PA and the PLO. Israel is often referred to by the Arab pejorative "the Zionist entity," and is glaringly absent from Palestinian maps, which portray its territory as part of a "Greater Palestine"—again, that is, from the Jordan River to the Mediterranean. When in 1998 Prime Minister Netanyahu protested this point, the PA's press responded contemptuously. "Which Israel is he talking about: that of 1948, 1967, 1982, or that extending from the Nile to the Euphrates? Let him define for us what Israel is so that we can add it to the map of the dictatorships that have had their day in history, only to vanish later without a trace."[14]

The new Palestinian school curriculum, introduced in September 2000, six years after the Palestinian Authority had assumed control of educational and cultural affairs in the West Bank and Gaza, conspicuously ignores Israel's existence in textbook maps, illustrations and narrative to such an extent that it fails to mention the long-standing Jewish-Palestinian conflict, instead referring to it obliquely as "external threats and provocations" to Palestinian national development. The 1993 Declaration of Principles is mentioned in the new textbooks only once, and even then not as a peace accord but rather as a document that enabled the return of "the largest part of the troops of the [Palestinian] Liberation Army to Palestine."[15]

Likewise, the PA's press and other media habitually refer to Israeli towns, cities, and regions as "occupied Palestinian land," often noting them by their Arabic names though many of these sites bear biblical names, predating Palestine's Arab occupation by millennia (for example, the Valley of Jezreel, called Bani Amr Valley in Palestinian media and textbooks). The Palestinian media constantly feature articles, programs, and documentaries glorifying the idyllic Palestine that had supposedly been destroyed by Israel and vowing to restore this lost paradise. The UN partition resolution of November 1947 is invariably denounced as an illegal act of international aggression, sending a clear message regarding the illegitimacy of the two-state solution. As a member of the Palestinian Council declared in a special program on PA television on the fiftieth anniversary of the UN resolution, "Our war with Israel and the Jews has not ended and will not end until the establishment of a Palestinian state on the whole of Palestine."[16]

As part of its effort to deny Israel's legitimacy, the Palestinian Authority has persistently denigrated Israeli and Jewish history, even repudiating any Jewish connection to the Temple Mount in Jerusalem or, by implication, to the land of Israel itself.

In a discussion on official PA television in June 1997, for instance, the prominent Palestinian historian Jarir Qudwa argued that the events described in the Bible took place in the Arabian peninsula, mainly in Yemen, and not in Palestine. This means that there is no Jewish historical association with Palestine, and that present-day Jews and Israelis have nothing to do with the ancient Israelites. "Most of the Ashkemaz Jews in Israel are descendants of the Khazars [an Asian people who converted to Judaism in the eighth and ninth centuries]," he claimed. "God is my witness that I have more Israelite blood in my veins than Ariel Sharon and Benjamin Netanyahu." According to Qudwa, the biblical Jewish Temple existed in Mecca, rather than in Jerusalem, while "the origins of civilization in Palestine dates back to our Canaanite forefathers who . . . drew the country's urban map more than 3,000 years ago."[17]

Additionally, during the Camp David summit of July 2000, several Palestinian negotiators denied the existence of King Solomon's Temple. Arafat himself told Clinton that the Temple had been located in Nablus rather than in Jerusalem, only to hear from the president that "not only the Jews but I, too, believe that under the surface there are remains of Solomon's temple."[18]

If the Temple signifies for the Palestinians the foremost ancient symbol of Jewish attachment to Palestine, the Holocaust is viewed as the most powerful modern-day justification for the existence of a Jewish state and has been similarly denied by the Palestinian Authority. By underscoring the horrendous scope of recent Jewish suffering, the Holocaust challenges the carefully nurtured image of righteousness adopted by the Palestinians as the hapless target of a Zionist grand design to dispossess them from their land, a historical wrong that they are entitled to redress.

Far from being the hapless victims of a predatory Zionist assault, the Palestinians were themselves the aggressors in the 1948 war, and it was they who attempted, albeit unsuccessfully, to "cleanse" a neighboring ethnic community. With the passage of time, however, Palestinian propaganda has managed to rewrite the history of the conflict to its own advantage. This has left the Holocaust as the foremost counterargument against the Palestinian claim to victimhood. The PA's official media has gone out of its way, albeit in a dual and often contradictory fashion, to minimize the Holocaust, if not deny it altogether. At the same time, the Palestinians are portrayed as the Holocaust's real victims for allegedly having to foot the bill for the West's presumed desire to atone for this genocidal act through the establishment of a Jewish state. (Aside from the actual absence of such "corrective policy" by the Europeans—Britain, as the occupying power of Palestine, was vehemently opposed to the creation of the Jewish state—if one were to accept the Palestinian denial of the Holocaust then there would have been no conceivable reason for the European nations to feel remorseful for something that had not even taken place.)

On numerous occasions, the PA's press and electronic media have reiterated their claim that the Nazi genocide did not take place, and that the number of Jews killed during the Second World War was nowhere near six million. Even Abu Mazen, the foremost symbol of Palestinian reconciliation, argued in a 1984 book that fewer than a million Jews had been killed in the Holocaust and that the Zionist movement was a partner in the mass slaughter of the Jews.[19] "The persecution of the Jews is a deceitful myth, labeled by the Jews as a Holocaust and exploited for garnering sympathy for them," ran a typical article in *al-Hayat al-Jadida*.

> They began to distribute horrific pictures of mass executions and fabricated the shocking story of the gas chambers, where Hitler allegedly gassed them. Newspaper columns began to fill up with pictures of Jews being cut down by Hitler's machine guns and of Jews being led to the gas chambers. In these pictures, they focused on women, children and old people and have exploited this to arouse sympathy for them, while demanding financial compensation, donations, and grants from all over the world . . . And while it is possible that Hitler's assault against the Jews hurt them slightly, the fact is that it has done them an important service, whose fruits they are reaping to this very day, and has constituted the main vehicle for winning American and European sympathy and for realizing their dreams and plans.[20]

Since Israel's very existence is based on a false pretense, then by extension, the Palestinian Authority has argued, there is no justification for the continued survival of this cancerous entity on Palestinian land. "Why have Jews from all over the world congregated in Palestine to establish their false state, while the real owners of the land are denied their right to national self-determination on their own soil? . . . Why was Israel not established in the United States or in Britain?" lamented *al-Hayat al-Jadida*, before calling "to renew the vow for the continuation of the struggle until *the liberation of the whole of Palestine* from the filth of occupation."[21] The newspaper's chief editor, Hafez Barghouthi, argued on Fatah's thirty-third anniversary that "Since the start of the revolution on January 1, 1965, to date, the struggle with the Zionist entity has continued, whether through the force of arms or by negotiations . . . This is a struggle that will not come to an end until the realization of the Palestinian people's legitimate rights on its national homeland."[22]

A poem read on the PA's official radio station addressed the same theme in more literary terms.

O my beautiful land, imprisoned in a cage and surrounded by wolves,
My shaded garden, the tormentors have destroyed you,

O Jerusaelm, O my city, the dogs have settled in thee,
With my notebook and pencil and the fire of my rifle I will shatter the cage,
I will kill the wolves and plant the flag,
The dogs will not bark in my heroic city.[23]

Children have occupied a place of pride in the PA's hate campaign. Like other modern dictators, from Adolf Hitler and Nicolae Ceauşescu to Saddam Hussein, Arafat is keenly aware that the road to absolute power has to begin with the education of the young, whose minds have not been "corrupted by backward ideas." From their first days at kindergarten, Palestinian children are inculcated with virulent hatred toward Jews and Israelis. They learn about an evil Jewish persona, traceable to biblical times, which accounts for the worldwide persecution of the Jews through the ages. They are indoctrinated with the idea that Jews are, and always have been, implacable enemies of Islam, people who "called Muhammad a liar and denied him, [who] fought against his religion in all ways and by all means, a war that has not yet ended until today." The Bible and the Talmud are singled out for particular scrutiny as the principal sources of Jewish moral depravity, the Bible being "full of texts that support the Jews' tendency to racial and religious zealotry" and the Talmud being a racist treatise obliging the Jews to seclude themselves from others even as they infiltrate and ruin the societies in which they live. As one school textbook puts it:

> It is said in the Talmud: "We [the Jews] are God's people on earth. . . . [God] forced upon the human animal and upon all nations and races that they serve us, and He spread us through the world to ride on them and hold their reins. We must marry our beautiful daughters with kings, ministers, and lords and enter our sons into the various religions, for thus we will have the final word in managing the countries. We should cheat [non-Jews] and arouse quarrels among them, then they will fight each other. . . . Non-Jews are pigs who God created in the shape of man in order that they be fit for service for the Jews, and God created the world for [the Jews]."

As they grow up, Palestinian children can join various youth organizations where they are further brainwashed with racist and anti-Semitic ideology. An increasingly important role in this systematic indoctrination is an extensive network of summer camps, established by the PA following its assumption of control of the Palestinian population of the West Bank in early 1996. Modeled on the Nazi youth organization Hitler Jugend, these camps have provided a carefully contrived mixture of ideological indoctrination and military training to thousands of Palestinian youth every year. All camps are named after "martyrs" or spectacular "acts of martyrdom" (i.e., terrorist attacks), and participants are thoroughly imbued with the virtues of death and martyrdom. In the words of a typical poem recited at the opening of a summer camp and broadcast on the PA's television:

> *We are your boys, O Palestine*
> *We will flood you with our blood . . .*
> *No one can stand against us on the battlefield . . .*
> *Let the rifle cry with joy . . .*
> *Fan the flames of fire, O son of Canaan, for your people is rising up.*[24]

Camp activities include such war games as charging Israeli outposts and kidnapping Israeli leaders while killing their bodyguards. At a graduation parade shown on PA television in August 2000, about a thousand Palestinian youngsters stood in neatly ordered platoons, cheering the mock kidnapping of an unsuspecting Israeli politician.[25]

Nor has Arafat been shy about utilizing the immense inflammatory potential of Islam, which has constituted the linchpin of the Middle Eastern social and political order for more than a millennium. The ease and rapidity with which the fundamentals of European anti-Semitism have been assimilated by the Muslim-Arab world testify to the preexistence of a deep anti-Jewish bigotry, dating to Islam's earliest days, and indeed to the Koran itself.

Reflecting the Prophet Muhammad's outrage over the rejection of his religious message by the Jewish community, both the Koran and later biographical traditions of the Prophet abound with negative depictions of Jews. In these works they are portrayed as a deceitful, evil, and treacherous people who in their insatiable urge for domination would readily betray an ally and swindle a non-Jew, along with tampering with the Holy Scriptures, spurning Allah's divine message, and persecuting

His messenger Muhammad just as they had done previous prophets, including Jesus of Nazareth. For this perfidy, they will incur a string of retributions, both in the afterlife, when they will burn in hell, and here on earth where they have been justly condemned to an existence of wretchedness and humiliation. "I never saw the curse denounced against the children of Israel more fully brought to bear than in the East," wrote an early-nineteenth-century Western traveler to the Ottoman empire, "where they are considered rather as a link between animals and human beings than as men possessed by the same attributes." To another nineteenth-century visitor to the region, the Jews' "pusillanimity is so excessive, that they flee before the uplifted hand of a child."[26]

Given the millennial disparagement of Jews in the Arab Middle East, it is hardly surprising that Arafat, himself a religious man deeply imbued with anti-Jewish prejudice since childhood,[27] has been using religious incitement as a primary tool to discredit his Israeli peace partners and, by extension, peace itself. In a message broadcast from his Tunis headquarters to a seminar at Ramallah's Bir Zeit University, shortly before the signing of the DOP, Arafat charged Israel with, among other things, "the violation of Islamic and Christian holy places, and the banning of our people's freedom to practice their religious rites." He repeated this in an address to the Arab League's one hundredth session later that month, and yet again at a 1995 UNESCO conference in Paris. A stone-faced Peres, who shared the platform with Arafat on that occasion, peremptorily denied the allegations.[28]

This rhetoric pales in comparison with the pervasive religious incitement institutionalized by the Palestinian Authority since its creation in the spring of 1994. Until then, mosques and religious courts in Gaza had been run by Egypt, while their West Bank counterparts had been administered by the Jordanians, under special arrangement with Israel, in force since 1967. In late 1994, Egypt handed over responsibility for religious affairs in Gaza to the PA, and King Hussein agreed to do the same in the West Bank, while maintaining his claim, as descendant of the Prophet Muhammad, to responsibility in Jerusalem. In reality, the PA's influence quickly spread to Jerusalem as well. As early as October 1994, Arafat appointed Sheik Ikrima Sabri to the highest Palestinian religious post—Mufti of Jerusalem—alongside the Jordanian appointee Abdel Qader Abdin. As a result, Abdin was all but ignored by the Palestinians, with preachers in the al-Aqsa mosque (who had previously had the texts of their Friday sermons vetted by the Jordanians) handing them instead to Arafat's officials for approval.

By controlling what was said at these Friday sermons, Arafat has found an extremely powerful tool of incitement. These sermons, which can run for up to an hour, are designed to teach Muslims about their religion and its main precepts, but under the PA they have concentrated far less on religious education than on anti-Israeli incitement. Week after week preachers have been using the pulpits to discredit the peace process and to instill hatred for Israelis and Jews. Worshipers have been taught that Jews are the "descendants of apes and pigs" and warned of Zionist machinations to divide the Palestinian people and spawn internecine strife. "The Koran repeatedly warns against the traps and plots of the 'people of the book,'" ran a typical sermon broadcast on the PA's official radio. "They relentlessly scheme in all times and places and this is what they are doing today and will do tomorrow against the Muslim camp."[29]

Israel has frequently been referred to as "the enemy," while the Oslo accords have often been derided as a devious plot to humiliate the Palestinians. "By what right do the Jews allow themselves to steal our lands or the lands of our fathers and grandfathers?" lamented a preacher in the West Bank town of Tulkarm. "What is taken by deception is illegal." A Gazan preacher took this theme one step further. "All the Muslims, and not only the Palestinians, are responsible for Jerusalem and al-Aqsa," he argued. "And not only these two places are holy, but the entire land of Palestine. Preserving the Holy Land can be achieved only through holy war [jihad]."

When in December 1994 Palestinian police shot and killed fourteen Hamas activists during the first bloody confrontation between the Palestinian Authority and its opponents, Ikrima Sabri in a sermon quickly blamed Israel for the massacre. "Investigations have shown that a third hand stirred up the trouble," he told worshipers at the al-Aqsa mosque. "Some of the ammunition used must have come from the Israeli army, because the Palestinian police do not use dumdum bullets." Another al-Aqsa sermon blamed Israel for the spread of illegal weapons in the Palestinian territories in an attempt to "turn the West Bank and the Gaza Strip into a second Lebanon."[30]

In making these false accusations Sabri was taking his cue from his paymaster, Yasser Arafat, who never tired of repeating the fantastic allegations that militant circles within the Israeli army and security services were both flooding the territories with weapons in the hope that this would lead to a Palestinian civil war and masterminding the homicide bombings against Israeli civilians.[31] One can easily detect a correlation between the vicissitudes in the PA's policy and the tone and direction of Friday sermons. When in the summer of 2000 Arafat chose to use the question of Jerusalem as the pretext for bringing about the collapse of the Camp David summit, Sabri quickly mounted a spirited propaganda campaign. "No stone of the *al-Buraq* wall [i.e., the Wailing Wall] has any relation to Judaism," he argued. "The Jews began praying at this wall only in the nineteenth century, when they began to develop [national] aspirations." Elsewhere he expanded this denial to include the entire country, claiming that "there is not a single stone in Palestine that proves the Jewish existence [in the land]."[32]

As Arafat launched his war of terror in September 2000, the Friday sermons shed whatever vestiges of restraint they'd had, embarking on an orgy of unmitigated anti-Jewish invective. In a sermon delivered on October 13, 2000, by Ahmad Abu Halabiya (former acting rector of the Islamic University in Gaza), on the day after the barbaric lynching of two Israeli soldiers in the West Bank city of Ramallah, Abu Halabiya demanded live on the PA's official television channel to

> Have no mercy on the Jews, *no matter where they are, in any country* [emphasis added]. Fight them, wherever you are. Wherever you meet them, kill them. Wherever you are, kill those Jews and those Americans who are like them and those who stand by them. They are all in one trench against the Arabs and the Muslims because they established Israel here, in the beating heart of the Arab world, in Palestine.

Sheik Ibrahim Mahdi, from the Sheik Ijlin Mosque in Gaza, had a similar message in one of his Friday sermons, broadcast on the PA's television on August 3, 2001:

> A young man said to me: "I am fourteen years old, and I have four years left before I blow myself up amongst the Jews." I said to him: "Oh son, I ask Allah to give you and myself Martyrdom."

The Prophet said: "The Jews will fight you, and [Allah] will establish
you as rulers over them . . . " We blow them up in Hadera, we blow them
up in Tel Aviv and in Netanya, and in this way, Allah establishes us as
rulers over these gangs of vagabonds. The Jews fight you, but Allah will
establish you as rulers over them. Until the Jew would hide behind a stone
or a tree, and the stone or the tree would say: "Oh Muslim, Oh servant of
Allah, a Jew is hiding behind me, come kill him, with the exception of the
Gharqad tree which is the tree of the Jews."

Blessings for whoever has raised his sons on the education of Jihad and
martyrdom; blessings for whoever has saved a bullet in order to stick it in
a Jew's head.

Ikrima Sabri was not to be upstaged by one of his subordinates. "They
think that they scare our people," he said in his Friday sermon on May
25, 2001, one week before a suicide bomber murdered twenty teenagers at a Tel Aviv discotheque.

We tell them: in as much as you love life—the Muslim loves death and
martyrdom. There is a great difference between he who loves the hereaf-
ter and he who loves this world. The Muslim loves death and [strives for]
martyrdom. He does not fear the oppression of the arrogant or the weapons of the blood-letters. The blessed and sacred soil of Palestine has vom-
ited all the invaders and all the colonialists throughout history and it will
soon vomit, with Allah's help, the [present] occupiers.[33]

This outright call for the indiscriminate slaughter of Jews and the destruction of the state of Israel was made by the highest-ranking Palestinian religious figure, appointed by the Palestinian Authority, and broadcast
on its official television and radio stations week after week. The tone and
substance of Sabri's sermon was not unique in any way. It afforded yet
another illustration of the guiding principle of Arafat's relations with Israel since the onset of the Oslo process: "Hate Thy Neighbor."

6

Terror Until Victory

The Palestinian people is willing to sacrifice its last boy and girl so that the Palestinian flag will fly over the churches and mosques of Jerusalem.

—Yasser Arafat, September 1995

At their first substantial meeting in Cairo, in October 1993, Rabin found Arafat totally impervious to the PLO's security undertakings. According to the DOP, following its withdrawal from Gaza and Jericho Israel would continue to exercise responsibility for external security, including the control of the border crossings with Egypt and Jordan, so as to prevent weapons smuggling and hostile infiltration. Now Arafat told Rabin that the Palestinians would be responsible for these borders and deploy their own soldiers there.

"You can have some police," said Rabin. "But, as party to the agreement, we are responsible for external security."

"No, no, Your Excellency, maybe we will let you have a few soldiers there!"

Rabin almost exploded. "We are responsible for external security!"

"Your Highness, Your Excellency, Your Highness—this is not external security! This is not external security!"[1]

It was thus left to Foreign Minister Peres, during a meeting later that month in the Spanish town of Granada, to convince Arafat to abide by his signed commitments. "Mr. Chairman," Peres said. "Rabin and I are aware of your difficulties, and we're interested in seeing you succeed. But you must appreciate that violence by Hamas, which we can foresee as part of their anti-peace strategy, will be met by our sharp response. We will not compromise over the operational side of controlling the border passages. . . . We're concerned about the smuggling of weapons," he stressed. "This is absolutely vital to our security."

"I cannot go for a Bantustan," Arafat protested. "Please look for another formula. You don't trust me!"

"We don't trust Hamas!"

"I cannot agree to this, given the opposition I face and the criticism of my associates. It's a matter of our honor. We will not permit security violations. We'll be tougher on this than you."

Old habits die hard. With violence constituting the essence of both its political philosophy and its operational ethos, if not its entire raison d'être, the PLO refused to distance itself from what its hallowed founding document, the Palestinian Covenant, stipulated as "the only way to liberate Palestine." When in the summer of 1974 the failure to entice the residents of the West Bank and Gaza into an armed struggle against Israel, and the consequent realization that Israel could not be defeated by military means alone, drove the PLO grudgingly to add political and diplomatic means to its arsenal, it nevertheless left "armed struggle" as its preferred instrument.[2] Even when on November 15, 1988, at the PNC's nineteenth session in Algiers, the PLO accepted Security Council Resolutions 242 and 338, opening an official dialogue with the U.S. administration, Arafat could not bring himself to renounce violence and terrorism with a straightforward statement. It was only when the UN took the unprecedented step of convening the General Assembly in Geneva a month later to hear the Palestinian leader that Arafat read a brief message at a hastily convened press conference, stating, "We totally and absolutely renounce all forms of terrorism, including individual, group, and state terrorism."[3]

It took Arafat only five days to disown this most public of pledges, which had led to the immediate start of the coveted dialogue with the United States. When asked by an Austrian interviewer whether the PLO's renunciation of terrorism meant that it would now be prepared to lay down its weapons, Arafat replied rhetorically. "How can we do so? We are facing daily aggression."[4]

Abu Iyad, Arafat's second in command and the chief PLO ideologue, was equally categorical. "When the sensitive Palestinian society hears the language of peace it understands that we will not give up the use of armed force for the attainment of this peace," he said. "We have the right to use armed force and we will use it whenever we can." He reiterated his pledge for the continuation of an armed struggle on numerous occasions, both during the PNC's session and in its wake, not merely in the form of the uprising in the West Bank and Gaza (intifada) but in other parts of "occupied Palestine," namely terrorist attacks within Israel's pre-1967 borders. Nabil Shaath, Arafat's political adviser, echoed the same pledge: "We will continue all forms of our struggle in the entire territory of historic Palestine until the establishment of a Palestinian state with Jerusalem as its capital. The armed struggle will not desist until then."[5]

When a group of PLO terrorists was captured by the Israeli authorities after landing by sea on a beach near Tel Aviv on May 30, 1990, the U.S. administration demanded that Arafat condemn the operation and punish the culpable organization (Palestine Liberation Front), whose head was a member of the PLO's executive committee. The Bush administration, was particularly incensed when it transpired that the group had intended to attack not only Israelis but also the American embassy in Tel Aviv. Arafat did neither, and the administration peremptorily suspended the dialogue. Shortly afterward Arafat dropped any remaining pretences to "moderation" by backing Saddam's Kuwaiti misadventure.[6]

Widely known in Israel as "Mr. Security," Prime Minister Yitzhak Rabin would seek to predicate the nascent peace process on the PLO's unequivocal and irrevocable renunciation of the use of violence, and in particular terrorism, as a political tool. Arafat had promised that much already in his letter to Rabin on September 9, 1993, which paved the way for Israel's recognition of the PLO and the signing of the DOP four days later. "The PLO commits itself to the Middle East peace process and to a peaceful resolution of the conflict between the two sides and declares that all outstanding issues relating to permanent status will be resolved through negotiations," he wrote.

> The PLO considers that the signing of the Declaration of Principles constitutes a historic event, inaugurating a new epoch of peaceful coexistence, free from violence and all other acts, which endanger peace and stability.

Accordingly, the PLO renounces the use of terrorism and other acts of violence and will assume responsibility over all PLO elements and personnel in order to assure their compliance prevent violations and discipline violators.

Arafat reiterated this commitment in another letter, on the same date, to Norwegian Foreign Minister Johan Jorgen Holst, in which he promised that upon the signing of the Declaration of Principles he would publicly state that "the PLO encourages and calls upon the Palestinian people in the West Bank and [the] Gaza Strip to take part in the steps leading for the normalization of life, rejecting violence and terrorism, contributing to peace and stability and participating actively in shaping reconstruction, economic development and cooperation."[7]

In the follow-up agreements on the implementation of the DOP, the PLO committed itself not only to forgo acts of violence against Israel but also to prevent any such acts by all groups and organizations under its jurisdiction. The May 1994 Gaza-Jericho agreement stipulated the establishment of a Palestinian Authority in these territories, which was to "take all measures necessary in order to prevent acts of terrorism, crime and hostilities . . . [and] such hostile acts directed against the Settlements, the infrastructure serving them and the Military Installation Area," as well as to take "legal measures against offenders."

The Palestinian Authority was also to ensure that no other armed groups would be established or operate in the Gaza Strip and the Jericho area, apart from the official police force, and that no organization or individual "shall manufacture, sell, acquire, possess, import, or otherwise introduce into [these territories] any firearms, ammunition, weapons, explosives, gunpowder, or any related equipment." In the September 28, 1995, Israel-Palestinian Interim Agreement on the West Bank and the Gaza Strip (Oslo II), the PA reiterated the pledge "to take all measures necessary in order to prevent acts of terrorism, crime, and hostilities," including the disarming of all illegal armed groups operating under its jurisdiction.[8]

These commitments were the culmination of months of secret Israeli-Palestinian negotiations in the Norwegian capital of Oslo. During these talks, Arafat indefatigably sought to convince his Israeli interlocutors that the only solution to their security concerns was the creation of a

Palestinian entity under his personal rule in the West Bank and the Gaza Strip. "Whatever they say about security, say yes, because Israelis are very sensitive about security," Arafat briefed Abu Ala, his chief negotiator to the Oslo talks.[9] Abu Ala complied. "We can put a stop to the violence, provided we can promise [our people] a different future," he told his Israeli counterpart, Uri Savir, during their second meeting on May 21, 1993. In a personal letter to the Israeli team a couple of months later, Arafat further argued that the arrival of the PLO leadership in the territories "is important in order to contend with possible actions of extremist groups interested in damaging the new agreement." He repeated this claim the following day in a meeting in Tunis with a Norwegian delegation headed by Foreign Minister Holst, where he emphasized the need for a strong Palestinian security force to control the situation in the territories, placing great importance on establishing himself there in order to "deal with Hamas." In a follow-up meeting with Holst the next week, after the Norwegian minister had passed his message on to the Israeli government, Arafat stressed fervently the imperative of his own presence in the territories, portraying himself as a catalyst to the creation of common Palestinian-Israeli interests.[10] Recalled one Israeli negotiator, "They told us, 'Once we come to Gaza, we will declare a curfew. We'll go from house to house searching for weapons. We'll search for Hamas—some we will kill, some put in jail, some reeducate—and we will do it better than you! Trust us!'"[11]

These promises all but vanished following the signing of the DOP. Already during the Oslo negotiations, Arafat sought to persuade the PLO leadership to support the crystallizing deal by promising to transform the territories into a new Lebanon. "Just as I ruled Lebanon from Fakhani," Arafat said, "I will rule the territories from Jericho."[12] Now that he had obtained Israel's blessing for the entrenchment of the PLO in the West Bank and Gaza, Arafat no longer felt obliged to indulge his new peace partner, despite the continuation of terrorist attacks on Israelis. "No one has the power to stop the intifada," he said on September 10, 1993, a day after making his public pledge to Rabin to renounce violence, adding a week later that "the intifada will end when the occupation ends." "Meanwhile, incidents are possible?" asked his interviewer. "Naturally, we must expect events, we do not have a magic wand, no more than the Israelis do. We must bear with incidents here and there."[13] He similarly evaded his undertaking to Holst to call, in his White House speech, for a halt to violence. It was only a week later that he issued such a statement from his Tunis headquarters, and even this came only under intense Israeli and Norwegian pressure.[14]

The same message was echoed by Abu Mazen, Arafat's second in command after Abu Iyad's death in 1991 and the person who signed the DOP on the PLO's behalf. Abu Mazen asserted that the intifada would continue as long as there is an occupation, while Hani Hassan, one of the PLO's foremost figures, declared that the organization would not give up the struggle against Israel before the end of the occupation. Yasser Abd Rabbo, head of the PLO's information department, categorically denied in an interview with Jordanian television on September 22, 1993, that "the mutual recognition document between Israel and the PLO contains any Palestinian pledge to stop violence."

"They interpreted this as an end to the intifada," the interviewer insisted. "Let them interpret as they wish," retorted Abd Rabbo. "The intifada is a popular movement that began as a result of occupation . . . It will not stop because of anyone's decision or after a word here or a word there that anybody can interpret as he wishes . . . It will end when the occupation is over."[15]

Since Israel's withdrawal from the territories according to the DOP was supposed to be implemented within several years, these statements amounted to a carte blanche for terrorist attacks over a protracted period of time in flagrant violation of the accord. After the DOP's signing, PLO officials were extremely reluctant to condemn terrorist attacks against Israeli targets. "I do not condemn them. No, I do not," Hakam Balawi, head of the PLO's internal security apparatus and a confidant of Arafat, told an Israeli interviewer on the day of the DOP's signing, in response to a spate of attacks by Hamas. "Today is Monday, not Sunday. Do not ask me about the past."[16]

Arafat was equally intransigent when asked to condemn a Hamas terrorist attack in early October, in which some thirty Israelis were wounded. "Have I asked Rabin to uproot the opposition on his side? If he respects their opposition to him, I also respect the opposition on my side," he claimed,[17] ignoring altogether the fact that opposition within

Israel to the agreement manifested itself in political protest and not in systematic and organized killing of innocent civilians. In mid-November 1993, intense pressure by President Clinton and Prime Minister Rabin forced Arafat to begrudgingly condemn the recent murder of an Israeli citizen by Fatah, the PLO's chief constituent group and Arafat's own organization.[18] Yet a few days later, following another murder of an Israeli civilian, a Fatah circular in Ramallah advocated the continued killing of settlers. The prominent West Bank politician Hanan Ashrawi commented, "This is the true reaction of the Palestinian people who began suspecting Israel's intentions and credibility."[19]

This state of affairs means that, unlike their Israeli partners, and in stark contravention of their own formal commitments, Arafat and the PLO leadership never considered the Oslo accords as signifying the end of the armed struggle against Israel. In the words of Hani Hassan, Arafat's longtime associate and a member of Fatah's Central Committee, "The armed struggle plants the seeds while the political struggle reaps the harvest."[20]

To judge by his behavior since arriving in the territories, Arafat's demand for controlling the borders of his autonomous entity was designed not to prevent the smuggling of weapons into the territories but rather to ensure their uninterrupted supply. On the day of his triumphal arrival in Gaza in July 1994 Arafat returned with Mamduh Nawfal, mastermind of the 1974 Maalot atrocity in which twenty-seven children were murdered, hidden in the trunk of his car. Three years later, when visiting the West Bank town of Hebron following its evacuation by the Israeli army in January 1997, hidden ammunition boxes were found in Arafat's personal helicopter, and his bodyguards were armed with an improved version of Kalashnikov assault rifles, smuggled from Egypt in violation of the Oslo accords.[21]

Not only did Arafat do precious little to curb Palestinian terrorism in the territories under his control, but following the establishment of the Palestinian Authority in mid-May 1994, terrorism spiraled to new and unprecedented heights. In the two years between that date and the fall of the labor government in May 1996, 161 Israelis were murdered in terrorist attacks, compared to 116 in the preceding twenty-four months.

Some three-quarters of these victims were killed in Israel's pre-1967 territory, nearly three times the number of similar fatalities in the preceding period. Until the outbreak of Arafat's war in September 2000, each of the years between 1994 and 1996 saw the largest number of terrorist fatalities since the original occupation of the territories in the Six-Day War of 1967: seventy-four fatalities in 1994, followed by sixty-eight in 1996 and fifty-one in 1995.[22]

This carnage did little to soften the Palestinian position. Muhammad Dahlan, the young and energetic head of the Preventive Security Service in the Gaza Strip, asserted that "our policy priority is the security of the Palestinians here." His West Bank counterpart, Jibril Rajoub, was more direct. "The opponents of the agreement with Israel," he said, "can continue the armed struggle."[23] Arafat was more diplomatic than his lieutenants, feigning ignorance whenever pressed by the Israelis to intensify his antiterrorism efforts. In what was to become the standard Palestinian pretext for inaction, Arafat claimed he needed more time to harness public support before acting more vigorously. "You fought against terror by force—and you failed," PLO negotiator Hassan Asfour told Savir when they first met in Gaza. "Arafat has a different strategy, and it will succeed. Trust him, strengthen him, and you'll see. We are negotiating with Hamas, and many of their people are coming over to our side." Abu Ala even told Savir in mid-1994 of an evolving agreement between Hamas and Fatah, which included an end to the use of violence and the acceptance of a central authority that would legitimize political pluralism.[24]

Arafat was talking with Hamas, though not with a view to curbing its terrorist activities but rather to neutralize its ability to endanger the Palestinian Authority. Even before the conclusion of the DOP Arafat had unsuccessfully sought to convince Hamas to join the PLO as its second largest constituent organization after Fatah.[25] Now that he had established himself in Gaza and Jericho, Arafat was busy courting the militant religious group. He did little to curb its terrorist attacks, let alone attempt to disarm it as required by the peace accords, or even to condemn its atrocities in a clear and unequivocal fashion. Far from trying to pursue and capture terrorists as he had promised the Israelis, Arafat preferred to encourage them to flee to safety in Sudan, an Islamic extremist stronghold, whenever Israel pressed him to root out the militants.[26] At the same time, he repeatedly underscored the need for "national unity" while seeking to free Hamas activists detained by Israel, including its spiritual leader Sheik Ahmad Yassin.

When in December 1995 the PLO reached an agreement with Hamas, aimed at facilitating the forthcoming Israeli withdrawal from the West Bank's populated areas, this did not provide for the suspension of terrorism in favor of politics. Allowing Hamas to uphold its commitment to the continuation of the "armed struggle" against Israel, the agreement obliged the organization to "avoid embarrassing the Authority" by forgoing terrorist attacks from territories under its full control (known as Area A). In return, the PA, which did not consider itself responsible for areas outside this zone, would withhold action against Hamas, release Hamas activists detained in its jails, and demand that Israel free Hamas prisoners it was holding, particularly Sheik Yassin. Removing any doubts about the cynical nature of this understanding, the chief PLO negotiator with Hamas, the PNC acting speaker Salim Zaanun said, "Everyone must understand that we are not the defenders of the Zionist entity [the standard pejorative term for Israel in Arab parlance]. If Israel wishes to spare itself Hamas's activities, it must speedily withdraw from the entire West Bank, and from wherever it remains in the Gaza Strip."[27]

Hamas leaders were greatly relieved. Aware of Arafat's violent track record, they feared the brutal repression of any opposition to the Oslo accords. Following the signing of the DOP, senior Hamas leaders confided to the Israeli military commander of Gaza their preference for Israel over the PLO, who they believed would pursue them more viciously.[28] As these fears proved unfounded, Hamas sustained its terrorist campaign. In April 1994, suicide bombings were introduced into Palestinian-Israeli relations when eight people were murdered while riding a bus in the town of Afula. Asked for his response, Arafat would not condemn the attack.[29] When in August 1994 a series of attacks left three Israelis dead and five wounded, the PA's minister of planning and international cooperation Nabil Shaath announced Arafat's readiness "to open a dialogue with our [Hamas] brothers," while Ghazi Jabali, head of the Gaza police, stated that the PLO would not take up arms against Hamas and blamed Israel for triggering the terrorist attacks by allowing the settlements to remain in Gaza. So did Sufian Abu Zaida, the PLO's liaison officer with Israel, who claimed that Hamas was merely responding to Israel's military provocations against it.[30]

Two months later, twenty-one Israelis were murdered on a bus in Tel Aviv. An incensed Rabin responded with the closure of the West Bank and Gaza, sealing them off from Israel. At a meeting with Arafat on November 2, Rabin bluntly told him, "We must continue to fight against terrorism. No other issue has such threatening ramifications, for both sides."

"Yes, we must fight the fanatics, who have a lot of money," Arafat retorted. "But instead of punishing them, you're indirectly punishing us. . . . Please," he implored Rabin, "stop the collective punishment. I know that after the tragedy in Tel Aviv, it was hard for you to announce that you're committed to the peace process. And I thank you for doing so. But I think it's worthwhile releasing Sheik Yassin. He will have an influence on the extremists. I know him. He will call for an end to the violence."

"We've checked. He is not prepared to do that," Rabin replied. "And in any case, it's vital that you yourself continue to combat terrorism. That's the key struggle."

General Uzi Dayan, head of the IDF Planning Division, passed on a similar message to the Palestinians at a secret meeting in January 1995. "If there's no change in this situation in Gaza," he warned, "I, as the person handling security issues, cannot recommend to Rabin that we begin detailed negotiations on an interim agreement. There simply cannot be flawed security in the West Bank."[31]

The Israeli pleas were to no avail. Shortly after Rabin's meeting with Arafat, two attacks in the Gaza Strip claimed the lives of ten Israelis. An additional nineteen people were murdered on January 22, 1995, when a bomber detonated himself at the Beit Lid junction in central Israel. In Gaza, thousands took to the streets to celebrate the massacre. Hamas militants, PLO activists, and PA policemen joined together in shooting into the sky to express their joy. In Jerusalem, the head of Shabak, Israel's security service, told the Knesset's foreign affairs and defense committee that Arafat had instructed his forces to avoid confrontation with Hamas and the smaller Islamic Jihad (which had carried out the Beit Lid massacre) as he considered himself president of all Palestinians. As a result, Hamas's terrorist infrastructure was openly being built throughout Gaza—bomb manufacturing, training, and indoctrination—and at times with the PA's active cooperation. Hamas activists, detained in mock arrests staged to appease Israel, were treated with deference, enjoying almost complete freedom and endless apologies from their captors. Arafat himself was also busy indulging the Hamas leadership. In a letter to Sheik Yassin and a senior Hamas terrorist imprisoned by Israel he wrote: "My brother Sheik Yassin, my holy brother Hadi Hunam, I cherish your participation in the struggle for the liberation of Palestine. It is due to you that Palestine is free."[32]

When Arafat called Rabin to express his condolences on the Beit Lid massacre, the prime minister was understandably furious. "Why didn't you publicly condemn the bombing?" he asked.

"Ahmad Tibi [Arafat's adviser] did."

"But why didn't you?"

Arafat did not reply. Instead he chose later to say that extremist Israeli security circles had masterminded the atrocity.

Nabil Shaath found a more imaginative pretext to absolve his boss. "[Arafat] really recognizes he is not a very good public speaker, particularly in English," he told the annual gathering of the National Jewish Community Relations Advisory Council (NJCRAC) in a satellite broadcast from Cairo. "Therefore, he has really been prevailing upon me and others who have more ability to do that explanation, to represent him. But I know in his heart and mind, he is absolutely set in this direction. And when he feels he can do it in a natural way, in a not-put-on way, in a way that really will express his real feelings of concern, that I know he does [have], I'm sure that he will do it."[33] Not surprisingly, Shaath refused to explain how Arafat, one of the most widely interviewed world leaders, had no such bouts of public shyness when it came to addressing the UN or the Nobel Prize Award ceremony, let alone inciting the Palestinian masses against Israel. While shying away from condemning the Beit Lid massacre, Arafat told a cheering crowd in Gaza of his sympathy for the attack. When news of the incident reached Israel, Arafat's spokesman Marwan Kanfani quickly denied that his boss had asserted that "all of us are suicide bombers," instead arguing that Arafat "only" said "All of us are martyrs."[34]

In the following months Rabin and Peres would hold several meetings with Arafat in an attempt to convince him that without a marked improvement in the performance of his security forces, there could be no interim agreement. A secret envoy, Yossi Ginosar, a former Shabak operative, who shuttled between Rabin and Arafat, provided another channel of communication.

At a secret meeting with the Palestinians shortly after the Beit Lid bombing, General Dayan opened a map of the West Bank town of Ramallah. "Let's, for a moment, theoretically transpose the present situation in Gaza to Ramallah after redeployment," he said. "Given the measures you're taking against terrorism today, if we were to pull back from Ramallah, which is five minutes away from Jerusalem, there would be no hope of stemming the flood of terrorism that might come from that city. Gaza is surrounded by a fence; the West Bank is not. Rampant terrorism from a place like Ramallah would promptly destroy the agreement."

The Palestinians were unimpressed. "It's your conception of security that's failed, not ours," claimed senior military official Abdel Razaq Yihya. "You want to impose your doctrine of security on us out of a narrow view [of] what security means. But you must understand that the answer lies in changing the psychological atmosphere. If you force something on us, Arafat will not be able to carry it out. If you appoint yourselves as arbiters of right and wrong, you will destroy the goodwill we have with our people."[35]

This claim had little to do with reality. Instead of preparing his people for peace, Arafat was fanning the flames of hatred, sending an unequivocal message that violence was a perfectly legitimate means of confrontation, regardless of its formal renunciation in the Oslo accords. On May 10, 1994, less than a week after the conclusion of the Gaza-Jericho agreement, he urged a closed meeting of South African Muslim leaders to support the Palestinian struggle until its ultimate triumph. "The jihad will continue and Jerusalem is not for the Palestinian people alone," he said. "It is for the entire Muslim *umma* [world community]. You are responsible for Palestine and Jerusalem before me . . . No, it is not their capital, it is our capital."[36]

On November 21, 1994, a month after the Tel Aviv bombing, Arafat told a large gathering in Gaza that "the Palestinian people continues its jihad."[37] Faisal Husseini, meanwhile, holder of the Jerusalem portfolio in the PA, warned Israel of "a new intifada, not only in Jerusalem and the occupied territories but also in the entire Middle East."[38] These threats were made in the midst of intensive negotiations with Israel over an interim agreement that would allow the PA to extend its control over the entire West Bank. As the talks neared their climax, Arafat steadily escalated his belligerent rhetoric in order to pressure the Israelis into concessions. On June 15, 1995, he praised two female terrorists, one of whom had participated in the massacre of thirty-eight Israelis near Tel Aviv in March 1978. "This is the Palestinian woman in all respects," he said. "This is the model woman in which we take pride and share their glory."

"We are all seekers of martyrdom in the path of truth and right toward Jerusalem, the capital of the state of Palestine," he told a public rally in Gaza a few days later, before repeating the PLO's battlecry for the destruction of Israel.

> The commitment still stands and the oath is still firm to continue this difficult *jihad*, this long *jihad*, this arduous *jihad* in the path of martyrs, the path of sacrifices, but this is a path of victory and glory.[39]

Arafat's lieutenants were no less explicit than their leader. In a speech at Ramallah's Bir Zeit University on October 23, 1993, a mere month after the signing of the DOP, Faisal Husseini told his audience, "Everything you see and hear today is for tactical and strategic reasons. We have not given up the rifle. We still have armed groups in the areas and if we do not get our state we will take them out of the closet and fight again."[40] He repeated the same threat two years later, warning that "should Israel continue to undermine the road to peace, we will have no alternative but to adopt the road advocated by the Palestinian opposition, namely the military option."[41]

Even Abu Ala, the architect of Oslo and the PLO's moderate face, did not consider violence as antithetical to the peace process. "If Israel does not honor the agreements," he threatened,

> the response to the continuation of the occupation will be more dangerous than the intifada . . . [T]he arms available . . . and the organization [are] better than in the past . . . The alternative to peace will be bad for the Israelis, something which they do not want. The Palestinian people will oppose the occupation, from children to adults, including the Palestinian police.[42]

Nabil Shaath, another supposed moderate and dedicated advocate of the Oslo process, was similarly disposed to threaten a return to the

"armed struggle" whenever he deemed Israel to be insufficiently accom-
modating of Palestinian demands. "If the negotiations reach a dead end,
we shall go back to the struggle and strife, as we did for 40 years," he
told a Nablus symposium in March 1996.

> As long as Israel goes forward [with the process], there are no problems,
> which is why we observe the agreements of peace and non-violence. But
> if and when Israel will say, "That's it, we won't talk about Jerusalem, we
> won't return refugees, we won't dismantle settlements, and we won't
> retreat from borders," then all the acts of violence will return.
>
> Except that this time we'll have 30,000 armed Palestinian soldiers
> who will operate in areas in which we have unprecedented elements of
> freedom.[43]

Speaking in similar terms, Marwan Barghouthi, Fatah's West Bank
general secretary and head of its armed militia, Tanzim, revealed that
the Palestinian security forces had been ordered to fire on Israeli soldiers should they try to enter territory under the PA's control, boasting
that the Palestinians possessed far more weaponry and a much larger
armed forces than allowed by the Oslo accords.[44]

Coming in the wake of a wave of suicide bombings that killed fifty-
eight Israelis in the span of one week, these statements could not but
prove to most Israelis the disingenuousness of the PLO's approach to
the peace process. Even Peres, who had assumed the premiership following Rabin's assassination on November 4, 1995, publicly criticized
Arafat for not trying to prevent attacks on Israelis, sending the head of
military intelligence, Major General Moshe Yaalon, to meet Arafat and
demand that he stop the wave of terror.

Arafat received the Israeli cordially, but when Yaalon asked him to
arrest Muhammad Def, the Hamas military commander who had masterminded the recent terrorist attacks, the PLO chairman feigned ignorance. "Muhammad who?" he asked. "Muhammad who?" Arafat's aides
could hardly keep a straight face.

Yaalon was stunned. Through his intelligence sources he knew perfectly well that just a week earlier Def himself had been sitting in the
very same chair chatting with Arafat. The intelligence chief left in anger.
Reporting to Peres, he pleaded with him never again to send him to meet
Arafat. The man is a liar, he argued. He may have signed a peace accord

with Israel, but he considered it no more than a piece of paper. When the opportunity arose, he would certainly resort to violence. He was not working against the terror infrastructure in the territories but was using it as a bargaining chip against Israel.[45]

The ignorance Arafat feigned in private was openly discussed by other Palestinian leaders. In an interview with the Israeli daily *Ha'aretz* on March 4, 1996, Minister of Justice Abu Medein presented the Palestinians as the real victims of the bombings and blamed Israel for their occurrence. "We believe that these people received the explosives from an Israeli source," he argued, "because such bombings do not occur in Syria, Jordan, or Egypt. It was a highly sophisticated device." In other words, the real target of Hamas's terrorist campaign was not Israel but the Palestinian Authority, with Israeli casualties merely a tool in the internal Palestinian struggle. "There is little doubt that the terrorist attacks were directed against the national aspirations of the Palestinian people, against our economy, our hopes, and the Palestinian Authority," he said. "Israel paid dearly with its blood for these attacks, and now we are going to pay a heavy price in terms of our future."

A similar message was passed to the Israelis in secret talks on security cooperation held between March 23 and April 17, 1996. "Your closure policy, from the time of Oslo onward, has created unemployment, bitterness, and despair that have driven thousands of Palestinians into the arms of Hamas," complained Palestinian negotiator Hassan Asfour. "Your policies are shortsighted, and you're not seeking real cooperation." He also claimed that Arafat had been unable to engage in an all-out battle against Hamas because he had so little to offer his people as long as the closure policy prevailed.[46]

The truth, of course, was that the closures had not led to a single terrorist attack, while Arafat was perfectly capable of pursuing and arresting those Hamas leaders responsible for terrorism or dismantling the organization's terrorist infrastructure. His reluctance to do so reflected not his impotence, as he liked the Israelis to believe, but rather his tacit acceptance of Hamas's ultimate goal of Israel's destruction. As the PLO's foreign minister Farouq Qaddoumi would admit candidly years later at the height of Arafat's terrorist war, "We were never different from Hamas. Hamas is a national movement. Strategically, there is no difference between us."[47]

Only a month before the March 1996 bombings, the PA had named a square in Jericho after Yahya Ayyash (alias "the engineer"), Hamas's archterrorist assassinated by Israel in January 1996. Arafat himself had eulogized Ayyash, while senior Palestinian officials including Ghazi Jabali participated both in his funeral in Gaza and in memorial services throughout the West Bank. At one point in the funeral procession, even Palestinian policemen carried Ayyash's body.[48]

With the March 1996 bombings closing the gap between Peres and his rival to the prime ministerial elections, Likud leader Benjamin Netanyahu, Arafat was suddenly driven to act. At a time when Asfour was busy making excuses for the PA's inaction, some nine hundred Hamas activists, including four of the thirteen men on Israel's "most wanted" list, were being rounded up. The PA's security forces conducted house-to-house searches in Ramallah, Bethlehem, and Gaza, where they raided the Islamic University, a Hamas bastion. Human Rights Watch reported routine violations of suspects' due process rights by the PA.[49]

Yet even this, the most intense antiterrorist effort in the PA's history, which led to the complete suspension of suicide bombings against Israel until after the 1996 elections, was essentially nothing more than a canard. On March 11, 1996, at the height of the clampdown, the Palestinian press reported that Arafat had decided to exempt Palestinians whose homes had been demolished by the Israeli army from new building taxes.[50] Since the only houses that were being demolished at the time belonged to homicide bombers, or to Hamas and Islamic Jihad terrorists, the message behind Arafat's move was clear. Few Israelis were impressed by Arafat's surge of activism. On May 29, 1996, Netanyahu defeated Peres by a narrow margin to become Israel's prime minister. Arafat's longtime strategy of terror had backfired for the first time.

7

Eyeless in Gaza

You don't find ready-made partners, you have to raise them . . . We
close our eyes. We don't criticize because for peace, we must produce a partner.

—Shimon Peres, May 1996

With the benefit of hindsight, the extent of the Israeli leap of faith in
Oslo appears nothing short of mind-boggling. There were no ultimate
goals set for the negotiating team, no road map to follow. There were
no serious discussions over the direction of the entire process, not even
awareness among the negotiators and their superiors of each other's vision of peace. "Future historians of the Oslo I negotiations will discover
that the members of the Israeli team complained that they had no idea
about the negotiations' final destination," wrote Yair Hirschfeld, an Israeli academic who led the early stage of the Oslo talks. This stood in
stark contrast to the Palestinian delegation, which knew full well its
ultimate goal was "a basis for a future Palestinian state."[1]

Yossi Beilin was even more forthcoming. Asked in a 1997 interview
whether Rabin, Peres, or himself realized upon embarking on the Oslo
process talks that it was inexorably heading toward the establishment
of a Palestinian state, he answered, "No. It is very interesting to note
that soul-searching deliberations on 'where the process is going' took
place only between the parties, not within them. Such debates were held
between the Palestinian negotiators and us, then between Labor and
Likud. But I don't remember a single serious penetrating discussion
within the Labor Party, or the cabinet, or the negotiating team about
the final-status solution."

The interviewer was astonished. "I cannot understand. In 1992 a government was elected. In 1993 you initiated the Oslo process. And yet, at no stage you asked yourselves where all this was heading?"

"No."

"You never spoke to Rabin about the long-term consequences of Oslo?"

"Never.

"And to Peres?"

"I didn't discuss it with him either."

"So you embarked on the most dramatic historical process and at no stage you told yourself, 'Just a moment, let's do some stocktaking, see where all of this is going'"?

"With Rabin, the abstention from discussing the ultimate solution was a policy. He pushed it to the sidelines, he suppressed it. After he died, I sat with Leah Rabin and I told her that if someone could have known what kind of a final-status agreement her husband had in mind she was that person. She said, 'I cannot really say. He was very pragmatic, hated to deal with something that will happen years down the road. He only thought of what would happen now, in the very near future. As far as I know, he did not have a clear picture of what the final-status agreement would look like.'

"Rabin thought that the process would move forward," added Beilin. "He envisaged something instrumental, a kind of autonomy that may or may not develop into a state. He did not have a clear picture."

"And yet, when the cabinet approved the Oslo accord in a quick and superficial session, with almost no discussion, weren't you disturbed?" the interviewer asked.

"It was amazing. Amazing. For dozens of years I had been arguing with these people, and they had been opposing, like lions, my proposals regarding the PLO . . . Then all of a sudden Rabin brings an agreement with the PLO and all are in favor."[2]

Arafat is a man and leader who has thrived on violence for more than forty years, and he has taken every opportunity to violate the Oslo peace accords. Why then did the Israeli government acquiesce in this wanton

and repeated violation of signed agreements? How was the PLO transformed from Israel's most implacable enemy into a trusted peace partner?
In Northern Ireland, the decommissioning of weapons by all paramili-
tary organizations was a prerequisite to the entire peace process. In the
West Bank and the Gaza Strip, the Israeli government saw the arming
of the PLO with dozens of thousands of weapons, despite its far worse
terrorist record, as the key to peace and security. From where did this
blind faith originate?

On one level the answer is that nobody likes to admit failure, much
less so politicians, least of all politicians who might be found out to have
gambled with their nation's fate. "We had books and books filled with
violations," one of the Israeli negotiators in Oslo told an American journalist. "I saw Rabin and Peres so angry at what they had to eat from the
Palestinians. But, had they talked back publicly, everyone in Israel would
have said, 'You chose them. You're saying that they violated all the agreements, that they can't be trusted. O.K. You made the mistake; so admit
that something must be done.'"[3]

For Foreign Minister Peres, however, such an admission would have
meant much more than an acknowledgment of a seismic error in a long
and distinguished political career dating back to the late 1940s. In his
eyes, Oslo was not merely the end of the Palestinian-Israeli conflict, it
was the peace to end all wars, the edifice of a "New Middle East" modeled on the European Community in which democratization, economic
cooperation, and individual prosperity would replace millenarian hatreds
and enmities. By joining the Oslo process, Arafat and the PLO had become Israel's partners in a momentous historical odyssey; and if they
occasionally forgot this fact, they had to be gently swayed back on course.
As long as the partnership remained intact, its ultimate success was a
foregone conclusion.

"I think what is really important for a peace process is the creation of
a partner, more than a plan," argued Peres. "Because plans don't create
partners but if you have a partner then you negotiate a plan. . . . When I
was thinking about the peace process," he continued, "I knew in my heart
that the greatest problem is how to transform Arafat from the most hated
gentleman in this country, and himself with an array of very strange ideas,
into a partner that we can sit with, and make him become acceptable to
our people—maybe not beloved but at least accepted."[4] But what if the

partner would not act out the role ascribed to him, what if his "array of very strange ideas" proves impossible to change? "We close our eyes. We don't criticize because for peace, we must produce a partner."[5]

Peres conceded that the effort to transform Arafat had been a daunting task. Not only because of the pervasive hostility among Israelis to the person who for decades had been openly seeking to destroy their state, but also "because his looks are not terribly attractive, and also because his speeches are very revolting, and because he represents everything that the people of Israel didn't like, and also because of his demands on Jerusalem—I mean, he makes our lives so complicated."[6]

This recalls Neville Chamberlain's purported deathbed remark "If only Hitler had not lied to me, everything would have been all right."[7] Obviously, had Arafat acted differently he would have made life much simpler for Peres. Yet as the late Yehoshafat Harkabi noted in the mid-1960s, for all its professed empathy with the Arabs the Israeli left never treated its Arab interlocutors as equals in the patronizing assumption that it knew what was in the Arabs' best interests.[8] Peres himself famously quipped that "The role of the word in the Arab world is different from its role in our world. For us a word is a commitment, for them it is an ornament."[9]

Yossi Beilin, Peres's longtime protégé and the foremost architect of the Oslo process, had for years sought a dialogue with "moderate" factors within the PLO, even at a time when this was specifically forbidden by Israeli law. Now that this dialogue had evolved into an "historic peace," Beilin, like Peres, made every effort to sanitize Palestinian intentions and objectives, along with ignoring or excusing flagrant violations of signed accords. Arafat's insistence on Jerusalem as capital of the prospective Palestinian state was thus dismissed as a dispensable bargaining tactic. "The Palestinians understand that we cannot give up [Israel's sovereignty over the city]," argued Beilin. "In the end, they will have to confront the difficult dilemma, from their point of view, of surrendering the demand for sovereignty in Jerusalem, just as they would have to give up the demand for Israel's withdrawal to the pre-1967 borders." He was similarly buoyant about the demilitarization of the future Palestinian state, since "I learned that the civilian Palestinian leadership has no interest in a strong Palestinian army, because it is keenly aware of the likely balance of forces between the Israel Defense Forces (IDF) and itself." Peres was equally dismissive of the cherished Palestinian ideal of the right of return. "The right of return is in my view an Arab dream that is bound to remain a dream," he commented as late as September 2001. "I thought then, just as I think today, that one can solve problems without giving up the dreams."[10]

As Ehud Barak was to learn at the Camp David summit of July 2000, the Palestinian insistence on Jerusalem as well as on Israel's total withdrawal from the West Bank and Gaza and the "right of return" was anything but a tactical maneuver. Nor did one have to wait for Arafat's war of terror to realize the extent of Palestinian determination to build a strong army and to test it in battle. Their scathing opinion of Israeli society's resilience, confirmed by numerous public statements over the years and the pervasive smuggling of weapons prohibited by the Oslo accords, was proof enough of this fact. As Arafat told an Israeli negotiator as early as 1996, "Are you Israelis capable of sustaining 500 fatalities? We can readily sacrifice 30,000 martyrs, or more. And let there be no doubt that we know what your main weakness is: [sensitivity to] human life."[11]

When in May 1994 Arafat told Muslim leaders in Johannesburg that the Oslo accords were a temporary arrangement designed to bring about Israel's eventual demise, Beilin brushed off these comments as "silly words" while Peres excused them as a reflection of the difficulty that Arafat had in reconciling himself to a new reality. "Unlike others on both sides of the political divide, I never had any illusions regarding Arafat," argued Beilin.

> I have never considered him an important world leader. I think he has committed numerous follies. He could have achieved a lot for his people many years ago, but his personal record includes almost every possible mistake. And in spite of this, to my deep regret, he has no substitute . . . If I had a "spare Mandela" with whom to negotiate, I would have done so immediately. But since I have only Arafat, for all the stupidities that he utters, I must negotiate with him.[12]

This approach makes the Oslo process probably the only instance in diplomatic history where one of the signatories to a peace accord was a priori amenable to its wholesale violation by its cosignatory. There have of course been numerous bilateral agreements where one, or both, parties acted in bad faith. In September 1938, to offer a notable example, Adolf Hitler signed the Munich agreement with the deliberate intent of using it as a Trojan horse for the destruction of Czechoslovakia, a strategy that Arafat emulated fifty-five years later in Oslo. Ironically, while there was little the Czechs could do given their marked military inferiority and their betrayal by the international community, at Oslo it was the stronger party that allowed the far weaker one to flaunt the agreement with impunity for the sake of "creating a partner," or, more precisely, of sustaining the facade of a partnership. As Peres commented on Arafat, "One should not forget that [he] is the first Palestinian leader who has been ready to reach an agreement based on compromise, and what counts are not words but actions on the ground."[13]

Yet even when these "actions on the ground" were set diametrically against the agreement, they were not allowed to stand in the way of "maintaining the partnership." When in late October 1993 an Israeli civilian was murdered by terrorists belonging to Arafat's Fatah, Beilin described it as "the swan song of Palestinian terrorism." He argued that "We must prevent terrorism and fight against it, while at the same time remain patient and understand that peace is stronger and that it is an interest of both sides." With the October 1993 murder heralding the start of a tidal wave of terrorism rather than its end, Beilin's upbeat prognosis was gradually replaced by a fatalistic acquiescence. "The terrorist attack in Jerusalem is neither the first nor the last [attack]," he told a group of visiting U.S. congressmen following the murder of four people in a homicide bombing on a Jerusalem bus in August 1995. "Those who argue that if we halt the peace process terrorism will stop, forget that between 1956 and 1967 there were relatively fewer casualties of terrorism. Do these people therefore support the return of the territories?"[14]

What Beilin forgot to tell his distinguished guests was that the relative calm between 1956 and 1967 was attributable to both Israel's destruction of the Gaza terrorist infrastructure during the 1956 Sinai War (and the attendant Egyptian abstention from rebuilding it in the subsequent decade) and the embryonic state of development of the Palestinian terrorist organizations, which started operating only in the mid-1960s. In terms of ferocity, the number of casualties, and the frequency of penetration into the heart of Israel, the current attacks had no equal in the country's history. The pre-1967 terrorist incidents occurred well before Israel had a peace agreement with the PLO, whereas now it was confronted with a terrorist campaign condoned and tacitly supported by its official peace partner.

Beilin also failed to mention that even by the criteria he had himself set out shortly after the signing of the DOP, these bombings would have constituted clear and incontrovertible proof of the total failure of the Oslo peace process.

"The greatest test of the accord will not be in the intellectual sphere," he told the Israeli daily *Maariv* on November 26, 1993. "Rather, it will be a test of blood."

"Meaning what?" asked the interviewer.

"If the accord will lead to a significant drop in the level of violence and terrorism, it will be a great success. If, heaven forbid, it will not bring about such a reduction, then it will be a scathing failure. This is why I am not wholehearted about the agreement."

"But in the meantime it has resulted not in the reduction of violence but in its intensification, hasn't it?" the interviewer persisted.

"The test will be in the months, or the first year or two, after the establishment of autonomy in Gaza and Jericho and the formation of the Palestinian police. After this period there can be no more excuses. If, heaven forbid, terrorism will not be defeated within a reasonable period of time, the Palestinians will no longer be able to feign innocence."

"And then what?"

"Should it transpire that they fail to stem terrorism, then [Oslo] will have to be regarded as a temporary agreement, and with all the difficulty involved—we will have no choice but to renege on it. This will only be a means of last resort. But if we realize that the level of violence does not subside, we will not be able to proceed, and will most certainly not implement the final-status agreement. And should there be no choice, the IDF will return to those places which it is about to leave in the coming months."

Following the establishment of Arafat's Palestinian Authority and the granting of autonomy to Gaza and Jericho, not to mention the formation of the Palestinian "police," terrorism skyrocketed to unprecedented levels. In the entire two decades preceding the Oslo accords, some four

hundred Israelis were murdered. In the decade attending the conclusion of the peace agreement, three times as many have lost their lives in
terrorist attacks—a sixfold increase. Beilin has never acted upon his own
"test of blood" by calling for an end to the process. Instead he has laid
the primary blame for this terrorist campaign on its Israeli victims rather
than on its true perpetrators.

Prime Minister and Minister of Defense Yitzhak Rabin, a man who had
devoted his entire life to Israel's national security, masterminded the
greatest victory in Israeli history, and under no circumstances compromised Israel's security, was uniquely qualified to sell the Oslo accords
to the Israeli public. Because Rabin was held in exceptionally high regard by the Israeli public (a claim Peres could never make), without his
endorsement the entire peace process would never have gotten off the
ground.

   Unlike Beilin, Rabin did not come to Oslo from an ideological stance
advocating peace through appeasement and self-abnegation. He was a
representative of the "activist" approach to Arab-Israeli relations, which
maintained that peace would be possible only when the Arabs realized
their inability to destroy Israel by force of arms. Having no illusions
about the imminent advent of a New Middle East, Rabin was driven
by his belief in the existence of a unique "window of opportunity" for
reaching agreements between Israel and its Arab neighbors, opened
by the end of the Cold War and the collapse of the Soviet Union, the
foremost champion of Arab radicalism. Such agreements, he hoped,
would substantially ameliorate the two most dangerous developments
confronting Israel on the eve of the twenty-first century: the spread
of Islamic radicalism and the regional drive toward the attainment of
nuclear weapons.[15]

   Rabin's first preference was to try to reach an agreement with Syria,
which he considered the key to regional peace. After the conclusion of
the Egyptian-Israeli peace treaty in 1979, Syria remained the most formidable enemy on Israel's borders and the only country that could con-
ceivably pose an existential threat to the Jewish state. Its leader, Hafez
Assad, was seen as a dangerous if rational leader who could be expected
to see the benefit of peace for his country's national interest and to live

up to his word. An agreement with Syria would pave the way for peace with Lebanon, which had long been under Syria's effective control, and eventually with the Palestinians, who could be expected to fall in line with their stronger Arab ally.

It was only upon realizing that Assad would not make the necessary leap of faith, and that the negotiations in Washington with the Palestinian delegation from the territories were heading nowhere, that Rabin begrudgingly agreed to accelerate the Oslo talks. Yet his fundamental distrust of the PLO drove him to make numerous attempts to establish a direct channel of communication with the Palestinian "inside" delegation in Washington, only to be repeatedly obstructed by Arafat.[16] Even when he understood that Oslo was "the only game in town," Rabin remained unhappy with the progress of the negotiations, going as far as to suspend them for a few days in early June 1993 without giving the Oslo team any explanation, so as to try and negotiate a better deal on his own. Efraim Sneh, a Labor Party parliamentarian and Rabin confidant who had conducted the secret overtures on his behalf with the Palestinians, was sent to London where he secretly negotiated a draft agreement with Nabil Shaath. Yet as this formula was more favorable to Israel than the one that was being devised in Oslo, conditioning inter alia Israel's recognition of the PLO on a six-month halt to terror attacks, Arafat balked outright. A disgruntled Rabin was thus forced to resume the Oslo talks, which ultimately blossomed into the Declaration of Principles.

During his 1992 election campaign, Rabin had promised to reach an Israeli-Palestinian agreement within nine months. With Oslo offering the only possible opportunity to make good on this pledge, Rabin seized the moment, regardless of its many risks and uncertainties. "Thus the Palestinians," Sneh concluded, "managed to reach the Israeli government through a channel that was more trusting, less cautious, more eager to reach an agreement, and better disposed to concessions."[17]

Rabin's lack of faith in Oslo was also influenced by his deep distrust of its two main architects. His deep enmity toward Shimon Peres, which he was to feel to his dying day, dated back to 1974 when the two had competed to succeed Prime Minister Golda Meir following her forced resignation in the wake of the 1973 Yom Kippur War. Rabin eventually won, but Peres, who would not reconcile himself to the defeat, used his position as minister of defense to undermine his superior at every opportunity, driving the embittered Rabin to describe him in his 1979 memoirs as "an inveterate schemer," an accusation that would haunt Peres. Rabin had a similar amount of spite for Beilin, whom he called "Peres's poodle," a comment that had a similarly damaging effect on Beilin's political career.

Unable to avoid having his nemesis as his second in command, Rabin was determined to reduce to a minimum Peres's role in the peace process. It has been suggested that Rabin initially authorized the Oslo talks as a ploy to keep Peres occupied while he was concentrating on the Syrian negotiations.[18] This, however, proved to be a gross underestimation of Peres's abilities, who quickly transformed Oslo into the foremost negotiating channel with the Palestinians. According to Mamduh Nawfal, a prominent PLO figure and a close associate of Arafat, Peres asked the PLO leadership to obstruct the Washington negotiations so as to force Rabin into approving the Oslo deal.[19]

Rabin thus embarked halfheartedly into the Oslo process. He initially decided not to go to Washington for the signing ceremony, so as to avoid shaking hands with Arafat. When Secretary of State Warren Christopher called to tell him that the president personally wanted him to attend, Rabin responded, "I will come; I have no choice." Shortly before the signing ceremony, as Israelis, Palestinians, and other guests were mingling in the White House, Christopher watched Rabin circle the Blue Room to avoid having to shake hands with Arafat. The Palestinian leader did not seem to notice.

During the signing ceremony, Rabin was uneasy, stiff, and reluctant. He could hardly bring himself to extend his hand in greeting to the beaming Arafat, whispering in evident relief to the far more relaxed Peres, who was next in line for a handshake, "I have gone through this hell, now it is your turn." Later, he told a group of Canadian Jewish leaders, "Of all the hands in the world, it was not the hand that I wanted or even dreamt of touching."[20]

Addressing the Knesset, the Israeli parliament, shortly after his return from the signing ceremony, Rabin admitted, "We did not know that all of this would be so difficult. There are hundreds of details we did not even imagine. I only hope that we will be able to reach an agreement on the security issue, which is the most important [aspect of the DOP], within the next couple of months." He told the parliamentarians that on his way back from Washington he made stopovers in Morocco and Egypt, where he told King Hassan and President Mubarak of his nagging fear that the PLO would not be able to rise to the challenge of evolving from a terrorist organization into a state builder. Both leaders tried to reassure their guest. Hassan expressed hope that the Palestinians would adopt the Israeli administrative system, while Mubarak sought to downplay the extent of the problem by claiming that "Three-quarters of a million Palestinians are hardly a small neighborhood in Cairo." Rabin remained unconvinced. "The PLO has never been responsible for a living community that needs to be fed, educated, and provided with housing and services."[21]

Rabin had more reason for skepticism following his first working session with Arafat in Cairo, on October 6, 1993. Emerging from their hour-and-a-half-long private talk, the two leaders held a session with the full delegations and President Mubarak where Rabin expressed his shock at having discovered "that we have got two different readings of the Oslo agreement." "We are facing conflicting interpretations of matters which I thought were clear," he said. "I wish I had met you [Arafat] before the signing, because there are matters which ought to have been made clear to you. There are some subjects on which I cannot compromise because they touch on the security of Israel."

Arafat interrupted. "Mr. Prime Minister," he said. "Don't forget that you are the one who is putting your hand on my territory." Rabin shot Arafat an angry glance, but maintained his composure. "Mr. Chairman, there is no need for such talk. We are two negotiating parties facing one another."[22]

A few weeks later, in November 1993, Rabin voiced new concern about his peace partner. "The PLO is a political and terrorist organization at one and the same time, rather than a sovereign state," he said. "Even the Hamas is better organized and less corrupt than the PLO . . . The PLO is an unclean organization since part of the money it receives goes to private pockets." Several months later, Rabin still referred derisively to Arafat as "chief talker . . . the master of survival, but the builder of nothing, so far."[23] As late as February 1994, Rabin was still highly skeptical of the PLO's commitment to peace. The organization gave its consent to the process, he told his ministers, "but only God knows how long this will last," adding that the PLO's agreement to participate in the process was the only thing it actually "gave," since thus far "we are always giving and they are taking."[24]

All this makes Rabin's failure to consult with the IDF or other security organizations during the peace negotiations, notably the Shabak, charged with the prevention of terror attacks in Israel and the territories, more troubling. When shown a copy of the agreement shortly before it became public, the IDF chief of staff, Lieutenant General Ehud Barak, warned, "Yitzhak, be careful, we have a lot of holes. It's like Swiss cheese." In an interview on the occasion of the Jewish New Year, Barak was even more skeptical, arguing that it would be impossible to sustain the fight against terrorism at its present level once the agreement came into effect. "There is a presumption regarding the efficacy of the Palestinian police, which does not yet exist, and its cooperative level," he warned, "and these are far from simple matters."[25]

Rabin later explained that he had not consulted with the military because he felt that it was important for this decision to be wholly political.[26] This claim is highly dubious since Rabin had no qualms about involving the army both in the subsequent negotiations on the Gaza and Jericho Agreement and in "selling" the accord to the political system and the Israeli public at large. For example, in an attempt to prevent the ultra-Orthodox Shas party from leaving his coalition in protest over the DOP, Rabin sent Barak and his deputy Major General Amnon Shahak to convince Rabbi Ovadia Yosef, Shas's spiritual head, that the Oslo deal was consistent with Israel's security concerns. How Barak managed to sell the "Swiss cheese" to Ovadia is not entirely clear, but the rabbi was sufficiently reassured to keep his party in the coalition.[27]

Having entered into a deal with a partner he detested and distrusted with no clear idea of its ultimate goals or long-term consequences, Rabin moved ahead like a man possessed, making his dissatisfaction known repeatedly yet refusing to do anything to stop the process.

By mid-October 1993, the prime minister was in a "disillusioned and depressed mood." Arafat not only failed to condemn the continued murder of Israelis in terrorist attacks or to distance himself from Hamas, but he assiduously sought to convince his Israeli partners to release the Hamas spiritual leader Sheik Ahmad Yassin. Instead of attempting to pressure Arafat to abide by his formal obligations, Rabin developed the oxymoronic thesis that Palestinian compliance could be ensured through noncompliance. Rabin believed Israel should not demand that Arafat adhere to his signed commitments, let alone criticize him in public for failing to do so, since this would only weaken the Palestinian leader. Instead, the Israeli government should try to boost his position through unilateral concessions on top of those agreed in the DOP, such as releasing larger numbers of Palestinian detainees and allowing the return to the West Bank of refugees who had fled during the 1967 Six-Day War. When in late October and early November 1993 three Israelis were murdered in terrorist attacks, one of them by Arafat's Fatah, Rabin stated that he did not consider Arafat responsible for preventing terrorist attacks by the peace agreement's Palestinian opponents. He similarly excused the PLO's open advocacy of the continuation of the Arab economic boycott against Israel as an understandable attempt to gain leverage for the negotiations.[28]

Arafat exploited this appeasing attitude by constantly testing Rabin's patience. In December 1993, for example, Rabin was so incensed with Arafat's behavior as to tell the Knesset that after the IDF pulled out of Gaza and Jericho, Israel would retain the right to preempt terrorist attacks from these territories by exercising its right to hot pursuit, "and for us, hot pursuit means the ability to chase them [not only] during an incident, but also in order to prevent an incident." As the Palestinians protested that the statement contradicted the DOP, Rabin quickly backed down and announced that "there will be no thwarting of terrorist actions."[29]

By the spring of 1994, as the IDF was leaving Gaza and Jericho, Rabin no longer believed that the PLO, unhampered by "High Court rulings and human rights organizations," would deal with Hamas terrorism far more effectively than democratic Israel ever could. Terrorism was a natural outcome of the Oslo accords, he asserted at the opening of the Knesset's summer session, though he expressed the belief that "even more acts of terrorism won't stop the peace train." In private Rabin was less upbeat, admitting that he had misjudged Arafat's interest in peace, yet still hoped that the process would succeed despite him. "You ask me whether Arafat will abide by all his commitments," he told a Labor Party Knesset faction meeting. "[The problem is that] among the Palestinians, Arafat's PLO is our only partner."[30] Rabin was essentially reduced to accepting a peace "partner" without any of the real fruits of peace.

Following Arafat's infamous Johannesburg speech of May 1994, not only did he ignore Rabin's demand for a retraction, but he repeatedly dismissed Oslo, much to Rabin's muted exasperation. When in August 1994 Arafat refrained from condemning Qaddoumi's call for Israel's destruction, Rabin responded with a strong tirade, only to quietly back down later. "These words contradict the agreement and it is inconceivable that we should act as if nothing has happened," he protested, adding that Israel would condition further progress in the peace process on the amendment of the Palestinian National Covenant. He also warned that the Palestinian failure to fight terrorism raised a big question mark over the entire process in general, and on the negotiations for an early empowerment agreement in particular. "It is true that it is impossible to prevent terrorist attacks altogether," he argued, "but we do not see a serious effort by the Palestinian Authority to restrain those opponents of the agreement who endeavor to undermine it through anti-Israel terrorist attacks—Hamas, Islamic Jihad, and, occasionally, other terrorist organizations."

Rabin repeated these warnings in subsequent weeks. On August 24, two Israeli technicians were murdered in the town of Ramle. Israel requested the extradition of the suspected killers from the Palestinian Authority, in accordance with the Gaza and Jericho Agreement. Arafat dismissed the request, claiming that the murder had been on criminal rather than terrorist grounds. An enraged Rabin countered that the Palestinian police was perfectly capable of fighting terrorism but that Arafat had not given it the necessary instructions: "We will not be able to put up for much longer with a situation in which we pass them information, and despite their clear knowledge of what has to be done they regularly fail to do it."

In mid-November 1994, following the kidnapping of a soldier in the center of Israel by Hamas, which then threatened to execute him unless the Israeli government gave in to a string of demands, Rabin delivered his toughest ever warning since the beginning of the Oslo process.

Conveyed through Secretary of State Christopher, the message was an ultimatum: either Arafat declared war on Hamas and made a serious effort to neutralize its military arm, Izzadin al-Qassem, or he would no longer be considered a peace partner by the Israeli government.[31]

These threats were to no avail. The early empowerment agreement, which authorized the transfer of some forms of civilian authority throughout the West Bank and the Gaza Strip, was signed on August 29, 1994, two weeks after Rabin threatened its possible suspension. The Interim Agreement of September 1995 was also signed, despite the Palestinian failure to amend the covenant or to declare war on Hamas. By the end of 1994, top Israeli military sources were saying openly that the autonomous Palestinian areas were undergoing a rapid process of "Lebanonization," with the numerous armed groups in Gaza becoming by the day far better organized and adept. Land and sea smuggling from Egypt, virtually inactive when Israel ruled the area, was bustling. With the Palestinian Authority's tacit approval, smugglers had turned the Gaza Strip into a huge arms cache, with the number of unlicensed weapons rising from hundreds to thousands. (Arafat acknowledged the existence of 26,000 such weapons but blamed Israel, which, he claimed, smuggled them into Gaza in order to instigate a civil war there.) Terrorists who a year earlier used primitive, homemade bombs were now using sophisticated TNT explosives and other standard military materials, which multiplied casualties by a factor of five. All this, in the opinion of Major General Uri Saguy, chief of military intelligence, had transformed Palestinian terrorism from a painful nuisance into a strategic threat of the first order and a danger to the entire peace process.[32]

On October 20, 1994, a week after delivering his toughest ultimatum yet to Arafat, Rabin stated that it would be a mistake to blame the Palestinian Authority for the continuation of terrorism. "The enemy must be defined. It is not Jordan or those Palestinians who want to live in peace with us," but rather the Islamic extremists who seek Israel's destruction. At a press conference with Arafat on January 19, 1995, Rabin went further, claiming that Israel did not expect watertight guarantees on the halt of all attacks from PA-controlled territories, since "even in areas under our control we cannot claim to have completely eradicated terrorism." Instead, Israel hoped for the development of better conditions for the prevention of terrorism and for cooperation with the Palestinians. An evidently relieved Arafat heartily concurred. "We do not have a magic wand for fighting terrorism," he said, "but we are doing our utmost."[33]

These words could not have been further from the truth. From the time of the establishment of the Palestinian Authority in May 1994, the number of terrorist attacks in the Gaza Strip had increased fourfold. During the first half of January 1995 alone, more than twenty attacks were recorded, some of which involved weapons given to the Palestinian police by the IDF. Three days after the Arafat-Rabin meeting, nineteen Israelis were murdered in a homicide bombing at the Beit Lid junction in central Israel, with Arafat telling cheering crowds in Gaza that "All of us are martyrs."

A deeply traumatized Rabin responded by closing the West Bank and Gaza and announcing his intention to erect a fence in order to separate Israel from the Palestinians, though not along the 1967 lines. Islamic terrorism, especially homicide bombings, constituted a strategic threat to Israel, he argued, and he demanded that Arafat prevent Gaza from becoming a terrorist haven, or otherwise "we will not be able to move forward unless we are confident that the personal security [of Israelis] is assured." The eternally optimistic Peres also questioned the prudence of negotiating with Arafat in view of his inability to assert his authority over practitioners of terrorism. "If he is too weak to do that or lacks the will, why should we negotiate with him at all?" he told the German weekly *Der Spiegel*.[34]

Yet for all his exasperation with Arafat, Rabin could not bring himself to break completely with the Palestinian leader. After the Beit Lid massacre, the Israeli president Ezer Weizman, himself a leading advocate of Israeli-Palestinian reconciliation, called for a halt in the implementation of the peace accords. Rabin was "livid," though several members of the cabinet quietly backed the suggestion and even Uri Savir, Oslo's chief negotiator, believed that "We need a profound change of direction to make the next stage a success."[35]

This was not the first time that Rabin rejected the idea of constraining Arafat's power. In 1994 he had declined a request by the two foremost "inside" Palestinian politicians, Faisal Husseini and Hanan Ashrawi, for assistance in the development of a democratic regime in the territories that would replace the corrupt and oppressive rule established by

Arafat and his Tunis cronies. The idea was to hold proportional elections for a legislative council, after which the winning party or parties would form a government. This was anathema to Arafat, who insisted on presidential elections where his victory was a foregone conclusion. Rabin turned the proposal down. "We should not dictate their electoral system," he told Beilin, who acted as mediator. "Besides, we too have direct elections for the premiership."[36]

Having ruled out the possibility of a potentially more democratic and less militant Palestinian regime, Rabin stuck with Arafat, whom he considered in a curious twist of logic as both a tacit supporter of terrorism and a peacemaker. Acknowledging that Arafat had made no serious effort to fight terrorism or to enforce law and order in Gaza, he argued in the same breath that "there is no alternative to negotiating with a partner who is ready to make peace . . . We must abide by our commitments provided Arafat can contain the terrorism emanating from the territories under his control."[37]

On April 14, 1995, Major General Shaul Mofaz, OC Southern Command, described Gaza as a hotbed of terrorism, adding that "if this is the maximum level of resolve and competence that Arafat and the Palestinian police can demonstrate, there is a huge question mark about their future ability [to fight terrorism] in the West Bank." The head of the military intelligence research department estimated that once the IDF withdrew from West Bank towns and cities the Palestinian Authority would lose all remaining incentives to fight terrorism. "There is nobody in the IDF intelligence who believes that Arafat is serious this time," a senior security source commented, responding to the arrest of hundreds of Islamic militants in early April 1995 following the first two homicide bombings inside Israel since the signing of the DOP. "All this talk of a showdown is purely for Israeli and American ears." A senior Palestinian police officer in Gaza corroborated this by revealing that the arrests were nothing but "a big show" and that most detainees had been released after their arrest, having promised not to engage in future acts of terrorism.[38]

Despite these warnings, in mid-August Rabin brought the Interim Agreement to the Israeli cabinet for approval, only to be confronted with harsh criticism, led by the cabinet's newest member, Ehud Barak. Having joined a few months earlier at Rabin's personal request, Barak argued that Israel would be making a grave mistake by failing to prolong its military redeployment in the West Bank until 1999, that is, until the latest stage of the final-status talks. Rabin was exasperated by what he considered an act of betrayal by his most prominent protégé. "Do you think that the Palestinians will sit quietly until then?" he angrily retorted.[39]

Barak's apprehensions were shared by Chief of Staff Shahak. On August 23, 1995, two days after four people were murdered and another hundred were wounded in a homicide bombing on a Jerusalem bus, Shahak warned the Knesset's foreign affairs and defense committee that "If the PA will not act decisively against Palestinian terrorism, everything we are doing now will fail." Two weeks later, as the Interim Agreement was about to be signed in Washington, the head of the military intelligence research department argued that "those who believed that the Palestinians will extradite terrorists should wake up to reality. The only reason for the improvement in the PA's fight against terrorism was the Israeli threat to halt the process." He added undiplomatically, "For Arafat, peace is shit."[40]

Ignoring the considered opinions of his most senior military advisers, Rabin signed the Interim Agreement on September 28, 1995. When questioned about the prudence of this move at a meeting with a group of American Jewish leaders, he exploded. "One should not waste any time on them," he told the Israeli press. "They are pariah Jews. They will be judged by Jewish history." On his way back to Israel, he continued to vent his fury at Jewish critics of the PA. "As far as the issues of war and peace are concerned, those who do not send their sons and daughters to do military service cannot, and have no moral right to, act against an elected government in Israel," he told a group of Israeli journalists on board his plane, before proceeding to condemn attempts by American Jewish groups to deny congressional aid to the PA as long as it failed to abide by its contractual obligations.[41]

These outbursts were more a reflection of Rabin's inner doubts about his latest move rather than an unwavering conviction in it. Only a few weeks later he confided to Nobel Prize laureate Elie Wiesel: "Initially I thought that Arafat was the solution [to the Palestinian-Israeli conflict]. Now I am convinced that he is the problem."[42]

8

The Tunnel War

We feel the Oslo agreement is impotent and deficient . . . We should be honest with ourselves and admit that Israel is the principal enemy of the Palestinian people. It was the enemy in the past, it is the enemy in the present, and will continue to be the enemy in the future.

—Yasser Arafat, May 1995

One person who needed no convincing that Arafat was the problem was Benjamin Netanyahu, the newly elected Israeli prime minister in 1996. As early as September 1993, Netanyahu warned that the Oslo agreement was nothing but "a prelude to a future war that the PLO is planning from a West Bank state."[1] In the Hebrew edition of his book *A Place Among the Nations: Israel and the World*, published in 1995 (the original English edition was published prior to Oslo II), he offered a far more scathing indictment:[2]

Oddly ignoring the PLO's explicit goal [i.e., the destruction of Israel], the Israeli government joined Arafat in signing the 1993 Oslo accords, thus effectively adopting the first stage of his "phased strategy"—Israel's virtual withdrawal to the 1967 lines and the laying of the groundwork for the creation of a Palestinian state in Judea, Samaria, and the Gaza Strip . . . It is not difficult to predict that once the Palestinian organizations receive these concessions from the Israeli government they will resume and intensify their terrorist campaign against the Jews, well before they start an all-out war. After all, the use of terrorism has allowed them to extract valuable assets from the present government. Why then shouldn't they believe that its continuation and intensification will not bring them further gains?[2]

Now that he had defeated the veteran Peres to become Israel's youngest ever prime minister at forty-six, Netanyahu was determined to slow
down what he believed to be Israel's inexorable slide toward complete
capitulation. Unable to disown the Oslo process altogether both because
democratic governments are bound by international accords signed by
their predecessors and because the Israeli public, for all its disillusionment with the Palestinian leadership, was loath to give up the promise
of peace, Netanyahu sought to balance these contradictory considerations by promising to adhere to the Oslo accords while proclaiming his
determination to bring "peace with security." Once elected, Netanyahu
quickly moved to demonstrate to the Palestinian leadership that while
the peace process would continue, the "rules of the game" had irrevocably changed to reflect a far greater measure of reciprocity. If the Palestinians wished Israel to continue implementing the Oslo accords, they
too had to keep their side of the bargain. A few months after forming
his cabinet, Netanyahu commented,

> I do not leave matter[s] to the other side's goodwill. That's precisely the
> difference between this government and its precursor, which put its faith
> in the other side, turned a blind eye [to its violation of the accords], mis-
> led the Israeli public, and brought upon us the most horrendous terrorist
> wave since the establishment of the state.
>
> We have taken a different line from the outset. We clarified to Arafat
> that the war against terrorism is not a passing episode stemming from ad
> hoc whims or political pressures. And we insist on action, not on words alone.
> This is in stark contrast to the Labor government's silly assertion that Is-
> rael would pursue the political track as if there were no terrorism and would
> fight terrorism as if there were no political process. Our policy is very clear.
> Should terrorism persist, we will not continue the political process.[3]

To Arafat, this was totally unacceptable. After nearly three years of constant indulgence, he was being asked to pay for what he had previously
received for free. To be sure, the Labor government had occasionally
taken strict measures to stem the mounting tide of Palestinian terrorism, notably the closure of the territories. Yet in its eagerness to maintain the facade of a partnership, it had been willing to acquiesce in the
face of systematic violations of the Oslo accords, going so far as to label
the hundreds of terrorist victims as part of the "price of peace."

Netanyahu was not only impervious to this kind of wishful thinking (it took him two full months after taking office to hold his first meeting with Arafat) but was likely to use the persistence of terrorist attacks as proof of Palestinian disingenuousness. Since Arafat saw the Oslo accords as the first step in bringing about Israel's ultimate demise rather than in securing its peaceful existence, he had no intention to start respecting his contractual obligations. Therefore Netanyahu had to be goaded into his predecessors' policy of surrendering land without a corresponding return, even if this involved the use of terrorism or other forms of physical coercion. "Netanyahu's clinging to old ideas will restore violence to the region for at least twenty-five years," warned Salim Zaanun, "after which either the Palestinian people will perish or be expelled from its homeland, or Netanyahu will be driven to the same conclusion as Rabin and Peres."[4]

This perception of "peace negotiations" constituted a material breach of the key principle on which the entire Oslo process was predicated, namely the complete and irrevocable exclusion of violence from Palestinian-Israeli relations. At no time, and under no circumstances would either party revert to physical force to promote its political ends. No differences, however profound, could possibly justify such a course of action. Unlike armed conflict, where belligerents seek unqualified victory and where one's gain is by definition the other's loss, conflict resolution is a mixed-motive interaction in which both sides are propelled toward a mutual goal, a give-and-take relationship rather than an imposed dictate.

As long as Israel was sufficiently pliant, Arafat was happy to sustain the pretence of cooperation, refraining from threatening his Israeli partners with direct violence, not least since they were more eager than he to sustain the process. With Netanyahu no longer willing to make disparate concessions, the real Palestinian position was abruptly exposed in all its cruel clarity. Out went Arafat's solemn pledge in his September 1993 letter to Rabin to commit the PLO "to a peaceful resolution of the conflict between the two sides" and the attendant promise "that all outstanding issues relating to permanent status will be resolved through negotiations." In came a naked threat of violence. There was no longer room for bargaining or negotiations. Either Israel accepted the Palestinian demands en masse, or, in the words of Abu Ala,

There will be no peace with Israel unless the Palestinian people in the Diaspora can exercise their right to repatriation or compensation . . . since the refugee issue is the root of the Palestinian question; no peace without the Palestinian people's right to self-determination, to defining their future, and to establishing an independent state with Jerusalem as its capital; and no peace if a single settler remains in the Palestinian territories or if a single stone remains in an Israeli settlement on Palestinian land.

What if Israel was to reject these demands, which after all were tantamount to its effective destruction? Abu Ala made no secret of the consequences:

Our options are clear. We can always go back to the previous situation. This means that we can go back to the previous intifada, to fighting, and to struggle. The region will never have rest unless there is just peace— one that resolves the Palestinian problem fairly and ends the Israeli occupation of Arab lands.[5]

Palestinian threats of violence began within days of the Israeli elections, well before Netanyahu managed to form his government. In a televised interview on May 31, the PLO representative to Germany said that he could not preclude the possibility of another terrorist wave "if we are unable to shape peace in a way that really allows us to live in peace." Hassan Asfour, one of the peace negotiators, said, "A return to square one will mean a return to the climate of war, intifada and resistance. If their choice is conflict, we will not remain passive onlookers. We are not so weak that someone can delude himself into attempting to impose his policies on us."[6]

Though Netanyahu had instructed his political adviser Dore Gold to inform Abu Mazen of Israel's full commitment to the peace process, Asfour's blatant threat was followed by a series of ground moves indicating Palestinian preparations for armed conflict. On June 11, a week before the formation of the Netanyahu government, Fatah's central committee established a twelve-member emergency group headed by Arafat, its aim to "revitalize the movement's activities and find ways and means to rearrange the internal situation." The heads of the PA's security services threatened that unless Netanyahu changed his position within a few weeks, they would suspend their fight against Hamas, while Fatah's youth organization had reportedly reached an agreement with Hamas on coordinated attacks against settlers. Arafat himself visited the Nablus prison in mid-June, where a senior Hamas operative was detained. He ordered the man released, and the two left together to attend Friday prayers at a mosque in downtown Nablus. By early July 1996, some seven hundred religious militants had been freed from Palestinian jails. When asked to comment on reports that the PA favorably viewed attacks by Hamas as long as the Netanyahu government did not change its policies, Faisal Husseini remarked that the Palestinian Authority would not impose discipline on the Palestinian people, let alone attempt to do so by force.[7]

By now, many members of the Palestinian leadership, including Abu Mazen, Abu Ala, Nabil Shaath, and Yasser Abd Rabbo, had threatened to resume the intifada and violence, while the PA-appointed mufti of Jerusalem, Ikrima Sabri, went a step further, urging the Palestinians to do so immediately. "For us there is really no difference between Likud and Labor. They are both heretics," he said in a Friday sermon. "There is no one who can deny that the Jews act deviously, as the Koran itself shows, and no one knows when they will be stopped . . . We must rise up against the occupation with all our might to achieve what we want. It is forbidden for us to sit quietly. If we are quiet we will not be victorious." Asked later whether he had issued a religious ruling against homicide bombings, Sabri retorted, "I never issued such a ruling, and the PA never asked me to do so."[8]

On July 28, Arafat gave his strongest endorsement since Netanyahu's election for the continuation of terror attacks, including suicide bombings. In a public speech in Gaza on the twenty-fifth anniversary of the "martyrdom" of two Fatah commanders, he heaped praise on "those pious martyrs who fell on the road to Jerusalem," lauding Yahya Ayyash, the Hamas archterrorist who had masterminded the murder of dozens of Israelis and who was subsequently killed by Israel in January 1996, as "the last martyr." "We follow those martyrs, we follow them to Jerusalem," he chanted ecstatically, before concluding on a chilling note. "I tell my brother martyrs: Everything is cheap for the sake of Jerusalem."[9]

At the end of August, Arafat called for the first "mass protest" against Israel since the signing of the DOP. He urged the Muslim masses to come by the thousands to the Friday prayer in al-Aqsa Mosque, and called upon the Christian minority to hold special prayers at the Church of the Holy Sepulcher the following Sunday. While none of these target audiences heeded his call, with fewer attending al-Aqsa than on ordinary Fridays, Arafat used a highly publicized visit to the Balata refugee camp in Nablus to send a pointed message to Netanyahu, whom he was about to meet for the first time the following week. "I am saying this to Israel. Should you fail to respect signed agreements, our people will have no other alternative [but violence]." Specifically addressing the younger members of the audience he continued, "Israel may have aircraft, but we have Palestinian kids . . . You, children of the rocks will keep up your resistance . . . With their spirit and their blood our future generations will continue the march [to Jerusalem], until the Palestinian flag is hoisted over its walls."[10]

Muhammad Dahlan, head of preventive security in Gaza, mimicked Arafat's threat in less prosaic terms. "Should the peace process deteriorate as a result of Netanyahu's policy, the Palestinian Authority might resort to armed force," he said on September 3, the day before Netanyahu and Arafat's scheduled meeting, adding that in such circumstances the Palestinians would use all weapons at their disposal, including those at the hands of their police force. Faisal Husseini, for his part, warned that a violent explosion was inevitable sooner rather than later, and that the PA could not be held responsible for its occurrence. "We are a party as long as the situation is similar to that of a chess game. However, if the Israelis want a boxing match, they will find additional partners."[11]

Against this backdrop, it was hardly surprising that Netanyahu and Arafat's first meeting was almost canceled a day before its occurrence when an article in the official Palestinian press derided the Israeli prime minister as "worse than a Nazi." After hectic contacts between Israeli and Palestinian officials, Arafat agreed to place a phone call to Netanyahu in an attempt to clear the air. "I do not accept any insult to anybody. How can I accept an insult to you, my neighbor and partner?" he asked, promising to initiate an investigation into the incident. Netanyahu reciprocated. "Mr. Chairman, I respect you as a leader. I will deal with you as a leader. We will make something together which makes those who oppose the peace process disappointed."[12]

Such words could hardly disguise the fact that their first initial meeting was a dialogue of the deaf. From the outset, Netanyahu sought to convince Arafat of the merits of his peace doctrine. "Our government is different from its precursor," he said. "We were elected on the basis of a different mandate. We promised to bring peace with security. We will base the process on reciprocity."

Arafat concurred. "Your government, and that of Yitzhak Shamir, started the process in Madrid. We established our first contacts with Likud during the negotiations between Menachem Begin and Anwar Sadat."

Netanyahu did not attempt to correct this skewed historical account. (In the late 1970s Arafat had turned down an American offer to join the Egyptian-Israeli peace process.) Instead he concentrated on obtaining Arafat's renewed commitment to fighting terror. "In security one must not go back. We saw what happens when one goes back."

"We are committed to security," Arafat retorted. "This is our strategic decision. We will act resolutely against terrorism." He elaborated on what the PA had done to combat terrorism thus far, and demanded the release of Palestinians imprisoned in Israel, including the Hamas leader Sheik Ahmad Yassin. He also complained about the adverse economic consequences of the continued closure. "The closure is only tied to security. We do not seek to economically oppress the Palestinians," Netanyahu answered, pointing out that a few days earlier his government had adopted certain measures to ease the Palestinian economic plight, which included a promise of establishing industrial parks along Israel's border with the West Bank and the Gaza Strip (the so-called Green Line).

Netanyahu left the meeting with a real sense of achievement, believing he had succeeded in putting Israeli-Palestinian relations on a new and more promising footing. In a news conference with the Israeli media shortly after his meeting with Arafat, Netanyahu made an impassioned plea for public support for the continuation of peace negotiations with the Palestinians. "In the context of the meeting, we set a framework or outline for the continuation of the negotiations between Israel and the PA and we set an order of priorities for all issues on the agenda," he said. "No longer [will there be] a situation whereby Israel gives and the Palestinian side takes. The giving and giving is over, and we are now switching to a give and take. If this seems to you to be self-evident, I tell you that this was far from being so."[13]

This upbeat prognosis could not be more misconceived. Arafat was no better disposed to a give-and-take relationship with Israel after his meeting with Netanyahu than he had been before it. Within days of the meeting, according to the Jordanian weekly *al-Hadath*, Arafat ordered the commanders of the various Palestinian organizations, notably Fatah's militia Tanzim, to brace themselves for a confrontation with Israel. He also instructed the PLO's intifada committee to revive a study on the intensification of the anti-Israel struggle that it had prepared in the summer of 1991 and had since been shelved. Envisaging a sustained and multifaceted confrontation aimed at debilitating Israel politically, militarily, socially, economically, and psychologically, the study recommended an escalation of fighting by shifting from rocks to more lethal weapons such as knives, Molotov cocktails, and firearms. It then called for a joint military effort by all Palestinian groups and organizations and the creation of unified national structures under the command of the Palestinian Authority that would take the struggle "to each and every town, village, refugee camp, and neighborhood in occupied Palestine," that is, in Israel itself and not only in the West Bank and Gaza.[14]

Arafat soon found a golden opportunity to make good on his threats, with the September 24 Israeli opening of a new entrance to an archaeological tunnel in Jerusalem. Arafat quickly capitalized on the move to stir a tidal wave of violence by condemning the decision as "a major crime against our holy places."[15] Dating to the Hasmonean era (second century to first century BCE), both historically and geographically the tunnel had nothing to do with the mosques on Temple Mount (or al-Haram al-Sharif, as it is known to Muslims). Located hundreds of yards from these religious sites, tens of thousands of tourists had gone through it since its first opening in the late 1980s with no impact on the mosques. Since the tunnel had no exit at its northern end, visitors were forced to double back through a narrow passageway. The opening of the new doorway thus enabled tourists to pass continuously through the tunnel, and it was expected to boost visits to the site with the attendant boon to the local Palestinian merchants.

The opening of the tunnel also took place within the context of an earlier Israeli-Palestinian deal. The *waqf*, a Muslim trust that administers the Islamic holy places, had been pressing for some time for prayer space in Solomon's Stables, a cavernous subterranean hall on the Temple Mount, thought to date from the time of King Herod's modifications of the Second Jewish Temple. In an agreement reached in January 1996, Muslims were permitted to use a defined space for prayer, and in return the Israelis would open a northern entrance to the Hasmonean tunnel. In accordance with this deal, Muslims prayed in Solomon's Stables during Ramadan (and have made significant modifications to the halls, in contravention of the agreement). When Israel went forward with the exit, the PA predictably reneged on its side of the agreement and unleashed a mass call to riot.[16]

Addressing a group of soldiers and policemen in Gaza on September 24, Arafat implored them to go out and fight Israel. "The Believers shall inherit paradise. They shall fight for Allah and shall kill and be killed," he chanted.

> Our Palestinian people will not stand idly by when their holy sites are being violated. . . . Oh our pure martyrs. Rest in peace, calm and assured. Our blood is cheap for the sake of the goal that had united us in the past . . . With Allah's will we shall meet again soon in the upper heaven.[17]

Arafat's inflammatory speech was broadcast that day by the PA-controlled media, as was a joint statement by the various Palestinian leadership bodies—the PA, the PLO Executive, and the Legislative Council—which urged the population to "move immediately and effectively to face this criminal scheme. We appeal to them all to shoulder their religious and national responsibilities in these serious circumstances and to confront these painful incidents and tragic dangers facing holy Jerusalem."[18]

This official incitement brought large numbers of Palestinians to the streets, but it did not produce the scores of "martyrs" Arafat desired. Anticipating mass public disturbances, the Israeli police went out of its way to pacify the situation, and thus there were no casualties during the first day of rioting.[19] An exasperated Arafat ordered the PLO security organs to engage the Israeli forces. Busloads of militant students were brought to the Israeli checkpoint outside Ramallah and to the strategic Netzarim junction, south of Gaza, where they joined thousands of rioters in attacking the soldiers with rocks and Molotov cocktails. To inflame spirits still further, the PA's ministry of information issued a statement protesting the "bloody massacre" allegedly committed by Israeli forces "against participants in the peaceful marches that overwhelmed all Palestinian cities and villages in protest of Israeli measures against Islamic and Christian holy shrines in the city of Jerusalem."

In reality, only a single Palestinian policeman had been killed in the clashes, but shortly thereafter Palestinian policemen opened fire on their Israeli counterparts, aided by sharpshooters using telescopic sights who had been positioned in advance in strategic sites. By the time fighting was over on September 27, fifteen Israelis and fifty-eight Palestinians lay dead, with hundreds more injured.[20]

For Arafat, this was a small price to pay. Just as his widespread practice of terrorism during the 1970s had brought him ever growing international recognition and acceptance rather than censure and ostracism, this latest spate of organized violence likewise paid handsome dividends. The international media willingly fell for the distorted Palestinian version of the crisis, turning aggressor into victim and victim into aggressor,[21] along with the Security Council, which passed a special resolution condemning Israeli behavior. The U.S. administration failed to veto the UN resolution and demanded Israeli gestures to the Palestinians, starting with the closure of the tunnel.

No less important, the tunnel war allowed Arafat to reassert his steadily deteriorating position among his subjects. Mutterings of discontent with the PA's oppressive and corrupt rule had been spreading throughout the territories during the previous months, and in August 1996 bloody riots broke out in the West Bank towns of Nablus and Tulkarm following the torturing to death of two religious militants by the Palestinian police. The shaken Arafat ordered the immediate release of scores of Hamas operatives from prison, had three policemen summarily tried and given long prison terms, and proclaimed a religious militant, shot dead by the Palestinian police, a martyr.[22] Now that he was ostensibly spearheading the campaign to protect Islam's third holiest shrine from "Jewish machinations," frantically liaising with Arab and Muslim leaders throughout the world, and urging the UN Security Council to condemn Israel, these domestic challenges were all but forgotten.

Last but not least, Arafat managed to box Netanyahu into a corner both domestically and internationally. Failing to recognize the conflagration's real causes, many in Israel and throughout the world came to regard the Israeli prime minister as a dangerous mixture of ideological dogmatism and political incompetence, of bluster and insecurity. Such views were held not only by sworn adherents of the Oslo process ("The past four years were the best in 4,000 years of Jewish history. Why stop it?" lamented Peres),[23] but also within Netanyahu's own camp. President Ezer Weizmann, who eighteen months earlier had urged the Rabin government to halt the Oslo process in response to Palestinian terrorism, invited Arafat to his private residence for a goodwill visit, while the heads of the security service (Shabak), still believing in the feasibility of Palestinian-Israeli antiterrorism collaboration, informed the media of their alleged opposition to the tunnel opening. Netanyahu's failure to take measures against this blatant act of insubordination by civil servants only served to reinforce the consensus that he was an indecisive leader whose bark was worse than his bite.

The tunnel war set an important precedent that would be repeated whenever the need arose. The greater the issues at stake the more ferocious Palestinian violence would be. The tunnel was but a handy pretext that could be disposed of once it had outlived its usefulness (the new exit has remained open since September 1996 to the benefit of tourists and local merchants, with the PA dropping the issue from its agenda after a few months).

On October 10, 1996, a week after returning from a summit with Netanyahu in Washington, where they agreed on the resumption of bilateral negotiations, and only two days after broadcasting comforting words to the Israeli public from President Weizmann's residence, Arafat made a militant address to the Palestinian Legislative Council. Having treated his audience to the standard Arab account of the Palestinian-Israeli conflict, he lauded the political gains of the tunnel war before warning the delegates to brace themselves for even tougher tests in the future. "We must be fully prepared and I hope you understand what I mean when I say fully prepared," he said. "A smart man needs only a hint. We must be fully prepared to confront all possibilities, which may be hard and difficult, Allah only knows."[24]

At a speech at the Deheisheh refugee camp near Bethlehem on October 21, Arafat was far more specific. "We know one word only: Jihad, Jihad, Jihad. Oslo I and II are agreed to as long as they lead to a Palestinian state, and in addition to that all options are open." Four days later, with Israeli security forces publicly warning against a possible suicide bombing, Arafat exclaimed in Gaza: "Let us pray to Allah that He shall grant us martyrdom."[25]

In January 1997 the Netanyahu government signed the Hebron Protocol, stipulating the redeployment of the IDF from the last major Palestinian town, something that the previous government had failed to do. It was a move that subjected Netanyahu to harsh criticism within his own camp. Yet the further withdrawal of Israeli forces from the West Bank (pullback from Gaza had been completed in May 1994) proved far more problematic as Netanyahu sought to transfer the minimum possible territory to the PA before the conclusion of the final-status agreement.

The September 1995 Interim Agreement divided the West Bank into three distinct areas in accordance with the degree of Palestinian sovereignty: Area A, namely the Jericho area and the seven main Palestinian cities of Jenin, Nablus, Tulkarm, Qalqilya, Ramallah, Bethlehem, and Hebron, which was to be under complete Palestinian control; Area B, comprising some 450 towns, villages, refugee camps, and hamlets, where the Palestinian Authority was to exercise civil authority and to protect the "public order for Palestinians" while Israel would maintain "overriding responsibility for security for the purpose of protecting Israelis and confronting the threat of terrorism"; and Area C, where Israel was to retain complete territorial jurisdiction with the Palestinian Authority maintaining "functional jurisdiction" over the Arab population in matters "not related to territory."

In accordance with the agreement, by the end of 1995 Israeli forces had been withdrawn from Areas A and B (with the exception of Hebron). This amounted to nearly 30 percent of the West Bank's overall territory and virtually its entire Palestinian population, which now came under the reign of the newly established Palestinian Authority.[26] On January 20, 1996, elections to the Palestinian Legislative Council were held, and shortly afterward the Israeli civil administration and military government were dissolved.

The further redeployment of Israeli forces "to specified military locations," as well as the transfer of internal-security responsibility in the various areas, was to be "gradually implemented in accordance with the DOP in three phases, each to take place after an interval of six months, after the inauguration of the [Palestinian Legislative] Council, to be completed within 18 months from the date of the inauguration of the Council."[27]

Since this timetable committed Israel to the withdrawal of its troops from most of the West Bank by September 1997, a year and a half before the conclusion of the permanent-status negotiations, it was widely resented by security people, including former prime minister Rabin, who had feared that once Israel surrendered its territorial assets it would be unable to ensure that the Palestinians would keep their part to the bargain.[28] For Netanyahu, whose long-standing conviction was that Arafat sought to transform the West Bank into a springboard for an assault on Israel in keeping with the PLO's so-called phased strategy, this timetable was nothing short of a disaster.

Netanyahu thus sought to extend the timetable as far as possible and tried to tie it to Palestinian compliance with the peace accords in the form of a Note for the Record, prepared by U.S. peace mediator Dennis Ross and appended to the Hebron Protocol. The note stipulated that all Israeli and Palestinian commitments "will be dealt with immediately and in parallel." In letters of assurance to Netanyahu and Arafat, Secretary of State Warren Christopher confirmed the extension of the redeployment timetable from September 1997 to "not later than mid-1998." In a follow-up letter, Ross clarified that "the U.S. understanding is that this range of time encompasses the months of June, July, and August 1998." No less important for Netanyahu was the U.S. State Department's official confirmation that the "further redeployment phases are issues for implementation for Israel rather than issues for negotiations with the Palestinians" and that the redeployment process "is an Israeli responsibility which includes its designating specified military locations."[29]

Armed with these assurances, on March 7, 1997, the Israeli cabinet decided to implement the next phase of withdrawal by transferring 9.1 percent of West Bank territory to various degrees of Palestinian control. Having just acknowledged Israel's right to determine unilaterally the scope of its redeployments, the administration gave its grudging consent, informing the Palestinians of its hope that Israel would "do more in the second and third phases." Arafat, however, was enraged because a week earlier the Israeli government had decided to build a 6,500-unit housing project in the Har Homa neighborhood in southwest Jerusalem. The Palestinians quickly denounced this action as a declaration of war. Now that Netanyahu had added insult to injury through the limited scope of his withdrawal, Arafat felt that the prime minister must have forgotten his September 1996 "lesson" and had to be given a timely reminder.

On the night of March 9, Arafat held a meeting in his office with Hamas leaders, his first meeting with the group in a long time, where he reportedly gave them "a green light" to resume terrorist attacks against Israel. Over the next few days, scores of Hamas terrorists were released from prison, including Ibrahim Makadme, a top member of the Hamas military wing, while the PA's preventive security organs were ordered to suspend their cooperation with Israel. The results were almost immediate. On March 21, a suicide bomber blew himself up in a Tel Aviv café, the first such attack in a year, killing three people and wounding forty-eight. Unmoved, Arafat flew off on an eight-day tour of the Arab world and South Asia, including his first visit in eight years to Iran, sponsor of the Hamas and Islamic Jihad terrorist groups, while Israeli security officials warned of further bombings. Marwan Barghouthi, commander of Fatah's Tanzim militia, used a discussion at the Legislative Council to offer his condolences to the family of the Tel Aviv "martyr," to the thunderous applause of fellow council members.[30]

On July 30, 1997, sixteen Israelis were murdered and 178 wounded in two consecutive suicide bombings in a Jerusalem market, while a month later five Jerusalemites were killed and 181 were wounded in three simultaneous bombings in the capital's main pedestrian mall. According to Major General Moshe Yaalon, head of military intelligence, there was no evidence that Arafat had personally authorized these specific attacks, but his glaring abstention from fighting terrorism was widely interpreted by his constituents as an endorsement to act. In mid-July, three Palestinian policemen were arrested en route to an attack on a Jewish settlement in the West Bank. In their interrogation they revealed the existence of other terrorist groupings within the Palestinian police and implicated senior security officials, including Ghazi Jabali, head of police in the Gaza Strip. Jibril Rajoub, the fearsome head of the Preventive Security Service in the West Bank, was found to be smuggling prohibited weapons in his private vehicle, while some of his subordinates were apprehended transporting Hamas terrorists in their official cars.[31]

In March 1997 Arafat also began reorganizing Tanzim, Fatah's militia, with a goal toward using it as a spearhead in a future military confrontation. Established in the early 1980s by Fatah youth, Tanzim was largely dormant during the early 1990s, though Arafat had never attempted to dismantle it as required by the 1995 Interim Agreement. Tanzim was reinvigorated following Netanyahu's election and was rapidly establishing itself as Fatah's military and terrorist arm.

Meanwhile Arafat continued to indulge Hamas. Numerous terrorists released from the PA's jails in the wake of the Hebron agreement, including senior commanders who had masterminded mass suicide bombings, remained free and active, and the organization's terrorist infrastructure was being steadily developed. At a two-day national-unity conference in late August 1997, with the participation of various "opposition" groups, Arafat was pictured cordially embracing Abdel Aziz Rantisi, a top Hamas leader, while Rajoub expressed his sympathy for Hamas and Islamic Jihad's anti-Israel campaign. Dahlan boasted that his preventive security organ was harboring many Hamas activists who were on Israel's wanted list.[32]

By now Israeli security forces had incontrovertible evidence that Fatah was making a sustained effort to set the territories ablaze under direct orders from Arafat. Their primary targets were Hebron and Nablus, which they hoped to turn into flashpoints of a general conflagration not unlike the tunnel war. (This replicated earlier violence in March 1997 when Fatah and Rajoub's men incited rioters to such an extent that Palestinian policemen, who were unaware of this connection, found themselves fighting against Rajoub's own security personnel.) At a meeting with the governor and the mayor of Nablus in July, Arafat complained that there were no demonstrations or rioting in the city as in Hebron. When told that the public was not at all motivated in this direction, he ordered the formation of special squads composed of Palestinian policemen that would open fire on Israeli targets without causing fatalities.[33]

In a particularly militant speech in Gaza on August 5, 1997, less than a week after the Jerusalem atrocity, Arafat openly told Fatah leaders to prepare for war against Israel. "In 1974 this movement received the banner of the revolution from the Vietnamese revolution," he boasted, before lauding the PLO's supposed military exploits: the 1968 battle of Karameh—"the first Arab victory"—and the 1982 Lebanon war, where "Sharon thought that he could collect us from the streets, but we sacrificed 72,000 holy martyrs and he failed to achieve his design." Invoking Fatah's historic battle cry—"The pledge is the pledge and the oath is the oath"—which is essentially the organization's commitment to the creation of a Palestinian state on Israel's ruins, Arafat told his listeners to brace themselves for ever more demanding challenges. "We have a bigger battle ahead of us than anything that came before," he proclaimed. "We are all living martyrs ready to renew our commitment to the path of the armed struggle on which we embarked many years ago." Faisal Husseini echoed this sentiment by warning that "war needs only one party to start it" and that the Palestinians would not be able to hold back until the present government's end of term, since "every day Netanyahu does something new."[34]

As it turned out, Husseini was only partly right. Arafat would indeed prove that it took just one party to start a war, but Netanyahu would not be the Israeli leader to fight it. Having moved the elections forward to May 1999 in the face of dwindling parliamentary support, Netanyahu was defeated by Labor candidate Ehud Barak, who became Israel's fourth prime minister in only four years.

9

Showdown in Camp David

Arafat proved to be one of the last of the historic leaders, because
he said no at the moment when no one says no to America.
—Freih Abu Medein, PA minister of justice,
comments on the Camp David summit

On Tuesday afternoon, July 11, 2000, in the scenic presidential retreat
of Camp David, Maryland, President Bill Clinton inaugurated the most
ambitious single effort to end the century-long feud between Arabs and
Jews over the Promised Land. Convened at the persistent urging of
Prime Minister Barak, the timing of the summit could not have been
more inopportune for Arafat. Ever since Netanyahu had insisted on reciprocity in the implementation of the Oslo accords, the Palestinian leader
had been busy preparing for a military and political confrontation with
Israel. While the 1996 "tunnel war" had driven Netanyahu to sign the
Hebron Protocol, and sustained pressure in its wake had produced the
1998 Wye Agreement that provided for further redeployments of Israeli
forces, Arafat had no intention of paying the price for these withdrawals,
such as clamping down on terrorism or curtailing the violent anti-Israel
incitement spread by his PA. The Palestinians had to reach final-status
talks while in control of the West Bank and the Gaza Strip, to obtain
the necessary springboard for the encroachment on pre-1967 Israeli sovereignty, and to fulfill Arafat's phased strategy, either through the implementation of the right of return or by other means. Since the Israelis
were acting to prevent this eventuality, they had to be faced with the
fait accompli of Palestinian statehood. The prominent Fatah leader Sakhr
Habash commented just days into the Camp David summit, "We will
establish our state not in order to declare war on Israel. We do not have

the military strength to fight Israel. Rather, we will be like Syria, part of whose territory is occupied by Israel, and then a new phase in the negotiations will have begun."[1]

From the initial days of the Netanyahu government, Arafat had repeatedly threatened that should the final-status negotiations fail to reach their desired goals by the designated date of May 4, 1999, a Palestinian state would be unilaterally proclaimed, with Jerusalem as its capital. "The Palestinian rifle is ready and we will aim it if they try to prevent us from praying in Jerusalem," he told a Fatah conference on November 15, 1998. "Whoever thinks he can toy with us regarding the 'Agreement of the Brave' should know that we are a people of giants."[2] When Netanyahu warned of a harsh response, including the annexation of certain territories to Israel, Arafat sought to mobilize the widest possible international support, to little avail. While expressing their sympathy for the idea of Palestinian statehood, the Americans and the Europeans were reluctant to give their blessing to what would effectively amount to a total renunciation of the Oslo process, built as it was on the idea of a negotiated settlement rather than an imposed dictate.

By the spring of 1999 the Netanyahu government seemed to be running out of steam. Right-wing parties were unhappy with Netanyahu's territorial concessions, and their leftist counterparts were critical of what they considered the government's unnecessary recalcitrance. The Israeli public was increasingly disenchanted with Netanyahu's overall performance. Barak, the Labor candidate, armed with a more appeasing political platform, appeared to be forging toward victory in the early elections that were called for in mid-May. The Palestinians were advised to await the results of the Israeli elections and remain committed to the Oslo process.

Arafat complied, only to be quickly disillusioned with the incoming prime minister. Though making an emotional pledge on election night to follow in Rabin's footsteps, to the cheers of thousands of ecstatic supporters, Barak had never been an admirer of the Oslo process. In his capacity as the IDF chief of staff, he had been not only overtly critical of the accord's security aspects but also suspicious of the PLO's ultimate objectives. ("The Hamas and the PLO are two sides of a national movement, espousing quite similar long-term objectives toward us," Barak stated about a year after the signing of the DOP.)[3] As a new minister in the Rabin cabinet, in

September 1995 Barak had famously abstained in the critical vote on the Interim Agreement, to the prime minister's public irritation. Three months later, as Labor braced itself for elections under Peres's leadership, Barak opposed the amendment of the party's platform to include support for the creation of a Palestinian state, arguing that he would rather have a unified political entity comprising Jordan and the West Bank.[4] Now that he had achieved his lifelong ambition to reach his country's top spot, Barak was reluctant to surrender any territories to the Palestinians before the conclusion of the final-status talks, so as not to lose these valuable bargaining chips. He went so far as to attempt to disavow the Wye Agreement, only to be goaded by the U.S. administration into its reaffirmation in a new document signed in the Egyptian resort of Sharm al-Sheik in September 1999.[5]

Unlike Netanyahu, who had shunned Arafat for as long as he could, Barak made a point of meeting the Palestinian leader on the very day he assumed the premiership. Yet his intention to avoid further redeployments before the final-status talks did not go unnoticed by Arafat. Neither did Barak's buoyant pledge to reach framework agreements with all Arab parties within eighteen months help dispel Palestinian skepticism, especially since he directed his energies vis-à-vis Syria on the assumption that once an Israeli-Syrian agreement was reached, the Palestinians would fall into line. Arafat thus renewed his dogged drive toward a unilateral proclamation of statehood, and in early July 2000 the PLO's 125-member Palestine Central Committee (PCC) announced its intention to declare the establishment of an independent state in the whole of the West Bank and the Gaza Strip on September 13, 2000, and to enforce its sovereignty over this territory as a nonnegotiable right.

The invitation to Camp David was thus seen as an unwelcome intrusion. Arafat told Clinton it would be a serious mistake to convene such a summit at this particular moment when the secret Palestinian-Israeli negotiations that had been transpiring for some time in the Swedish capital of Stockholm and other locations had failed to make any tangible progress. Weeks of intensive preparations would be required for the summit to have any conceivable prospect of success.

"Should the summit convene on the basis of the proposed agenda, I will not be responsible for the reaction of the Palestinian people," Arafat told Clinton at a White House meeting on June 15. "I will myself leave the territories and move to Cairo or Tunis, leaving Barak, the liar, to grapple with the consequences of his move." He added, "I am not going to negotiate, I will only come [to Camp David] for signing [an agreement]."[6] Clinton remained unmoved. In another phone call to Arafat, he informed him that he had just contacted Barak, who for his part promised to make new proposals that would enhance the summit's prospects of success. The skeptical Arafat made a final, spirited attempt to dissuade Clinton. Realizing that the president had made up his mind, Arafat gave his grudging consent on condition that neither party would be blamed in the event of failure. He had little hope of Israeli flexibility but did not wish to clash with Clinton, with whom he had established a particularly close relationship during the Netanyahu years, over matters of form. Arafat preferred instead to keep his ammunition in reserve for the moment of truth.[7]

When this moment arrived, within days of the opening of the summit, it was profoundly disillusioning for the Israelis and the Americans. The Palestinians had no illusions from the start of the Oslo process, and certainly since the Netanyahu years, that the Israelis would submit to their "minimum demands" without intense political and military pressure. Ignoring the overwhelming evidence accumulated over the previous years that Arafat's opening position was also his final one, American and Israeli peacemakers were confident of their ability to bring an end to the century-long conflict in the span of a week or two. In the words of Shlomo Ben-Ami, internal security and foreign minister in the Barak cabinet and a chief peace negotiator: "That the Palestinians would agree to less than 100 percent was the axiom of Israeli politics since 1993."[8]

"The Palestinians used to tell U.S. officials: You would be making a grave mistake in believing that Yasser Arafat will sign an agreement that falls short of the minimum level of Palestinian national rights," wrote Akram Haniya, an adviser of Arafat and editor of the PA daily *al-Ayyam*, in what can be considered the official Palestinian version of the Camp David talks.

The response was always a mixture of doubting, suspicious looks, and smiles expressing [superior] knowledge and confidence in their ability to achieve results. The Palestinians would tell them: "The army of the contemporary Palestinian revolution that Fatah launched came from the refugee camps outside Palestine and any agreement that fails to include a just solution to the refugee problem will be an invitation for a more violent revolution from the refugee camps." The response used to be silence and refusal to listen to anything that contradicted the foundations of their conception.[9]

While repeatedly reassuring their Palestinian constituents that there would be no concessions whatsoever on the "right of return," Arafat and his lieutenants had been deliberately evasive in their dealings with their Israeli partners so as not to alarm them prematurely over how entrenched the PLO position actually was. Most Labor negotiators were thus misled to believe that the Palestinian insistence on the right of return was a mere bargaining ploy that could be accommodated at the right price. Even the notoriously paranoid Barak, whose perennial distrust led him on one occasion to interrogate his brother over a suspected leak of a minor political story to the media,[10] fell victim to this doublespeak. At one time he claimed that had he been given four hours on his own with Syria's president Hafez Assad, he would have convinced him to make peace with Israel. Now that he had talked Clinton into the Camp David summit, Barak was confident that he could induce Arafat into a deal. A secret meeting with Abu Mazen on June 11, in which he received a detailed exposition of the Palestinian red lines, did little to daunt Barak's determination. If all else failed, he believed he could still paint Arafat as the recalcitrant party.[11]

On the plane carrying him to Camp David, Barak described how he was going to address the Temple Mount issue. "You will be in charge of al-Aqsa Mosque and all Muslim holy places on Temple Mount," he would tell Arafat. "The Palestinian flag will be flying over these sites. You will have a safe passage from your part [of the city] to the mosque. Let's assume, for example, that the Saudi crown prince or the King of Morocco pay you a visit. You will be able to take them in the safe passage up to the mosque without meeting a single Israeli soldier on the way, and you can then pray together. You are the only apparent ruler of the area."

Through such a formula Barak hoped to dilute the fact that the Palestinians would not receive full legal sovereignty over Temple Mount, only an ex-territorial status similar to that granted to embassies. This is precisely how he envisaged the overall Camp David settlement: bypassing the explosive symbolic issues through practical solutions. According to Barak, his team had done extensive preparatory work on Jerusalem, the major stumbling block, and had developed creative ideas that could satisfy the Palestinian demands while allowing Israel to retain its sovereignty over a unified city. Thus, for instance, it would be put to Israeli opponents of a compromise that those Arab neighborhoods that had been outside East Jerusalem's municipal control before the 1967 war (such as Shu'afat and Qalandiya) did not constitute a part of "historic Jerusalem" and could therefore be transferred to the Palestinians. Similarly, it could be pointed out to the Palestinians that the new Jewish neighborhoods in East Jerusalem were established on unpopulated "no-man's-land" and could thus remain under Israeli control. The idea was to reshuffle the various Jerusalem neighborhoods like a pack of cards, then redivide them, so as to end up with a similarly large city, with a more cohesive Jewish majority and symbolic Palestinian control over the Muslim holy sites.

The other issues, in Barak's opinion, were much simpler: "Arafat talks about 95 percent [of the West Bank], we talk about 85 percent. An agreement will be found somewhere in the middle. The Jordan valley will pass to Palestinian sovereignty after an interim period of 15 years, with Israel having a strategic say over this area. The refugees will return in very limited numbers over a prolonged period of time (20 years). The Palestinians understand that they cannot repatriate large numbers of refugees in a short span of time. Jerusalem was and remains the core problem. The [first] weekend [of the summit] will be relaxed. The first crisis will erupt on Sunday. On Monday the Americans will present their bridging paper. By Wednesday the time for decision will have arrived."[12]

There was only one problem with this outline. Arafat was not talking about 95 percent of the territories but instead demanded 100 percent, along with refusing to compromise one iota on any of the other disputed issues: borders, Jerusalem, and the refugees. In stark contrast to his Israeli counterparts, Arafat had never viewed the negotiations as a give-and-take process in which both sides were supposed to make painful concessions and meet somewhere in between, but rather as a redress of an historical wrong in which Israel was to give the Palestinians what was rightfully theirs without getting anything meaningful in return. If Barak was interested in an agreement, he had to accept the Palestinian position, fully and without equivocation. As Abu Mazen offered shortly after the summit, "Personally I cannot move one step forward. The other party has to come our way on all the issues on which it procrastinates."[13]

Arafat was equally unimpressed with Barak's creative ideas about Jerusalem. As a first step, the Palestinians were to have full sovereignty over East Jerusalem, including its Jewish neighborhoods and al-Haram al-Sharif. In Arafat's mind, he was the last in a distinguished line of immortal Muslim defenders of Jerusalem, from Caliph Omar ibn Khattab (the city's occupier in 638 CE) to Saladin (who took Jerusalem from the crusaders). "I will not sell Jerusalem . . . If anyone thinks that I can sign away Jerusalem, he is deluding himself," Arafat told Clinton. "I am not just the leader of the Palestinian people. I am the permanent vice president of the Islamic Summit. I am also defending the rights of the Christians. I will not sell Jerusalem."[14]

Within days, the Israelis had come a substantial distance toward the Palestinian position. They accepted the creation of a Palestinian state in the entire Gaza Strip and 92 percent of the West Bank (compared with their initial proposal of 85 percent), and agreed to discuss "a satisfactory solution to the issue of the refugees," which they had hitherto attempted to avoid. More important, Barak broke the prevailing Israeli consensus since the Six-Day War of 1967 regarding Jerusalem's position as the nation's undivided capital by accepting the city's partition in accordance with an American bridging formula. This granted the Palestinians sovereignty over the Old City's Muslim and Christian quarters while the Jewish and Armenian quarters would be annexed to Israel. The Palestinian state would also have "functional sovereignty" over Jerusalem's internal Arab neighborhoods (including Sheik Jarrah, Wadi Juz, Salah al-Din, Ras Amud, and A-Tur) and full sovereignty over its external suburbs. As for the main bone of contention, the Palestinians were to be granted "custodial sovereignty" of the Haram by the Security Council and Morocco (chair of the Islamic Conference's Jerusalem Committee), while Israel would retain "residual sovereignty."

At about 1 A.M. on July 24, Palestinian negotiator Saeb Erekat brought Arafat's response to Clinton. He valued the president's efforts and hoped for their continuation, but they were "in contradiction to international references." "I will accept no Israeli sovereign presence in Jerusalem," Arafat insisted, "either in the Armenian quarter, or in the al-Aqsa mosque, or on the Via De La Rosa, or in the Church of the Holy Sepulcher. They can occupy us by force, because we are weaker now, but in two years, ten years, or one hundred years, there will be someone who will liberate Jerusalem."[15]

Why did Arafat reject the opportunity to establish a Palestinian state in the lion's share of the disputed territories, with East Jerusalem as its capital? If he deemed the scope of the Israeli proposals too limited and was unwilling to accept less than 100 percent of the West Bank (the entirety of the Gaza Strip was already in his pocket), then why did he not continue the negotiations or, at the very least, propose a symbolic counteroffer? Given Barak's desperation for a deal, and the widespread public readiness in Israel for far-reaching concessions in return for an agreement that would end once and for all the conflict with the Palestinians, there is little doubt that Arafat could have extracted further substantial concessions. Instead, Arafat preferred to turn down the first proposal for Palestinian statehood since the UN Partition Resolution of November 1947.

About a year after Camp David, and several months into the Palestinian-Israeli war, a revisionist account of the summit was contrived by Western commentators sympathetic to the Palestinian cause and die-hard Israeli supporters of Oslo, which sought to absolve Arafat of culpability for the summit's failure. "It is a terrible myth that Arafat and only Arafat caused this catastrophic failure," argued Terje Larsen, an architect of the Oslo process turned UN special envoy to the Middle East. "All three parties made mistakes, and in such complex negotiations, everyone is bound to. But no one is solely to blame." He added, "It was a failure of psychology and of process, not so much of substance."[16]

Larsen's assertion is at odds with his own prognosis from four years earlier, given in confidence to a senior Israeli negotiator. Larsen then argued that Arafat constituted the foremost obstacle to peace, and that the process would be more stable and successful if he disappeared altogether from the political scene.[17] Now that he was out to publicly exonerate the person he privately derided, Larsen added his voice to the "revisionist narrative" that focused almost exclusively on Barak's alleged psychological mistakes, notably his detached and impersonal demeanor

during the summit and his failure to establish a close working relationship with Arafat. "There was . . . one dinner in which Barak was on the
right side of Clinton and Arafat was on the left," Nabil Shaath told the
New York Times journalist Deborah Sontag, "but Chelsea sat to the right
of Barak all evening, and she received his undivided attention. Why the
hell did he insist on a summit if he did not intend to meet his partner
for a minute?"[18] A senior Palestinian source carried this theory a step
further. "Had Barak embraced Arafat, negotiated directly with him rather
than through the Americans, and shared a cabin with him and Clinton
for two or three days," he told an Israeli journalist, "an agreement would
have been reached."[19]

These revisionists also tend to downplay the scope and significance
of Barak's concessions, while casting Arafat in a far more pragmatic role.
"It is hard to state with confidence how far Barak was actually prepared
to go," wrote Hussein Agha and Robert Malley in the most extensive
revisionist account of the summit. "[S]trictly speaking, there never was
an Israeli offer. Determined to preserve Israel's position in the event of
failure, and resolved not to let the Palestinians take advantage of one-
sided compromises, the Israelis always stopped one, if not several, steps
short of a proposal." In contrast, Agha and Malley found the Palestinians quite flexible.

> While insisting on the Palestinian refugees' right to return to homes lost
> in 1948, they were prepared to tie this right to a mechanism of imple-
> mentation providing alternative choices for the refugees while limiting
> the numbers returning to Israel proper. Despite their insistence on Israel's
> withdrawal from all lands occupied in 1967, they were open to a division
> of East Jerusalem granting Israel sovereignty over its Jewish areas (the
> Jewish Quarter, the Wailing Wall, and the Jewish neighborhoods) in clear
> contravention of this principle.[20]

The problem with this version is that it runs contrary to accounts from
Palestinian negotiators and sources close to them (like Akram Haniya)
in the wake of the summit, which invariably praised Arafat's intransigence in the face of heavy American and Israeli pressure, despite extract-
ing substantial gains from Israel. "Arafat proved to be one of the last of
the historic leaders, because he said no at the moment when no one says
no to America," declared Freih Abu Medein, the PA's minister of jus-

tice. Sheik Ahmad Yassin, Hamas's spiritual leader, had nothing but praise for his political foe. "I welcome his steadfastness," he said in Gaza. "There is no choice but the choice of resistance. What was taken by force must be returned by force."[21]

"We gained some concessions from the Israelis yet indicated no readiness to concede anything in return," boasted Muhammad Dahlan, the young and energetic chief of the Preventive Security Service in Gaza and a member of the Camp David negotiation team. "We have no intention of compromising on any of our basic demands, particularly on the issues of Jerusalem and the refugees."[22] Hassan Asfour, Dahlan's fellow negotiator, concurred. "We worked at the negotiations very seriously and succeeded in breaking the Israeli concept of Jerusalem," he said.

> This is a political gain for the Palestinians. It is true that this does not meet our ambitions and rights, but it broke the notion of a united Jerusalem as Israel's eternal capital. This is a political achievement. It is one of the results of the first battle—the battle for Jerusalem. The second battle has to do with the concept of Palestinian borders and the return of Palestinian refugees, especially the refugees in Lebanon.[23]

Arafat himself was no less explicit. "We told the Israelis: [We demand] not only al-Haram al-Sharif, the Holy Sepulcher, or the Armenian quarter, but the whole of Jerusalem, the whole of Jerusalem, the whole of Jerusalem," he told a mass rally in Gaza upon his return from Camp David, flatly contradicting Agha's and Malley's later apologetics. "And those who don't like this can go drink from the Dead Sea."[24] He similarly contradicted the revisionist claim of Palestinian flexibility over the right of return by asserting that "the return of the refugees to their homeland and their dwellings [in Israel] in accordance with Resolution 194 is sacred." Abu Mazen echoed this view. "It should be noted, and this is what we clarified to the Israelis, that the right of return means a return to Israel, not to a Palestinian state," Abu Mazen wrote in the London daily al-Hayat in November 2000. "This is because it is Israel that expelled them and because their property is there."[25]

Contrary to Agha's and Malley's claim, the Palestinian negotiators in Camp David knew exactly how far Barak was prepared to go. An official Palestinian report on the course of the negotiations, issued about a month after the Camp David summit, detailed Barak's offer to withdraw from

85 percent of the West Bank (and 100 percent of the Gaza Strip) and his demand for control of the Jordan Valley for a period not exceeding twelve years. In return, Israel agreed to complete Palestinian sovereignty over the borders and crossings with Egypt, and to the dismantling of all Israeli settlements in the Gaza Strip as well as a gradual evacuation of sixty-three settlements in the West Bank, including Hebron.

These demands were flatly rejected by the Palestinian team, which insisted on Israel's complete withdrawal to the pre-June 1967 borders. Once this principle was accepted, slight modifications of up to 1.5 percent of the West Bank might be considered, but only in exchange for twice as large a chunk of Israeli territory, so that the total area of the prospective Palestinian state would be larger than the combined territory of the West Bank and Gaza. This included the addition of 145,000 dunums to the Gaza Strip and another 50,000 dunums from other areas near Latrun and around Qalqilya, Tulkarm, Jenin, and the Jordan River, in return for Israel's annexation of some 116,000 dunums. This was a total of 79,000 dunums in excess of pre-1967 borders.

After some haggling, the Israelis accepted the principle of land exchange and agreed to increase the size of the future Palestinian state from 85 percent to 92 percent of the West Bank (including the expansion of the Gaza Strip area by 1 percent). While this concession fell short of the Palestinian demands, it was nevertheless lauded by the report as a major achievement that refuted once and for all "the story about turning the lands of the Palestinian state into cantons and reserves."

As for the refugees, the Palestinians put the following demands on the negotiating table:

- Israel's admission of its political, legal, and moral responsibility for the creation of the refugee problem and its public apology to the Palestinian people.
- Recognition by Israel of the Palestinian right of return, including the compensation of those who do not wish to return, and its acceptance of a mechanism and a timetable for exercising this right.
- Israel's compensation of the returnees for the properties it confiscated on the basis of the Law of Absentees.
- The creation of an international fund, to which the donor states will contribute, for the compensation of those refugees who did not wish to return.

According to the report, Israel refused to accept political or moral responsibility for the problem but would express sympathy for the plight of the refugees from a humanitarian point of view. Israel also agreed to a limited repatriation within the framework of family reunification, but refused to pay any compensation for the Absentees Fund, demanding instead that the hundreds of thousands of Jews expelled from the Arab states as a result of the 1948 war be compensated for their lost properties. Notwithstanding these polarized positions, the report viewed the discussion of this issue as a success. First, because of President Clinton's support for giving the Palestinian refugees the option of return, and, second, because "Israel's traditional recalcitrance on the issue of refugees was effectively undone by the proposed compromise solutions, which recognized the right of return."

In contrast to its relatively upbeat description of the border and refugee issues, the report described the negotiations over Jerusalem as the most ferocious and difficult. Having their demand to defer this issue rejected by the Palestinians, the Israelis put forward a mixture of complicated proposals aimed at preserving their control and sovereignty over the city. These revolved around partitioning Jerusalem into districts and suburbs, and contained confusing and vague concepts about sovereignty, custodianship, and job distribution. The proposals even went as far as to suggest a divided control of al-Haram al-Sharif, whereby the Palestinians would have sovereignty over the site itself while Israel would have sovereign rights below the surface. This proposal was designed to allow the Israelis "to excavate for the remains of the alleged Temple, although excavations for the past 70 years have confirmed that there is no trace of it."

All these suggestions were rejected by the Palestinian delegation, which insisted on keeping Jerusalem an open city, with Israel controlling the Old City's Jewish quarter and the Wailing Wall and the Palestinians maintaining complete sovereignty over East Jerusalem, including the Jewish neighborhoods built there after the 1967 war.[26]

The general details of the report were confirmed by a "high-ranking source in the Palestinian delegation to Camp David," who told the Egyptian magazine *al-Musawwar* that at the summit Arafat was presented with a coordinated U.S.–Israeli proposal that included the following components:

- Complete Israeli withdrawal from the Gaza Strip, including the settlements, as well as from 92 percent of the West Bank.
- Shared control of the Old City of Jerusalem, whereby the Muslim and Christian quarters would be under Palestinian sovereignty and the Jewish and the Armenian quarters under Israeli sovereignty.
- The al-Aqsa mosque would remain under Israeli control but its actual management would be given to the Palestinians, who would have access to the mosque via a flyover connecting it to Ramallah.
- A minimum of $30 billion in compensation to the refugees and the provision that an agreed-upon number of them would be able to return to the Palestinian state within a fixed time frame.
- Israel agreed to absorb a symbolic number of refugees in the framework of family reunion, but refused to acknowledge any political or historical responsibility for the creation of the refugee problem, let alone concede the Palestinian right of return.

Arafat rejected the proposal, telling Clinton in an emotional plea, "By accepting that deal, I will be betraying my people, my nation, and my creed. It is not in my capacity, or the capacity of any Palestinian leadership, to leave al-Aqsa and Jerusalem under Israeli sovereignty or waive the refugees' right of return."[27]

The minute details of Israeli concessions, and the lack of interpersonal chemistry between Arafat and Barak, had little to do with the summit's final outcome. The Camp David summit reached a dead end not because of inadequate preparation or ineffective communication between Israelis and Palestinians, but because it exposed the intractable gaps between the two parties. Even if Arafat and Barak had managed to establish an immediate rapport, they would have remained miles apart on the core issues of the conflict. It is not that the Palestinians did not know how far Barak was actually prepared to go, but that no matter how hard he tried, Barak could never go far enough to satisfy the Palestinian "minimum demands."

"The question is not whether Arafat made mistakes, or whether these were justified," argue Agha and Malley. "The question is whether his behavior can be explained by factors other than his presumed inability to put an end to the conflict."[28] A close examination of Arafat's behavior, from the onset of the Oslo process through Camp David, shows that his failure to make the anticipated leap of faith at the summit stemmed not from his inability to put an end to the conflict, but from his reluctance to do so on any terms other than his own. These extend well beyond Israel's withdrawal to the pre-1967 borders and the Jerusalem question. Even if these two weighty issues were resolved at Camp David, the negotiations would still have been unable to settle the right of return. No Israeli government could yield to the Palestinian demand on this issue without signing away its country's national existence. The Palestinian leadership would not accept the end of the conflict without granting the millions of 1948 refugees and their descendants the "right of return" to territory that is now part of the state of Israel as well as their financial compensation for their losses and suffering. While Arafat had previously gone to great lengths not to scare his Israeli partners with premature right of return discussions, at Camp David and in its aftermath the Israelis were confronted with the full extent of Arafat's desire for the first time.[29] "It is not a matter of Jerusalem alone," said Abu Ala, the chief Oslo negotiator and speaker of the Palestinian Legislative Council. "The refugee issue is actually more complicated than that of Jerusalem. Jerusalem is deep in the heart of each of us, but the refugee issue is a right claimed by the Palestinian citizen."[30]

The right of return was not only enshrined in the new Palestinian draft constitution drawn up in the wake of Camp David in anticipation of a unilateral proclamation of statehood,[31] but in the months following the summit, Israelis were surprised and disturbed to find hundreds of Palestinians bused into Israel by the Palestinian Authority, roaming their neighborhoods in search of the homes they had fled some fifty-two years ago.[32] The message was clear. There would be no end to the conflict without the implementation of the right of return, in other words, the destruction of Israel through demographic subversion.

Here was the source of the Camp David failure. For Arafat the summit was not a vehicle for conflict resolution, but yet another opportunity to implement his phased strategy. Arafat was opposed to the summit from the outset, but not for the need of adequate preparations. Having negotiated with Israel for seven years, including fifteen substantive sessions in Stockholm and Israel shortly before Camp David, the Palestinians were extraordinarily familiar with the Israeli position. Had Barak not insisted on an end to the Palestinian-Israeli conflict, Arafat would have readily cashed in his concessions in return for further ambiguous pledges regarding a Palestinian-Israeli "peace." Yet there was absolutely no way for Arafat to peacefully sign away the conflict without attaining the destruction of the state of Israel, through either geographic or demographic means. Since he had no doubt that this would not happen in Camp David, Arafat preferred to avoid the summit altogether, instead confronting Israel with the reality of a Palestinian state within the 1967 borders, forcing its withdrawal to these lines under combined military and international pressure, and then enter into negotiations with the debilitated Jewish state over the final-status agreement. With Israel overwhelmed by millions of refugees, the end of the conflict would become synonymous with the end of the Jewish state.

Along with geographic and demographic subversion, the Palestinians were also not above religiously subverting Israel's legitimacy during the Camp David summit by denying Jerusalem's holiness for Judaism and the Jewish people. Arafat himself told Clinton that the Temple of the Mount had existed in Nablus and not in Jerusalem, and that as a religious man Arafat would not allow his name to go down in history as the person who had "confirmed the existence of the so-called Temple underneath the mountain." He was followed by Erekat, who expressed doubts regarding the Temple's very existence, and by Abu Ala, who asserted that Jewish claims about the Temple were nothing but a plot to allow Israel to gain sovereignty over the holy site with a view to destroying the mosques.[33]

These sweeping denials of Judaism's core values were not simply a bargaining chip in the struggle for sovereignty over Temple Mount/al-Haram al-Sharif, but reflected a fundamental rejection of the Jewish attachment to the land of Israel and, by extension, of Israel's right to exist. The *Jerusalem Post* offered the summit's epitaph:

> Just as for 2,000 years of exile Jerusalem symbolized the Jewish yearning for a return to Zion, Palestinian recognition of the Jewish connection to ancient Jerusalem would recognize the moral and historic right of Israel to exist in this land.
>
> Accepting the Jewish connection to Jerusalem is tantamount to abandoning the Arab notion that the Jews are squatters on a land that is foreign to them, sort of Crusaders with computers who will go as quickly as they came . . . Without recognizing Israel's ancient connection to Jerusalem, the Palestinians can cling to the notion that Israel exists only by might, not by right.[34]

10

Countdown to War

As long as Israel occupies any part of our land, in Tel Aviv or Jaffa
or Haifa, we have not liberated our homeland.
—a sixteen-year-old participant in the PA's
summer camp, August 2000

"If the Israelis can make compromises and you can't, I should go home,"
Clinton told Arafat just before the Camp David talks ended, and depriv-
ing the president of any opportunity to ensure his legacy as the man who
helped broker a lasting peace between Israelis and Palestinians. "You
have been here fourteen days and said no to everything. These things
have consequences; failure will mean the end of the peace process."[1]

In public the president was more diplomatic, yet no less pointed as
to who was responsible for the summit's failure. "Prime Minister Barak
showed particular courage, vision, and an understanding of the historical
importance of this moment," he told a White House news conference
announcing the end of the talks. "The prime minister moved forward
more from his initial position than Chairman Arafat, particularly surrounding the question of Jerusalem." A few days later, in a special interview on Israeli television, Clinton elaborated.

I kept telling the Palestinians, and I will say again to the world, that you
cannot make an agreement over something as important as a city that is
the holiest place in the world if it is required of one side to say: "I completely defeated the interest of the other side." If either side gets to say
that at the end, there won't be an agreement. There can't be.[2]

Arafat felt betrayed. In his understanding he had received Clinton's
unequivocal assurance prior to the summit that there would be no blame

apportioned in the event of failure. Now he found himself singled out as the only culprit. To be sure, the Arab League quickly blamed the summit's failure on "Israel's intransigence," while thousands of Gazans were ordered into the streets to greet Arafat upon his return. Children wearing black T-shirts and khaki military trousers lined the roads leading to his headquarters in Gaza City. Vans with loudspeakers roamed the streets urging residents to receive "the Saladin of his generation," while the media circulated stories about Arafat's heroic stand in Camp David in "a siege climate that was harder than the siege of Beirut." A hastily organized opinion poll found 68 percent of Palestinians supported Arafat's performance in Camp David, especially his handling of the refugee problem.[3]

Yet Arafat knew that without redeeming himself in the eyes of the international community, these contrived manifestations of support at home would achieve little, especially since successive opinion polls during the 1990s showed that most residents of the territories desired peace. Now that Israel's rejection of "minimum Palestinian national rights" had received the blessing of the leader of the free world, the tables had to be quickly turned on Barak. Openly rejecting Clinton's warning to refrain from declaring statehood, Arafat embarked on a whirlwind world tour that took him to seventeen capitals in eighteen days, in an attempt to harness international support for the unilateral proclamation of a Palestinian state on the date designated by the Palestine Central Committee (PCC), September 13, 2000.

Arafat placed major importance on bringing the full weight of the Arab world behind the Palestinian struggle. Like all Palestinians, Arafat put little trust in pan-Arab rhetoric, knowing that when push came to shove, the Arab regimes would always choose self-serving interests over that of the Palestinian cause. However, he had always considered the entanglement of the Arab states in the conflict with Israel as a vital force multiplier. "From the start of Camp David we warned that this summit's failure would not be a failure of yet another round of negotiations but would spell the end of a long process to which the Palestinians had given all they could," wrote Hassan Kashef, director-general of the PA's ministry of information and a regular commentator in the Palestinian media. "The Palestinians have given peace every possible chance. They have acted with maximum patience and restraint despite the Israeli attempts to evade implementation of all signed agreements. Under the circumstances, the Palestinian people should now seek the Arab nation's support. The weight of a unified Arab nation upholding its rights to its lands and to the holy city of Jerusalem should back the Palestinian people."[4]

Such support was not forthcoming. Appreciative as they were of the Palestinian stand in Camp David, the conservative Arab states, headed by Egypt, the PLO's foremost patron since its expulsion from Lebanon in the early 1980s, would not give Arafat the concrete support he asked for. The Egyptians ducked the Palestinian request for an Arab summit to discuss the situation and cautioned against a unilateral proclamation of a Palestinian state lest this trigger a harsh Israeli response, instead advising the continuation of pursuing Palestinian goals through negotiations. The Palestinians' staunchest European backers, not to speak of the less committed nations around the globe, all gave similar responses. "Over ninety-five percent of friendly states have advised the leadership to take its time and to exercise caution in choosing the timing [of a unilateral proclamation] and coping with reactions to that timing," Nabil Amr, minister of parliamentary affairs in the PA, revealed in late August.[5]

The PCC thus decided to postpone the proclamation of an independent state, leaving it to the Palestinian leadership to fix a new date for this move. "We have already postponed the declaration for a year, 17 months now, because of U.S. and European promises," Salim Zaanun explained. "There are no pledges from either party now. There are, however, U.S. threats and a warning from Europe. They told us that they could not assist us. Our people must face the fact, be creative, and resist any measures that may be taken against us as a result of the proclamation of Palestinian statehood."[6]

Presenting its decision as a considered response to "the advice by fraternal and friendly countries" and further proof of the Palestinian commitment to peace, the PCC nevertheless warned that this was not an open-ended gesture but one that required reciprocation from the Israelis. The United States, the European Union, and other states that had advised the Palestinians into additional negotiations were now required, more than ever before, to make a serious effort to turn this new opportunity into a success. "It is true that this position entails the risk of the interim stage becoming a fait accompli," commented the PA daily *al-Ayyam.* "However, this risk is small, since the deep-rooted elements of the conflict in the region and the lack of an agreement and terms of reference are likely to make this fait accompli unsustainable. Thus, in the end, it will be unavoidable to choose between confrontation and agreement."[7]

With his image severely tarnished by the Camp David summit, and denied the minimum Arab and international backing for a unilateral proclamation of a Palestinian state, Arafat felt increasingly pressured to act. Though allowing the continuation of discreet talks with Israel (in August and September, Israeli and Palestinian negotiators conducted nearly forty negotiating sessions), he held little hope for a breakthrough. He knew that he would not back down from the "minimum conditions" he had set for himself at the onset of the Oslo process, while suspecting that Barak, with his newly gained international aura as a courageous man of peace, would not improve on his Camp David offer without adequate reward. Confronted with sharp criticism in Israel and the Jewish world for his concessions over Temple Mount, Barak backed down from his Camp David position and asserted that no foreign sovereignty would be allowed over Judaism's most sacred site.

In Arafat's perception the "armed struggle" had invariably brought the Palestinians their greatest historical achievements, either on its own or in conjunction with other tools such as politics and diplomacy, and his decision to embrace the Oslo process did little to change this position. As demonstrated by the 1996 tunnel war, the PLO continued to view violence as a legitimate means despite its formal renunciation of this option in the Oslo accords. Now that Barak had not only failed to comply with the Palestinian demands but also mustered substantial international support for his position, a far greater measure of physical coercion had become a necessity if Arafat were to regain the political momentum.

Before the start of Camp David, Arafat openly talked of his intention to resort to violence should the summit fail to meet his "minimum demands." "No one can threaten us," he warned on the eve of his departure for the United States. "We are fighting for our land . . . We will sacrifice our souls for Palestine . . . and those who have forgotten this fact should remember the battle of Karameh [1968], the battle of Beirut [1982], and the seven years of the intifada . . . We are ready to wipe the slate clean [i.e., abandon the peace process] and start from the beginning."[8]

Other members of the Palestinian leadership quickly followed suit. "In the past we sacrificed 100,000 martyrs and we are now ready to sacrifice another five or six thousand," argued Freih Abu Medein. "We therefore say to the Israeli generals who are thirsty for Palestinian blood: it is true that this blood is precious to us, but we will have no qualms about sacrificing it."[9] Khaled Musmar, deputy head of the National Guidance Directorate, agreed. "We are all seekers of martyrdom," he said. "So it was in the past and so it will be in the future: either our people's will is realized or all of us will be martyred." He then explained why the Palestinians were destined to prevail over their Israeli adversaries: "They love life as much as we love martyrdom."[10]

Faisal Husseini, holder of the Jerusalem file at the PA and one of its foremost moderates, warned that the peace process would grind to a halt if the Palestinian demands for Jerusalem and the right of return were rejected. Though peace was the preferred Palestinian option, he cautioned, it was by no means the only one. Were Israel to remain recalcitrant, the Palestinians would be forced resort to other options.[11]

An article published in al-Ayyam shortly before the Camp David summit clarified what these "other options" were. "The Palestinians will not lose much by a military battle to assert their rights, supported by public opinion in the West, the Arabs and the Muslims," it argued.

> The East is looking forward to the moment when the Palestinians can have a state. The success of the Palestinians in breaking the vicious circle will lead to the establishment of a Palestinian state, and if they lose the battle the situation will not be much different. Why go so far? One year ago, Israeli proposals on the area of the [Palestinian] state referred to 40 percent, while today the talk is about ninety-plus percent or one-hundred-minus percent.[12]

Threats of violence continued throughout the course of the Camp David negotiations. Were the summit to fail, the entire peace process would reach a dead end, argued Muhammad Ghunaim, a Fatah Central Committee member. In such circumstances, the Palestinian leadership would adopt "alternative means to defend the interests of its people and to restore its occupied territories." An independent state would be declared by the Palestinian people, who would also determine its borders and its guiding principles, first and foremost the right of return for the refugees. Once the state's territory had been defined, Israel's military and civilian presence there would be considered a hostile encroachment of Palestinian sovereignty and met by "struggle from the Palestinian masses with all the means at their disposal." An unnamed senior PLO official echoed this threat. "It must be understood that the proclamation of a Palestinian state is an act of struggle," he said. "We will not content ourselves with raising the flag but will enforce our sovereignty on the entire territory, including the settlements." But what if Israel were to respond harshly to such a move? Any such response would be considered a declaration of war, warned Marwan Barghouthi, commander of Fatah's Tanzim militia. "The Palestinian people are prepared to fight with all means to defend their land and achieve all their rights."[13]

As early as July 27, two days after the end of the Camp David summit, Muhammad Dahlan spelled out the broad contours of the Palestinian strategy in the coming weeks. "We don't want a confrontation and we don't seek one," he said. "Yet the agreement we have signed with Israel is due to expire on September 13. One hour after that date we are not committed to anything vis-à-vis Israel . . . If we do not reach an understanding by September 13, the Palestinian leadership will be free to make the decision it deems to be in the best interest of the Palestinian people."[14] A week later, Dahlan argued that failure to reach an agreement would inexorably lead to confrontation. "The Palestinian people . . . knows how to defend itself, its rights to this land, and its political integrity," he said, adding that "the potential for resistance and steadfastness is now much greater than it was when the Palestinian leadership was in exile. Now we have the necessary mechanisms and institutions in place . . . We also have the ability and the will to resist." While conceding that the military balance of power favored Israel, he nevertheless believed that "the Israelis will think many times before committing themselves to a confrontation with the Palestinian people. We will attain an independent Palestinian state with Jerusalem as its capital even if this requires blood."[15]

Threats of violence were not confined to hardened men of war like Dahlan. The quintessential representatives of the political process within the Palestinian leadership did not shy away from threatening Israel with wholesale violence should it fail to submit to Palestinian demands. "When we are convinced that a peace agreement is not possible, no doubt our people and the leadership of the Palestinian people will have other alternatives," Abu Ala told a press conference in Ramallah after the Camp David summit. "I am not calling for violence, but I don't know how the people will react."[16]

The affable and soft-spoken minister of planning and international cooperation Nabil Shaath concurred. "The proclamation of a state is the only nonviolent card that we hold," he told the French daily Le Monde. "For want of such cards, the only recourse is to violence." The Palestinians might be convinced to postpone the date of such a proclamation, though not forgo it altogether, if Israel "made concessions concerning both Jerusalem and the refugees."[17] Since these issues had constituted the breaking points of the Camp David summit, Shaath knew that Israel was highly unlikely to make further concessions without a Palestinian *quid pro quo*, unless the readiness for a temporary abstention from violating signed agreements could be considered one. Shorn of its diplomatic niceties, Shaath's message was simple: Israel either submitted to Palestinian demand or incurred their wrath.

Hassan Kashef had no time for such niceties. Writing in *al-Ayyam* on July 24, the day before the end of the Camp David summit, he called for a national campaign "to prepare the people and their national authority to defend the state, should it be proclaimed on September 13, and to seize the rest of our rights to our land and sovereignty." These preparations had to be comprehensive, and they had to include all components of national power, both civilian and military. "I have heard a fellow official complain about our weak abilities to store food supplies," he wrote.

> Based on our own experience, and that of others, the solution is simple and does not require building huge depots. Each Palestinian household is capable of storing its requirements in basic food supplies for several months. Each house has a place to store a few sacks of wheat, rice, sugar, and a quantity of candles and lamps working on gas or kerosene. If all houses became stores, securing the needs of their inhabitants, the leadership will be freed of this big burden and will be able to focus on other essential needs.

As for armed confrontation, Kashef advocated using the guerrilla tactics that, in his opinion, had served the Palestinians well during their long years of struggle. "It would be utterly wrong to prepare ourselves as a regular force with barracks, fixed positions, and depots," he argued.

> This is precisely what the Israeli military establishment would like us to do. This establishment puts trust in its military superiority and air supremacy. To ensure our superiority we must thus return to our national instincts as a fighting people versed in the art of the intifada, and in sheltering its combatant groups defending their people and independence. This solution also applies to the command centers. Every house in the homeland is open and ready to become a command center.[18]

Before his departure for Camp David, Arafat met with Fatah commanders in the territories to discuss the operational consequences of the summit's inevitable failure. In the following days, as the negotiations were taking place, plans were drawn up, training intensified, weapons distributed, and Fatah activists placed on high alert, instructed to prepare for a possible confrontation with the IDF.[19] At the same time, the PA's ministry of supplies held meetings with the main wholesalers in the Gaza Strip to discuss the provision of basic food products in anticipation of a military confrontation with Israel. Condemning the meeting as bordering on incitement to violence, the Israelis protested to the Authority. They also expressed their concern at the vast rise in purchases by Palestinian wholesalers of supply commodities that were normally imported from Israel or via Israeli ports and the rush among ordinary people to stockpile basic commodities in anticipation of a prolonged struggle. The Palestinians were unfazed. Nationwide stockpiling of basic commodities and petrol continued apace, at both the individual and the institutional levels, and emergency services were being readied to handle large numbers of casualties.[20]

As the Camp David negotiations neared their conclusion, the Palestinian media launched a sustained militant campaign that continued until the outbreak of hostilities in late September. The public was barraged with a daily diet of speeches, interviews, sermons, documentaries, and short clips detailing Israel's alleged aggressive designs and the PA's resolve to defend Palestinian rights.

This incitement was accompanied by systematic military preparations. In late July, anti-tank trenches and trap holes under major roads in the West Bank and Gaza were being dug and filled with explosives, while Palestinian security forces were being deployed in potential flash points. In the West Bank, Israeli security forces detected increased military activity in such spheres as training, planning, and assignment of objectives. At the Palestinian police training facility in Jericho, security forces were practicing the taking over of Israeli vehicles, including buses (the road on which the bus traveled was blocked, the vehicle was then surrounded and its passengers abducted). From mid-September onward, there was a noticeable rise in the number of infiltrations by Palestinian policemen into Area B, where Israel had overall security control, aimed at gradually indicating that this area constituted an integral part of the future Palestinian state. These encroachments were accompanied by increased requests by the PA for entry of Palestinian policemen into Area B to carry out detention of offenders. Though these requests were made within the framework of the Oslo accords, their unusually high volume indicated an overall increased Palestinian presence in these areas.[21] Meanwhile, General Ghazi Jabali, head of police in the Gaza Strip, told a public rally in Rafah that "the Palestinian police, together with all honest members of the Palestinian people, will be at the forefront once the hour of confrontation arrives." He added, "President Arafat and all the sons of the Palestinian people are potential martyrs."[22]

The clearest indication of Arafat's intentions was the feverish effort, begun in secret in early 2000 with the help of Egyptian and Jordanian military experts, to transform his existing security forces into a 100,000-strong army. By the time of the Camp David summit, an embryonic division had reportedly been established in Gaza with hundreds of Palestinian security operatives having undergone military training in Algeria, Morocco, Egypt, Libya, Yemen, and Pakistan. Once back in the territories, they quickly passed their training on to thousands of their peers as well as civilian members of Fatah. This included fighting in built-up areas, charging fortified army posts, firing anti-tank man-borne missiles, and occupying Jewish settlements.

The newly established military infrastructure consisted of a skeleton army, with a well-defined echelon of command, a training and

recruitment system, and a rudimentary military industry for local manufacture of small firearms, hand grenades, and other ammunition. According to some reports, the army staff was supposed to include twenty
generals, some of whom already stood at the head of the PA's various
security branches.

The Palestinian security force, which was to number 24,000 under
Oslo, had been inflated to an estimated 45,000, making the PA areas the
most heavily policed territory in the world, with an officer-to-resident
ratio of 1:40. (The ratio for police officers and sheriff's deputies to residents in the United States is 1:400.) Similarly, the Palestinians were in
possession of approximately 40,000 illegal weapons, beyond the 11,000
Kalshnikovs, 4,000 pistols, and 240 mortars that were allowed under the
terms of the Oslo agreement. Since its creation, the PA had been amass-
ing stocks of weapon systems that were prohibited by the accords, such
as anti-armor weapons, rocket-propelled grenades, and anti-tank missiles.

Yet the attempt to create a regular army was by far the most flagrant
violation of the Oslo accords. Predicated as they were on the idea of a
demilitarized Palestinian entity, Oslo allowed for the existence of "a
strong police force" but not a conventional military. That Arafat chose
to flaunt his commitments when the final-status agreements were close
at hand sent an unmistakable message to his own people and to Israel
alike that the newly created Palestinian state would never relinquish
the military option. Upon the unilateral proclamation of statehood on
September 13, 2000, Arafat instructed his officials, he would like to be
addressed by the title "President and Commander in Chief of the Palestinian Armed Forces."[23]

Palestinian children were also being drawn into the war effort. During the summer of 2000, thousands of teens were in military camps,
participating in three-week sessions that included arms training, physical fitness, martial arts, and other fighting skills. The trainers came from
the officer corps of the various security branches, and the would-be soldiers were trained in carrying out defined missions such as capturing a
piece of territory and storming Israeli settlements. A particularly popular drill involved the kidnapping of an Israeli leader by masked commandos, ending with his bodyguards sprawled dead on the ground.

The PA had run these camps since the early days of its existence, yet
the images of young teens charging mock military positions marked by

the Israeli flag, chanting "death to Israel," and screened on official Palestinian television shortly after the most ambitious attempt ever to put an end to the conflict, was a potent harbinger of things to come. "As President Arafat says, this is the generation that will plant the Palestinian flag on the walls of Jerusalem," said a PLO official in charge of a number of such camps. "We joined the Palestinian national movement when we were their age, and we are creating a continuum between our generation and theirs."

What this continuum meant for most kids was demonstrated in a response from a typical sixteen-year-old participant. Asked how he defined Palestinian freedom, he said it included the liberation of Jerusalem, and then the rest of the territory constituting the state of Israel. "As long as Israel occupies any part of our land, in Tel Aviv or Jaffa or Haifa, we have not liberated our homeland."[24]

In laying the ground for a confrontation with Israel, the Palestinian leadership was consciously modeling itself on what came to be known as the "Lebanese precedent." During the 1999 election campaign, sensing the deepening disillusionment among Israelis with their country's protracted military presence in southern Lebanon, Barak promised "to bring the boys home by agreement" within a year of taking office. Without concessions from either Syria or the militant Hizbullah organization, the IDF hastily vacated its outposts in south Lebanon and redeployed behind the international border in the dead of the night on May 24, 2000, under sporadic, but sometimes heavy, Hizbullah mortar and rocket fire.

While Barak presented the withdrawal as a glowing success that ended, without a single casualty, two decades of inconclusive military involvement in Lebanon, the move was widely seen in the Arab world as the defeat of the formidable Israeli army by a small but determined guerrilla force. Hamas and Islamic Jihad quickly applauded Hizbullah's achievement as proof of the indispensability of the armed struggle for forcing Israel's withdrawal from occupied Arab lands, as did the PA daily *al-Hayat al-Jadida*, which claimed the lesson to be learned from the Israeli withdrawal was that the Palestinians would not regain their rights unless they followed the Lebanese example.[25] Thousands of Gazans celebrated the withdrawal with placards reading "Lebanon Today, Palestine

Tomorrow." An opinion poll held by the Palestinian Center for Political and Survey Research shortly after Camp David found that 63 percent of respondents wanted to see the Palestinians follow the same route taken by the Hizbullah. "We don't enjoy sacrificing people," stated Marwan Barghouthi. "But we understand that the Israelis left Lebanon under Hizbullah pressure. So why shouldn't this be repeated here." On another occasion he warned, "If by September 13 the Israelis will not have withdrawn from Jerusalem and the border passes as they did in Lebanon, then it should be borne in mind that the Palestinian people, which fought in the intifada, does not at all fear another confrontation."[26]

The day following the withdrawal, Arafat expressed the hope that this move would "reinvigorate the political process and lead to Israel's complete withdrawal from the territories and its implementation of the international resolutions pertaining to the Palestinian issue, as it implemented UN Resolution 425 with regard to Lebanon."[27] In private he was far more direct, telling Shlomo Ben-Ami a few days before Camp David that he doubted the summit's value, as Hizbullah had set a powerful precedent of coercing Israel into submission through the use of armed force. Ben-Ami's warning that the Palestinian situation was fundamentally different from that in Lebanon had absolutely no effect on Arafat. "How do you think all this makes me look?" he complained to Dennis Ross, the chief U.S. peace envoy. "Hizbullah does not negotiate and receives everything. I sit at the negotiating table and get nothing." Prior to his departure from Camp David, Arafat told two of the Israeli negotiators, "We can see to it that the Hizbullah precedent is replicated in the territories." Dahlan repeated the same threat during the summit: "The only way to negotiate with you is through the Hizbullah procedure."[28]

A major factor intensifying PLO anxiety toward the end of September 2000 was an imminent American bridging paper designed to help the parties recapture the momentum of the peace process. While low-key Palestinian-Israeli talks continued after Camp David, at times with American mediation, these discussions were geared more toward redeeming Arafat's tarnished image in the eyes of the administration than to obtaining concrete results. Ad hominem attacks on the Barak government in the Palestinian media continued regularly, while the negotiations failed to break new grounds, so much so that Arafat avoided Barak during their stay in New York in early September for the UN Millennium Summit. Despite Barak's tireless efforts to meet, finally he had to chase Arafat into an elevator. He shook his hand, then let his advisers spread the word that the two leaders held "a brief meeting."[29]

During his meetings with President Clinton and Secretary of State Madeleine Albright, Arafat once again insisted on full sovereignty over East Jerusalem, "our holy capital." When Albright mentioned Jewish reverence for Jerusalem, the site of their ancient Temple, Arafat erupted. "In history all things happen. But this does not confer sovereignty. There are Roman antiquities in Gaza. Does it give Italy any claim to sovereignty over Gaza? When you are talking to me, don't use the term Temple Mount but rather al-Aqsa," he shouted at the astonished secretary of state before angrily leaving the room.[30]

In late September, Israeli and Palestinian negotiators were summoned to Washington, where the Americans reportedly extracted further Israeli concessions and were about to set them down in a bridging paper that would point the way forward.[31] Yet the Palestinians remained apprehensive that the impending document would be further apart from their position at Camp David, especially with regard to full sovereignty over Temple Mount, where the Americans were believed to have drifted from their Camp David position toward the idea of Security Council sovereignty. "More than one billion Muslims and Arabs, supported by the Christian world, are unanimous that the Palestinians must have sovereignty over al-Aqsa mosque," wrote *al-Quds*. "Yet the proposals leaked from the U.S. document seek to circumvent this unanimity and defy the resolutions of international legitimacy through the notion of international and Security Council sovereignty over the Islamic holy sites. The suggestion of a Security Council sovereignty is no more than a ploy to hide Israel's continued domination of these places."[32]

In these circumstances, a drastic action that could forestall the imminent U.S. paper before the Palestinians would be again branded as an obstacle to peace became a pressing necessity, and what could provide a better rallying call than the defense of Islam's third holiest site against Jewish machinations. Already during the Camp David summit the PA warned of Israeli designs on Jerusalem, and by early August the Palestinian media were rife with rumors of Israel's alleged intention to build a synagogue inside al-Aqsa.[33] Arafat, addressing a special meeting of the Islamic Conference's Jerusalem Committee in early September, made a more fantastic claim by charging Israel with planning the construction of a Third Temple on the ruins of al-Aqsa and the Dome of the Rock. He also declared that there would be no solution to the city's future status other than that established by Caliph Omar upon his occupation of Jerusalem in 638—an arrangement based on Muslim domination and Jewish and Christian subservience.[34]

Other prominent members of the Palestinian leadership echoed this incitement. "The Jewish belief that Jerusalem is sacred to them, and their claims about al-Haram al-Sharif, give them absolutely no right to sovereignty over a single inch of land in Holy Jerusalem," wrote Bassam Abu Sharif, Arafat's adviser. "The Jews have ancient places of worship in Iraq, Yemen, Morocco, Egypt, Lebanon, Syria, and European countries. Do these give Israel a right to demand sovereignty over these cities and countries?"[35]

Yasser Abd Rabbo, the PA's minister of culture and information, was equally scathing. "The Israelis say that beneath the noble sanctuary [the Esplanade of the Mosques] lies their Temple," he argued on September 26. "Looking at the situation from an archaeological standpoint, I am sure there is no Temple. They have dug tunnel after tunnel with no result. But even if we accept that the Temple did exist, is it allowable these days for anyone to go back to a 3,000-year-old past to lay current claim? . . . All this should come to an end."[36]

There was of course nothing new about this dismissal of Judaism's deepest beliefs and the historic Jewish attachment to Palestine. Such denial is deeply entrenched in the Arab and Muslim worlds and has played a focal role in the indoctrination of Palestinian society by Arafat's PA; it also resurfaced ominously at the Camp David summit. Yet resorting to such inflammatory rhetoric by the Palestinian leadership, shortly after making Jerusalem the breaking point of the summit, and on the eve of a planned visit by Ariel Sharon, head of the Likud opposition party, to Temple Mount, was nothing short of wholesale incitement. Just like the tunnel war, Sharon's visit gave Arafat all the pretext for violence he needed and had been waiting for since Camp David. The alleged protection of al-Aqsa had always provided a potent rallying call for anti-Jewish violence. In 1929, Hajj Amin Husseini, the mufti of Jerusalem and the effective leader of the country's Arab community during the British mandate (1920–48), used this pretext to trigger large-scale pogroms, in which some 140 Jews were massacred, while in 1996 Arafat had used the alleged threat to the mosque resulting from the opening of an adjacent underground tunnel to unleash wholesale violence against Israel. He was not going to let this latest opportunity for bloodshed slip from his fingers. "Jerusalem's defense requires blood," stated the PA's official mouthpiece, *al-Sabah.*

> The time of victory and martyrdom has come . . . The Jerusalem campaign is the Mother of all Campaigns . . . We will move forward and proclaim a general intifada for Jerusalem. The time of the intifada has come, the time of the intifada has come. The time of the jihad has come, the time of Jerusalem has come, and Jerusalem is calling us.[37]

11

Why War?

I knew that the end of September was the final deadline for the explosion, but when Sharon visited the al-Aqsa Mosque, this was the most appropriate moment for the outbreak of the intifada.
—Marwan Barghouthi, September 29, 2001

On Friday, September 29, 2000, Jews throughout the world celebrated New Year's Eve. A relaxed and festive mood swept Israel as public places gradually closed and people made their final preparations for the holiday. The previous day, Ariel Sharon and other members of the opposition Likud party had made a high-profile visit to Temple Mount, accompanied by the mayor of Jerusalem, Ehud Olmert, yet there was no precipitation of trouble in its wake, perhaps because of the surprisingly mild Palestinian response to the visit.

In a series of interviews published in the weekend papers, Barak was in an upbeat mood. "I am optimistic," he said. "We are at the beginning of the road. The Jewish state is 52 years old . . . If you look at the big picture, this is a success that has no precedent in history—a nation that returns to its land after 2,000 years."

Barak was particularly effusive about the congenial dinner party he had held for Arafat a few days earlier in his private residence in Kochav Yair, the first meeting between the two since the failed Camp David summit. "The meeting was very good, warm, and open," he said. "We talked about responsibility, the significance of the [present] opportunity, the alternatives, the time frame that remains, the importance of leadership. It was very open. We even spoke of his childhood memories, where he grew up . . . He told us about his experience in a Syrian prison, he was jailed there once." At one point Barak took a phone call from President Clinton and, within earshot of the Palestinian leader, theatrically proclaimed, "I'm going to be the partner of this man even more than Rabin was."[1]

For those Israelis who didn't read the holiday papers until Saturday or Sunday, these words must have seemed surreal. During the weekend, a tidal wave of Palestinian violence engulfed not only the territories but also large parts of Israel itself.

Violence broke out in Jerusalem late Friday afternoon, when thousands of agitated Palestinians coming out of al-Aqsa Mosque after the prayers began throwing rocks and other objects at the police and on Jews praying at the Wailing Wall. Before long the confrontation spread to other West Bank towns as well as to the Gaza Strip, involving numerous running clashes between Palestinian youths, militia gunmen, and security forces and the Israeli army and police. The following day, to the astonishment of most Israelis, violence spread into Israel's pre-1967 territory, when its Arab citizens joined their brothers in the territories. Main road arteries were blocked by stone-throwing mobs, while thousands of Jewish holiday makers, spending their vacation in the Galilee, found themselves in the midst of violent riots. Shops, banks, and other public places were ransacked, while rioters throughout the country clashed with the police. In Nazareth, thousands of Arabs marched in the streets chanting, "With our souls and our blood we will redeem Palestine." Jaffa and Haifa, for decades the epitome of Arab-Jewish coexistence, were likewise rocked by violent demonstrations.

Palestinian explanations of the origin of the confrontation vary in accordance with who exactly was asking for an explanation. To their own constituents, as well as to Arab audiences, it was portrayed as a premeditated Israeli assault, the latest link in a long chain of unprovoked atrocities aimed at perpetuating the occupation of Arab and Palestinian lands. Saeb Erekat complained upon the outbreak of hostilities that "a war is being waged against us, and the Palestinian people are facing a savage onslaught," while Arafat charged Israel with exacting a painful revenge on the Palestinians for their courage and steadfastness. "Most of the Israeli political and military leaders admitted that they had been planning for more than a year to ignite this fire," he told a special Arab League summit, convened in Cairo in November 2000.

Our people, who were worshipping in al-Aqsa, countered Sharon with their chests and naked fists, and prevented him from conducting this dangerous visit, forcing him to leave the holy place. The Israeli government, however, did not forgive the Palestinian worshippers their stand, and committed a new massacre during Friday prayers in the al-Aqsa mosque compound on the very next day. We all saw the bloody chapters of this massacre on the media.[2]

To Western audiences, likely to be more skeptical of Arafat in the wake of the failed Camp David summit, the eruption of violence was portrayed as a spontaneous explosion of rage sparked by Sharon's Temple Mount visit. On the day of the visit, the Arab League condemned the event as a "desecration of al-Haram al-Sharif" that was certain to trigger a violent reaction.[3] Professor Sari Nusseibah, the Oxford-educated president of al-Quds University, took a similar stance. "A lot of this is Sharon's fault," he told *New Yorker* editor David Remnick.

He knew just how to elicit the kind of reactions from us that would then be a justification for going one step further . . . Things move from one stage to another in a kind of inevitable way, leading to the point where people felt they had no way to react other than . . . this.[4]

Far from capturing the Palestinians by surprise, Sharon's visit was meticulously coordinated with the Palestinian Authority. According to Internal Security Minister Ben-Ami, Jibril Rajoub (the powerful head of the Preventive Security Service in the West Bank) had personally reassured his Israeli counterparts that the visit would pose no problem as long as Sharon did not enter the mosques. Rajoub later claimed that the riots started when Sharon tried to enter the Dome of the Rock, but then decided against it. In fact Sharon never attempted to enter the mosques, and had absolutely no reason to do so, but scrupulously observed the agreed-upon arrangements with the Palestinians.[5]

Notwithstanding violent incitement by the Palestinian media and outright calls by Fatah, Hamas, and Waqf officials for mass demonstrations against the intended "desecration of al-Haram al-Sharif,"[6] the actual turnout on Temple Mount on the day of the visit was far lower than expected. There were minor clashes between Israeli policemen and rock-throwing Palestinian youths, yet these were limited in scope and intensity and resulted in thirty lightly wounded Israeli policemen and four injured Palestinians. Not a single Palestinian was killed.[7] It was only on the next day that serious violence erupted in anything but a spontaneous manner.

Marwan Barghouthi, the dashing commander of the Tanzim militia, which sparked the hostilities and has carried out much of the fighting ever since, offered a deeper and more complex explanation of the war's origin than that of a simplistic "explosion of rage." Sharon's visit was merely the last straw in a long string of negative developments that had been stretching Palestinian patience to its limits. "We can no longer bear the occupation," he said.

> The intifada erupted because of the continued implementation of the Israeli policies of expanding Jewish settlements and building new ones, keeping more than 2,000 Palestinians in jail, carrying out projects aimed at the Judaization of Jerusalem, and the desecration of holy Islamic sites through such measures as Sharon's recent visit to al-Aqsa mosque. So long as these reasons exist and the occupation of Palestinian territories continues, the intifada will go on as well.[8]

The problem with this analysis is that since the beginning of 1996, and certainly following the completion of the redeployment from Hebron in January 1997, 99 percent of the Palestinian population of the West Bank and the Gaza Strip have not lived under Israeli occupation. All of the Gaza Strip's residents and nearly 60 percent of West Bankers—in the Jericho area and in the seven main cities of Jenin, Nablus, Tulkarm, Qalqilya, Ramallah, Bethlehem, and Hebron—have lived entirely under Palestinian jurisdiction. Another 40 percent of West Bank residents live in towns, villages, refugee camps, and hamlets where the Palestinian Authority exercises civil authority but, in line with the Oslo accords, Israel has maintained "overriding responsibility for security." Only 2 percent of the West Bank's population—tens of thousands of Palestinians—continue to live in areas where Israel has complete control, but even there the Palestinian Authority maintains "functional jurisdiction." As the virulent anti-Israel and anti-Jewish media, school system, and religious preaching can attest to, during these years any presence of a foreign occupation has been virtually nonexistent.

Arafat's war was an unwelcome development to ordinary Palestinians in the midst of a healthy recovery after several years of a deep economic crisis. Between 1994 and 1996, the Rabin and Peres governments had imposed repeated closures on the territories in order to stem the tidal wave of terrorism in the wake of the Oslo accords. This led to a steep drop in the Palestinian economy. With workers unable to get into Israel, unemployment rose sharply, reaching as high as 50 percent in Gaza. The movement of goods between Israel and the territories, as well as between the West Bank and Gaza, was seriously disrupted, slowing exports and discouraging potential private investment.

The economic situation in the territories began to improve during the Netanyahu government, as the steep fall in terrorist attacks led to a corresponding decrease in closures. Real GNP per capita grew by 3.5 percent in 1997, 7.7 percent in 1998, and 3.5 percent in 1999, while unemployment was more than halved. By the beginning of 1999, according to the World Bank, the West Bank and Gaza had fully recovered from the economic decline of the previous years and their position continued to improve well into the summer of 2000. GDP grew by 6.1 percent during the first half of 2000, and job creation in the territories continued to significantly increase, both in the public and the private sectors. Economic activity was particularly vibrant along the West Bank "fault line" in the Sharon and the Lower Galilee, where Israelis continued to frequent Palestinian towns and villages by the thousands for shopping and services, one of the many unspoken dividends of peace.

A burgeoning economy explains the lack of appetite for confrontation with Israel following Camp David, and, later, the initial mild response to Sharon's visit. Upon Arafat's return from the summit, Tanzim barely managed to muster some two hundred youths in Ramallah for what was supposed to be a "mass welcome for the returning Saladin." Likewise, the attempt to organize a commercial strike in East Jerusalem in protest against Barak's positions ended up in embarrassing failure. The frenzied reception in Gaza involved only a tiny fraction of the one-million-strong population and necessitated careful orchestration by Fatah.

Palestinian officials were thus forced to concede that the vast majority of East Jerusalem's Arab population preferred the continuation of Israeli rule to Palestinian sovereignty. "I estimate that close to 70 percent of the Arab residents want to remain under Israeli rule because of the economic benefits," Fadal Tahabub, a member of the Palestinian National Council and himself a resident of East Jerusalem, told a local

Israeli newspaper. These attitudes were so prevalent that Faisal Husseini, holder of the Jerusalem file at the PA, urgently summoned journalists from the three main Palestinian dailies to put out several messages
to East Jerusalem's Arab residents. Don't worry about losing Israeli National Insurance rights in the event of a change of sovereignty. Don't
worry about losing your freedom of movement in the west of the city
or the rest of Israel. Don't be concerned about forfeiting Israeli salaries for the significantly lower wage scales of the Palestinian Authority. Husseini, who was not at Camp David himself, promised that the
proper solutions would be found for all these issues in the event of an
agreement.[9]

Neither a result of simmering frustration with the Israeli occupation,
nor a spontaneous reaction to Sharon's Temple Mount visit, the sudden outbreak of hostilities was a deliberate attempt by Arafat to force
Israel to top its Camp David proposals without receiving anything in
return. It was a strategy of following peaceful concessions with bloody
terrorist attacks that had in the past routinely served Arafat well. Having carefully laid the groundwork for war since Netanyahu's term in office, and more specifically since the announcement of the Camp David
summit, Arafat used Sharon's visit to cast himself as "defender of Islam's
third holiest shrine." He sought to rally the Arab and Muslim worlds
behind him, divert international attention from the Camp David fiasco,
and regain widespread sympathy through the ubiquitous scenes of Palestinian rock-throwing youths confronting an ostensible Israeli Goliath.
This would allow him to extract further concessions from Israel without any reward, should the negotiations be resumed, or better yet pave
the road toward a unilateral proclamation of a Palestinian state.

Having learned of the initial muted response to Sharon's visit (there
were scores of Palestinian security operatives on the Temple Mount
compound at the time, including members of Arafat's personal guard,
Force 17),[10] Arafat used the Friday prayers, a traditional platform for anti-
Jewish incitement, as the springboard for his new war. In a particularly
militant sermon, the al-Aqsa preacher urged worshipers to "eradicate the
Jews from Palestine." "Should we respond [to Sharon's visit] only by
throwing rocks, or [only] by condemnation?" he asked rhetorically, before

sending the frenzied worshipers to stone the Israeli police on the mount, using stockpiles that had been prepared in advance. Under a barrage of heavy rocks, the Israeli police opened fire and thus provided Arafat with his first batch of martyrs. Meanwhile, official Palestinian television began screening archival footage of the intifada, the Palestinian uprising of the late 1980s and early '90s, while the Voice of Palestine radio played militant songs urging the Palestinians to rise up and take to the streets.[11]

Prior to the prayer service, Arafat gave direct orders to Barghouthi and his deputy Hussein Sheik to get their people out with stones, and later with guns, firing at Israeli army positions, the perimeter fences of Jewish settlements, and vehicles traveling on the major roads.[12] No inducements were necessary. Tanzim was well versed in the initiation of violence and his commanders, Barghouthi in particular, were spoiling for a fight. The militia had played a prominent role in the September 1996 tunnel war, as it did in the violent clashes of May 2000, on the fifty-second anniversary of the Nakba, as Palestinians call their 1948 defeat.[13] With Arafat's approval, thousands of Tanzim activists confronted Israeli troops with rocks and petrol bombs throughout the territories while scores of others, together with Palestinian policemen, were involved in shooting battles with the Israeli army. The desperate Israeli attempts to secure a cease-fire ran once again into Arafat's doublespeak, personally promising Barak to do his utmost to pacify the situation while instructing his chain of command to kill the largest possible number of Israelis. He threatened Israel with continued war yet denied the very participation of his security forces in the fighting.[14]

On the evening of Friday the twenty-ninth, Barghouthi summoned his militia leaders to his office in al-Bireh, outside Ramallah, to assess the first day of the clashes and the means for their continuation. A statement calling for a general uprising was then faxed to Fatah offices around the West Bank.[15] A week later, at a meeting in Arafat's Ramallah headquarters, Fatah leadership adopted a war strategy that envisaged a protracted confrontation aimed at wearing Israel down along the Lebanese model. The "public" war was to be conducted under the watchful eye of the world media and to involve mass clashes between Palestinian protesters and Israeli soldiers, portraying the war as a popular uprising by an oppressed nation against a brutal occupier. The "secret," albeit increasingly central, war involved armed attacks on Israeli targets throughout the territories, such as civilian and military vehicles, settlements, and so on. The Palestinian media were to continue to build up patriotic sentiments by instilling the willingness for sacrifice in the public at large, particularly in its younger members.[16]

A militant Barghouthi pressed to step up the struggle by encouraging Hamas to carry out suicide bombings in the West Bank and Gaza.[17] He was supported by the usually more cautious Rajoub, who raised the specter of terrorist attacks in Israel itself. "I think that it will not be diffi-cult to transfer the battle to their territory and their residential areas," he told *al-Jazira* satellite television a day after the outbreak of hos-tilities. "We will study each step at the right time in the light of the circumstances which we think will serve our people."[18] Accompanied by the incorporation of the Hamas and the Islamic Jihad into a newly es-tablished National Islamic Committee to coordinate the Palestinian struggle, and with the release of dozens of known Islamic terrorists from the PA prisons shortly after the outbreak of hostilities, Rajoub's state-ment sent a chilling signal as to what lay ahead.[19]

"The outbreak of the intifada did not come as a surprise to the Pal-estinian leadership," Imad Faluji, the PA's minister of post and com-munications, revealed. "The Palestinian Authority began preparing the present intifada and bracing for it since the return from Camp David at the request of President Yasser Arafat, who envisaged the intifada as a complementary measure to the Palestinian steadfastness in the nego-tiations, and not as a protest over Sharon's visit to al-Haram al-Sharif."[20]

Two of Fatah's foremost ideologues, Sakhr Habash and Othman Abu Gharbiya, also corroborated this account. Habash described Arafat's Camp David performance just over a week before he launched his war of terror. "Brother Abu Ammar [Arafat's nom de guerre] spoke in the language of a true believer, as a man who foresees the option facing him and the great Palestinian people: confrontation." Why confrontation? Be-cause Arafat realized that "the Israelis were incapable of delivering a real peace, the peace of the brave, which he had always desired."[21]

A couple of months after the outbreak of hostilities, Habash elabo-rated further as to why the failed summit had led inexorably to the outbreak of the intifada. In his account, Camp David proved conclu-sively that the Barak government was not a genuine peace partner and that the Americans were not going to pressure Israel to move in the

Palestinian direction. This drove the PA and the primary Palestinian organizations, first and foremost Fatah, to the conclusion that armed resistance constituted the only viable option with which to achieve their strategic goals.

Habash and Abu Gharbiya readily acknowledge that the intifada "was not a reaction to Sharon's provocative visit to al-Haram al-Sharif: this was only the spark." Rather:

> It accumulated in the depths of our people and channeled into an explosion in the face of the Barak government's procrastination, for a year and a half, over a fundamental problem—that of independence. Independence was the core issue of the intifada that broke out in al-Aqsa and spread to the rest of the cities, camps and villages in the West Bank and the Gaza Strip, as well as to Palestinian cities and villages within the Green Line [i.e., pre-1967 Israel].

Far from being a hasty response to Sharon's visit, the latest confrontation was a premeditated and meticulously prepared "War of Independence and Return," the culmination of decades of sustained Palestinian struggle in general, and the intifada of the late 1980s in particular. "The two uprisings are complementary parts," argued Habash. "The first broke out under exceedingly difficult conditions, while the second erupted amidst negotiations over a final-status agreement . . . The role of the second intifada is thus the attainment of independence, while that of the first intifada was the proclamation of independence."[22]

Mamduh Nawfal, a leading PLO thinker and a prominent Arafat adviser who was smuggled into Gaza in the trunk of Arafat's car upon his arrival in the Strip in July 1994, likewise corroborated the PA's role in the "spontaneous" eruption.

> The intifada was neither a mass movement detached from the Palestinian Authority nor an instinctive popular uprising. Quite the contrary in fact. It was started by a deliberate decision by the highest echelons of the Authority before being transformed into a popular movement. This happened immediately after Sharon's al-Aqsa visit, when the Authority's political and security bodies met and decided to protect al-Aqsa. Yasser Arafat viewed the visit as a flashpoint that could inflame not only the Palestinian land but also the situation beyond Palestine's borders. Accordingly, decisions about concrete preparations were made, and the

Authority's various forces held meetings in which they decided to move their fighters toward al-Aqsa on Friday.

"This movement was militarized from the first day," Nawfal continued.

The [intifada] began with blood and bullets already at the al-Aqsa compound on [September] 28 and 29, and continued this way to date. If we go back to the history of the movement, we will discover that not a single day has passed without arms or armed men playing a role in the confrontation. Armed clashes began on Friday, September 29, and continued with the appearance of armed personnel in the demonstrations and their participation in the shooting at settlements adjacent to the [Arab] towns, steadily moving toward full-fledged participation of the Authority's organs in the fighting. But even the armed men, who participated in the fighting from the start, were not unattached to the Palestinian Authority, its organs, or the ruling party [i.e., Fatah]. This is because weapons are primarily in the hands of the Palestinian Authority's organs and the ruling party, and are not readily available to the public at large apart from a specified number of people who received them at one time or another.[23]

Barghouthi, who more than anyone else came to epitomize Arafat's terrorist war, was similarly candid. In March 2000, four months before the Camp David summit, he made the case for renewed confrontation as a means to impose Palestinian demands on Israel. "Whoever thinks that the issues of the final-status agreement—such as the refugees, Jerusalem, settlements, and borders—can be resolved by negotiations alone is deluding himself," he said. "The negotiations over these issues must be accompanied by a campaign on the ground, that is, a confrontation. We need dozens of campaigns like the [1996] al-Aqsa Tunnel . . . You don't fight the settlements by pleading, but through the force of arms."[24]

Once hostilities broke out, Barghouthi, whose Tanzim militia carried most of the fighting, grew more outspoken. Asked by an Egyptian interviewer whether he believed that Arafat wished to stop the war, he responded, "The continuation of the intifada serves the interests of the Palestinian Authority, which has reached a deadlock in the negotiations. Experience shows that negotiations are ineffective in the absence of real resistance on the ground because the Israelis will only listen to themselves, while the United States is totally biased in favor of the Jewish state."[25]

In another interview, Barghouthi proudly admitted his critical role in starting the war. "I knew that the end of September was the final deadline for the explosion, but when Sharon visited al-Aqsa Mosque, this was the most appropriate moment for the outbreak of the intifada," he said.

> The night prior to the visit I participated in a panel discussion on a local television station and seized the opportunity to call on the public to go to al-Aqsa in the morning, for it was inconceivable for Sharon to visit al-Haram al-Sharif as a matter of course and walk away peacefully. I finished and went to al-Aqsa in the morning. . . . We tried to create clashes, albeit without success because of the differences of opinion that emerged with others in the al-Aqsa compound at the time. . . . After Sharon had left, I remained for a couple of hours with some other people, and we discussed the manner of response throughout the entire country and not just in Jerusalem. We contacted all [the Palestinian] factions . . . I prepared a leaflet in the name of Fatah's Higher Committee, coordinated with the brothers (e.g., Hamas), in which we called for a reaction to what happened in Jerusalem.[26]

The ferocity of Arafat's war was aptly matched by the totality of its objectives. In contrast to its attempts to convince world public opinion of the confrontation's limited objectives—the end of Israeli "occupation" in the West Bank and the Gaza Strip—the Palestinian leadership and its tightly controlled media have gone to great lengths to inform their people of the war's ultimate goal: the destruction of the Jewish state.

The War of Independence and Return—the name given to this confrontation in Palestinian internal discourse—specifically set the right of return as one of the war's twin goals. "The way to achieve peace is as clear as the sun in the sky: a full Israeli withdrawal of its army and its settlers from all Palestinian land occupied since June 4, 1967, and the implementation of resolution 194," Arafat said.

> Resolution 194 has to be implemented for peace to be achieved for those Palestinians who live expelled from their homes. Theirs is a sacred right, and it is the responsibility of the international community to secure this right of the Palestinian refugees . . . Yes, this is the only road to peace, the peace of the brave . . . We will continue in this way until the day we raise the Palestinian flag over Jerusalem, over Jerusalem's mosques and Jerusalem's churches.[27]

Starting with Camp David, and intensifying after the outbreak of hostilities, an endless stream of political statements, press reports, and
media broadcasts encouraged, indeed incited, Palestinians to sacrifice
their lives for the sake of the "greater good." Israel was vilified on a daily
basis and presented as a mortal threat to the existence of the Palestinian people and the "Arab Nation" at large. Clips lauding Saladin, the
legendary medieval router of the crusaders, and containing violent scenes
of confrontation between Israeli troops and Palestinian rioters, were
screened on PA television every day in what was increasingly portrayed
as a millenarian struggle over existence and destiny between two mutually exclusive communities. "Since Omar [the caliph who occupied Palestine in 638 CE] and Saladin we haven't given up our original rights in
Jerusalem and al-Aqsa, our Jerusalem, our Palestine," ran a typical commentary on the PA's official television.

> If time constitutes the [criteria of] existence, then Israel's temporary
> existence is only fifty-two years long while we, the Palestinian Arabs, have
> lived here for thousands of years, and we, the indigenous population, will
> eventually expel the invaders, however long it will take.[28]

The Palestinian official media also used classic anti-Semitic libel, such
as the blaming of the Jews for the murder of Jesus, to underscore the
Manichean nature of the Arab conflict with Israel. "Our struggle today
against the Other is an eternal one. It can be said to have started 2,000
years ago and continues to date," argued a Palestinian artist on the weekly
interview program *Good Morning Jerusalem*, on which he presented his new
paintings, among them a picture of Jesus with two Israeli soldiers standing at his sides.

> I demonstrate this through the figure of Jesus, who came to the world with
> a message of justice and the other side did what they did to him. The
> [present-day] Palestinian demands that same right and is being treated
> in the same manner. In this painting I demonstrate the following idea:
> the Israeli soldiers are wearing army uniforms while Jesus has nothing
> except for the truth. When they searched him at the entrance to Jerusa-
> lem, they found a stone, a piece of bread, and fish and he was handcuffed.
> This is the Palestinian from the beginning of the struggle until its end—
> if it will ever end.[29]

In carefully edited interviews with "ordinary people," grassroots messages were screened around the clock after the failure of the Camp David negotiations. Some were fatuous praise: "We are telling Arafat: You are the leader. Move forward until the liberation of Jerusalem and the whole of Palestine—from Ras Naqura [in the north] to Rafah [in the south]." Others were more explicit: "We want the liberation of all Palestinian territories—whether occupied in 1967 or in 1948 . . . All the martyrs fell so that Palestine shall live and that the Palestinian people will be able to adhere to his land and his rights . . . We will fight until our last drop of blood for our country and homeland."[30]

Children were also fed an enhanced diet of Palestinian propaganda. "Today I chose a really nice drawing for you of the map of Palestine," a presenter told her young viewers before explaining the country's geography, in which Israel did not exist.

> Let us all look at it together . . . A drawing of Palestine. It is so beautiful. There is Acre, Haifa, Jaffa, Tiberias . . . [all Israeli cities]. Palestine is so beautiful! Our country is so beautiful! . . . You can see how pretty our land is, how very pretty it is. And to all of our loved ones, who are on the map, whether they are from Acre, Haifa, Jaffa, or Nazareth . . . [all Israeli cities] we bid everyone a welcome.

In another episode of the same program, the hostess presented a similar drawing of the map of Israel and the Palestinian Authority areas shackled together, before telling her audience, "[This is] a picture of the map of Palestine with chains around it, and with Allah's will, my dear ones, these chains will be freed one day and Palestine will remain ours forever."[31]

Arafat had sold the West Bank and Gaza residents the belief that concessions compromised the very existence of Palestinians. According to the draft Palestinian constitution presented to Arafat in July 2000, Palestine was the exclusive preserve of the Palestinian people—"the deposit of the Palestinian people throughout its various generations, and its national rights are the joint legacy of all Palestinians. They are obliged to preserve it, to pass it from one generation to another, and to defend it."[32]

This was translated into a concrete combat order titled "The Campaign Has Started," issued to the PA security forces upon the failure of the Camp David summit, and which anticipated the outbreak of hostilities by a couple of months. "[This is] a call from the negotiating team, headed by the Commander and Symbol Abu Ammar [Arafat], to our heroic Palestinian people," it read.

> Be prepared. The Jerusalem campaign has started. This is the meaning of the return of the Palestinian delegation from Camp David to the homeland without compromising any of the declared and fundamental Palestinian positions: there will be no peace without Jerusalem, the eternal capital city of the State of Palestine. Nor will there be stability or security in the entire region unless Israel complies with the requirements of international legitimacy.[33]

Though in Palestinian parlance the "requirements of international legitimacy" had always been a code language for Israel's destruction, Sakhr Habash took the trouble to clarify its meaning at this particular historical juncture. "*Experience shows that without the establishment of a democratic state on the whole of Palestine there will be no peace,*" he stated in a public speech delivered on Arafat's behalf, a few months after the outbreak of hostilities.

> We are going through stages of struggle that will enable us to drive Zionist society into ridding itself of Zionism since there can be no coexistence between Zionism and the Palestinian national movement. The Jews must rid themselves of Zionism, which has immersed them in a string of confrontations that do not serve their interest. Instead they should be citizens of the future state: the democratic state of Palestine.[34]

12

Violence Pays

I want you to bring me an agreement, as long as it will not be humiliating.
> —Ehud Barak to Foreign Minister Ben-Ami,
> December 2000

Arafat's deliberate use of violence, instead of resulting in censure or global outrage, reconfirmed his international stature, as it had so many times in the past. At the end of the 1960s, as PLO terrorism was increasing, the UN General Assembly adopted a resolution recognizing the "inalienable rights" of the Palestinian people. In November 1974, on the heels of a string of deadly terrorist attacks on Israeli civilians, including the murder of eleven Israeli athletes during the 1972 Munich Olympics, Arafat became the first nonstate leader to address the General Assembly. Twenty-two years later, in September 1996, Arafat's unflinching sacrifice of dozens of Palestinians seriously undermined the domestic and international standing of the Israeli prime minister Benjamin Netanyahu. Now that Arafat had unleashed a war of terror on his peace partner, who had just offered the Palestinians an independent state in most of the West Bank and the Gaza Strip, a wide-ranging and diverse cohort of apologists, from the Arab states and from Europe, exonerated the Palestinian leader of any wrong-doing and instead pointed an accusing finger at Israel.

Arafat, who only months prior had been loathed and detested throughout the Arab world for wreaking havoc on those societies that had sheltered and protected the Palestinians, from Jordan, to Lebanon, to Kuwait, was given a new lease on life; the traitor who had sold out to the "Zionist entity" by signing the Oslo accords was now seen as fully rehabilitated.[1] As world attention focused on the new regional conflagration, Camp David was relegated to the fringes of collective memory, with Arafat's intransigence all but forgotten. Barak's conviction that the political credit he had won would shore up Israel's position in future, turbulent days was shattered as he was increasingly cast in the role of the regional villain. "After the collapse of the Camp David summit in July, [Arafat] is said to have concluded that the Palestinians no longer had 'a partner for peace,'" wrote the influential *Economist* magazine, as if it had been Barak who had walked away from a generous peace settlement. "He has little faith in Mr. Barak, whose skill at expanding Jewish settlements, while receiving diplomatic accolades from America and Europe, has long infuriated him. And he is believed to be greatly disillusioned with President Clinton, whom Mr. Arafat had believed to be genuinely 'sensitive' to the Palestinian cause."[2]

Yet it was television that provided the foremost boon to the Palestinian cause. With international coverage of the confrontation limited to a relatively small number of major flash points, notably the Ramallah-Jerusalem fault line, and unscrupulously manipulated by the PA so as to disallow the filming of anything it did not wish to be shown, the Palestinians were instantaneously portrayed as the underdog as pictures of clashes between ostensibly unarmed civilians and soldiers were shown throughout the world. Palestinian gunmen shooting at Israeli soldiers from behind stone throwers escaped the camera's gaze, as did daily firings on Jewish civilians and residential areas by Tanzim forces, yet millions of viewers throughout the world were horrified by the heartbreaking scene of the death of twelve-year-old Muhammad Dura, caught with his father in the crossfire between Palestinian gunmen and Israeli soldiers near Gaza and filmed by a French television crew. The feeble remonstrations by the IDF that the boy was killed by Palestinian fire (a fact corroborated some eighteen months later in an independent investigation undertaken by a German television company) were to no avail. The picture of Dura's death instantaneously became the foremost Palestinian icon and the most potent symbol of their victimization by Israel. (In a macabre twist, in its broadcasts to its Palestinian subjects the PA has turned Dura from a victim into a role model, preparing a special TV clip in which a young actor portraying the dead Dura urges Palestinian kids to emulate him and "martyr" themselves: "How fresh is the fragrance of the martyrs . . . I am waving to you not to bid farewell but to say: 'Follow me.'")[3]

Media outlets, commentators, and politicians throughout the world eagerly subscribed to the notion that the Palestinian violence was fully understandable in the light of Sharon's "provocation." Speaking in Cairo following a meeting with Egypt's foreign minister Amr Musa, EU Middle East peace envoy Miguel Moratinos condemned the raging violence and offered his condolences to the bereaved Palestinian families. No mention was made of Israeli casualties.[4] At a meeting with Jacques Chirac, the French president, on October 4, Barak was peremptorily reprimanded and told that "Israel is to be blamed for the violence. It all started with a serious provocation by Sharon which seems to have been coordinated with you."[5] A Security Council resolution, passed on October 9, similarly put the blame for the violence on "the provocation carried out at al-Haram al-Sharif in Jerusalem on 28 September 2000" and criticized "the excessive use of force against Palestinians." To Israel's dismay, the U.S. administration, while strongly censuring the resolution as "one-sided," stopped short of vetoing it.[6] An international fact-finding commission, headed by former U.S. senator George Mitchell, was specifically instructed by President Clinton in his letter of appointment of December 6, 2000, to "strive to steer clear of any step that will intensify mutual blame and finger-pointing between the parties." Though stressing in its final report that "violence will not solve the problems of the region" and that "there is only one way to peace, justice, and security in the Middle East, and that is through negotiation," the committee refrained from singling out which party had started the war, let alone offering any criticism of the Palestinian armed escalation, but instead reverted to bland assertions about the failure of both sides to "fully appreciate each other's problems and concerns."[7]

The Israelis were stunned. "A World Gone Mad," proclaimed a *Jerusalem Post* article lamenting what it believed to be the unbearable short-term international collective memory. "It isn't that our 'partner for peace,' after signing no less than five agreements renouncing violence in the last seven years, initiated a shooting war," the article stated. "That has happened before, in the fall of 1996, and it will doubtless happen again as long as Yasser Arafat continues to walk away from such conflicts with diplomatic gains . . . Nor is it that—unlike 1996, when the world blamed Palestinian violence on Netanyahu's 'intransigence'—the current round of fighting follows the most far-reaching concessions any Israeli prime minister has ever offered." What the *Post* author found totally inexplicable was "the fact that the Western world seriously considers Ariel Sharon's visit to the Temple mount sufficient justification for a bloodbath." This was a guaranteed recipe for the continuation of the war.

> As long as the world is prepared to justify Palestinian violence on the most spurious of pretexts—even at a time when Israel's government is offering unprecedented far-reaching concessions, and to the point that it even blames Israel for shooting back—the Palestinians have no incentive to refrain from violence. On the contrary: they have learned that starting a war is an excellent way to achieve diplomatic gains in the form of increased pressure on Israel.[8]

Enthused by the extent of international indulgence and mindful of Barak's growing desperation for a cease-fire, the Palestinians were raising the ante by the day. While at the outbreak of hostilities Rajoub had promised to stop the shooting if Israel would apologize for the earlier deaths (something that the Israelis refused), a few days later the PA insisted on the withdrawal of all Israeli forces from their newly gained positions and the appointment of an international committee to investigate "the massacre on al-Haram al-Sharif."[9] Several weeks later, the Palestinian conditions had become much more far-reaching. "If Israel were to withdraw unilaterally from, say, 92 percent of the West Bank," suggested Shaath, "the Palestinians would declare an independent state in these territories. Israel and the Palestinians would then negotiate the permanent borders and other issues state-to-state."[10] In other words, the Palestinians would gain the territorial concessions made by Barak in Camp David, without giving anything in return, apart from stopping the war they had started in the first place.

For Barghouthi, even this was not enough. "Fatah will continue its struggle and fight until the end of the occupation, the realization of the right of return, and the establishment of a state with Jerusalem as its capital," he said. "The Israelis have to choose either peace and security or occupation . . . The condition for peace in this region is an independent Palestinian state with Jerusalem as its capital, return of the Palestinian refugees, and liberation from occupation."[11]

When Arafat met with Barak on October 4, 2000, in the residence of the U.S. ambassador to Paris, within the framework of an American attempt to engineer a cease-fire, he toyed with the Israeli prime minister. Asked by Barak to rein in Barghouthi and Hussein Sheik, Arafat feigned ignorance. "Who?" he asked. "Who?" Barak repeated the names, this time with a pronounced Arabic inflection, and Arafat again said, "Who? Who?" Some of his aides couldn't keep themselves from laughing. Arafat dropped the pretence, and agreed to call them later.[12]

A few days later, Arafat treated UN secretary-general Kofi Annan to a similar spectacle. As Annan came out of their meeting to inform reporters of Palestinian readiness "to lower the level of violence," a Fatah leaflet was simultaneously circulating throughout the West Bank and Gaza calling for the continuation of the fighting, while scores of Islamic terrorists were being freed from PA prisons.[13]

Arafat could afford such maneuvers. Overwhelmed by the magnitude of Palestinian violence—during the first two months of hostilities there were no fewer than two thousand terrorists attacks of various types (rock throwing excluded)—and disturbed by the erosion in his domestic political standing, Barak quickly extended his Camp David concessions. Already in the discussions in Washington in September 2000, shortly before the outbreak of hostilities, the Israeli negotiators agreed to increase the territory of the prospective Palestinian state to 95 percent of the West Bank (compared to 92 percent in Camp David), and to drop the demand for Israeli sovereignty over the Jordan Valley. They also agreed to Palestinian sovereignty over Temple Mount/al-Haram al-Sharif, provided that Israel was granted sovereignty over the earth beneath the surface of the holy compound. The Palestinians, who refused to recognize any Jewish connection to Temple Mount, again dismissed the proposal out of hand.[14]

Once violence erupted, Barak instructed the military to explore the possibility of an interim agreement based on Israeli recognition of a unilaterally proclaimed Palestinian state and subsequent negotiations over the outstanding issues. The report, classified TOP SECRET and submitted to the prime minister on October 25, recommended that Israel persist in the quest for a final-status arrangement, as any interim agreement would not resolve the core problems and would only postpone the moment of truth.[15] Barak concurred. On December 21, 2000, an Israeli team headed by Foreign Minister Shlomo Ben-Ami met a Palestinian delegation that included Yasser Abd Rabbo, Saeb Erekat, and Muhammad Dahlan in the American airbase of Bolling. By now, Barak had called general elections for the premiership (according to the existing Israeli law at the time, such elections could be held separately from the parliamentary elections), and was desperate for an achievement that would salvage his tottering position. "I want you to bring me an agreement, as long as it will not be humiliating," he told Ben-Ami. The foreign minister, one of the leading doves in the cabinet, needed no inducement. Without consulting Barak, he offered the Palestinians complete sovereignty over al-Haram al-Sharif in return for an undertaking not to carry out excavations in the space beneath the compound, as this area was sacred to Jews.

Ben-Ami's Israeli counterparts were startled. At a stroke the foreign minister had granted the prospective Palestinian state control over Judaism's most sacred site, without any quid pro quo. The Palestinians again demurred, prepared to forgo the excavations but not to concede the site's holiness to Jews. "I am neither an historian nor a theologian," Abd Rabbo retorted. "What made this episode particularly galling," Ben-Ami recalled a year later, "was not the refusal itself but the way in which it was spelled out—with such contempt, such patronizing dismissal. At this moment it dawned upon me that the Palestinians were no Sadat. That they would not move in our direction even at the emotional and symbolic levels. At the deepest level they are not prepared to recognize that we have any right to this land."[16]

Ben-Ami's ideas were ultimately incorporated into a new peace plan submitted by President Clinton to the Palestinian and Israeli negotiators on December 23. This plan envisaged a mutual declaration at the end of the Palestinian-Israeli conflict on the basis of the following:

- Transfer of 94–96 percent of the West Bank and all of the Gaza Strip to the Palestinians, together with Israeli territory adjoining the Strip to make up for the remaining 4 to 6 percent that would be annexed to Israel.
- On Jerusalem, "what is Arab should go to the Arabs, and what is Jewish to the Jews." In the Old City, Israel would control the Jewish quarter, including the Western Wall and a corridor in the Armenian quarter leading from the Jaffa Gate to the Wall. The Palestinians will be granted sovereignty over the Muslim and Christian quarters, and part of the Armenian quarter. Israel will also retain control over the Mount of Olives and the City of David.
- The surface of Temple Mount would be under Palestinian control. The area underneath the Mount, believed to hold the remains of the First and Second Temples, will have a special status respecting Jewish rights to the site.

• The right of return of the Palestinian refugees would be applied to the prospective Palestinian state, not to Israel. In addition, some refugees would be resettled in the Arab host countries, third-party countries, or inside Israel—in line with Israeli policy. An international fund of $30 billion would be established for either compensation or to cover repatriation, resettlement, and rehabilitation costs. Israel would be asked to recognize the suffering of the Palestinian people as a result of the 1948 war, and to take part in the international rehabilitation effort.

• An international force would supervise the implementation of the agreements. Israel would have three years to withdraw, with the international force gradually taking over. At the end of this period, Israeli forces would remain at specific locations in the Jordan Valley for another three years, under the supervision of the international force. Israel would maintain three early-warning stations in the West Bank for a period of ten years, as well as emergency supplies at a number of points in the Jordan Valley in case of a threat from the east.

• The Palestinian state would be nonmilitarized.[17]

Though this plan contained substantial concessions to the Palestinians on top of those offered in Camp David, after three days of deliberations the Israeli government announced its acceptance, with a number of minor requests for clarification.[18] Arafat dragged his feet for a week and more before giving his response to Clinton in person on January 2, 2001. There are contradictory accounts as to what happened at the White House meeting. Palestinian apologists have reported that Arafat agreed to the American peace plan. Arafat himself was more elusive, saying in a subsequent interview that he had suggested that the president immediately summon Israeli and Palestinian negotiators for marathon talks since in his opinion a deal could be reached in two weeks. According to Dennis Ross, Clinton's special envoy to the Middle East, who attended the meeting, Arafat rejected "every single one of the things he was supposed to give," including Israeli sovereignty over the Wailing Wall:

He rejected the idea on the refugees. He said we need a whole new formula, as if what we had presented was nonexistent. He rejected the basic ideas on security. He wouldn't even countenance the idea that the Israelis would be able to operate in Palestinian airspace.

You know when you fly into Israel today you go to Ben Gurion. You fly in over the West Bank because you can't—there's no space through otherwise. He rejected that. So every single one of the ideas that was asked of him he rejected.[19]

None other than Arafat's close associate and adviser, Mamduh Nawfal confirmed Ross's account. In an article published in the PA daily *al-Ayyam* a fortnight after the White House meeting, Nawfal commended the outgoing president's warm attitude to Arafat, and also praised Clinton's readiness to move beyond previous American ideas with regard to the refugees and the Jerusalem problems, and for acknowledging that "there can be no solution without the establishment of an independent and sovereign Palestinian state on 95 percent of the territories occupied in 1967, with Jerusalem as its capital." Yet he described the American peace plan as based on Israeli ideas that had been "cleverly wrapped in U.S. papers so as to camouflage and sell them to the Palestinians at a high price in dollars and not in shekels." Palestinian negotiators, who had seen through this ploy, refused to buy these ideas.

They told both Israelis and Americans that though these were significant and valuable proposals, they were nevertheless far from the international legitimacy resolutions on the Palestinian-Israeli conflict. These proposals do not offer a drastic and permanent solution to this conflict and are favorable to Israel and its strategic interests and unfair to the Palestinians. Some of them even pose grave danger to the interests and national rights of the Palestinians because they undermine and replace UN resolutions 194, 242, and 338.[20]

Another article in *al-Ayyam* denounced Arafat's invitation to Washington as "a last-ditch attempt by U.S. President Bill Clinton to shatter the Palestinian stance rejecting his proposals—which are Israeli in origin," and urged the Palestinians to brace themselves for the post-Clinton era "by escalating the action on the ground and developing the forms and methods of the intifada, as well as raising the level of confrontation, fortifying our masses, and providing them with the factors for steadfastness to continue their struggle."[21]

*   *   *

In tandem with this "escalating action on the ground," Arafat agreed to Clinton's request for another Palestinian-Israeli summit meeting. Considering the U.S. plan as a basis for further gains, instead of the end result of the negotiations as envisaged by the American president,[22] there was little he could lose by such an exercise. As at Camp David, Arafat was not coming to this summit to negotiate but rather to coerce Israel into accepting more of the Palestinians' "minimum demands." Barak's desperation for a cease-fire had already produced a significant erosion of his Camp David stance, and his weak position in the run-up to the Israeli elections on February 6, 2001, where he was trailing far behind Ariel Sharon, the Likud candidate, was seemingly conducive to further Israeli concessions. In the best-case scenario, Arafat could make substantial gains, such as Israel's withdrawal to the 1967 borders and complete sovereignty over East Jerusalem, in return for an interim agreement that would boost the Palestinian position in the next stage of the negotiations. At worst, the Israeli concessions would constitute the starting point for future negotiations, as had been the case previously at Camp David. Either way, the Palestinians would emerge as the stronger party, having ostensibly given peace another chance without conceding any ground, let alone signing away the end of the conflict.

When the two sides met at the Egyptian resort of Taba, on the Red Sea, between January 21–27, 2001, as in Camp David there were no real negotiations but rather a steady Israeli retreat, which, according to the Palestinian account, "moved considerably beyond the positions they had presented at Camp David as 'red lines' beyond which they could not go 'without jeopardizing the state.'"[23]

The first substantial concession was the Israeli acceptance that "in accordance with the UN Security Council Resolution 242, the June 4, 1967, lines would be the basis for the borders between Israel and the state of Palestine."[24] Since this resolution does not actually demand Israel's complete withdrawal from the territories but rather from some of them, the Barak government was not only adopting a highly generous position about its implementation but it uncritically endorsed the Arab misinterpretation of the resolution's provisions. Yet this, too, failed to satisfy the Palestinian negotiators. They rejected the annexation of settlement blocs to Israel as envisaged by the Clinton plan, on the grounds that this "would cause significant harm to the Palestinian interests and rights." Nor did they agree to contiguity between and among the Israeli settlements, or to Israel's annexation of a number of neighborhoods on the fringes of Jerusalem, such as Maale Edumim and Pisgat Ze'ev. Though accepting the principle of land swap, they rejected the territory offered by Israel in the vicinity of the Gaza Strip, insisting instead on receiving Israeli territory contiguous to the West Bank, including Kochav Yair, Barak's hometown.[25]

Another significant Israeli concession related to its effective acceptance of the right of return, though not the actual return of all Palestinian refugees to Israel itself. The person to finally break this most sacred of Israel's taboos was Yossi Beilin, the minister of justice, who had been appointed by Barak to discuss the refugee problem in Taba. As the chief architect of the Oslo process, Beilin was anxious to salvage his brainchild from the claws of disaster, forgetting altogether his own assertion in November 1993 that should Palestinian terrorism persist after the creation of the PA, the peace process would have to be stopped dead in its tracks.[26]

In October 1999 Beilin told Barak that the apparently intractable issue of the right of return could be surmounted through the devising of a formula that "will allow the Palestinians to avoid declaring the abolition of this right, because this is beyond their capacity for concessions, without obliging Israel to acknowledge it, as this would imply a readiness to absorb whoever wished to return."[27] As no such solution was reached in Camp David, Beilin was instrumental in prevailing over the objections of the government's attorney general who questioned the legitimacy of a peace agreement signed on the eve of the elections, under intense military pressure, and without a parliamentary majority. Once in Taba, Beilin was determined to do everything within his power to reach an agreement. Without asking or receiving Barak's permission, Beilin submitted to his Palestinian counterpart Nabil Shaath a "non-paper" on the solution of the refugee problem. Having expressed Israel's "sorrow for the tragedy of the Palestinian refugees, their suffering and losses," the non-paper suggested that "a just settlement of the refugee problem in accordance with the UN Security Council Resolution 242 must lead to the implementation of UN General Assembly Resolution 194 [of December 11, 1948]." It continued:

Since 1948, the Palestinian yearning has been enshrined in the twin principles of the "Right of Return" and the establishment of an independent
Palestinian State deriving the basis from International Law. The realization of the aspirations of the Palestinian people, as recognized in this
agreement, includes the exercise of their right to self-determination and
a comprehensive and just solution for the Palestinian refugees, based on
UN General Assembly Resolution 194, providing for their return and guar-
anteeing the future welfare and wellbeing of the refugees, thereby addressing the refugee problem in all its aspects.[28]

For the first time in the history of the Palestinian-Israeli conflict, a senior member of the Israeli government officially recognized the Palestinian "right of return," correctly viewed by both Israelis and Palestinians
as implying the destruction of Israel through demographic subversion.

Beilin's proposed implementation of this right differed from the traditional Palestinian stance. While the latter insisted on the return of the
refugees to territory that is now part of the state of Israel, Beilin suggested a number of options: repatriation to Israel, to Israeli swapped
territory, to the future Palestinian state, to third countries, as well as
resettlement in the Arab host countries.[29] Yet once the right of return
to Israeli territory had been recognized, the guard sheltering the Jewish
state from demographic subversion was dropped. The Trojan horse, to
borrow Faisal Husseini's phrase, would have been brought into the city,
and it would have been a question of time before the soldiers hidden in
its wooden body would use the opportunity to subvert the enemy's territory. If the principle were accepted, it became simply a question of
numbers, and, to judge by the record of the Oslo process especially since
Camp David, the Palestinians could be expected to progressively erode
the Israeli position. Indeed, while Beilin emphasized that "the wish to
return shall be implemented in a manner consistent with the existence
of the State of Israel as the homeland for the Jewish people,"[30] according to Hani Hassan, a senior Fatah leader and Arafat's adviser, "at the
Taba talks the Israelis [i.e., Beilin] proposed the return of 200,000 Palestinians." Beilin himself told a fellow Israeli negotiator in Taba, "I see
no problem in absorbing even 200,000 Palestinian refugees. We will in
any case be relinquishing control over 200,000 Arabs by transferring East
Jerusalem to the Palestinians." The proposal was ultimately rejected by
Arafat since "the refugees are not a matter for bargaining or trading."[31]

Beilin was certainly aware of the fundamental difference between the Jerusalem Arabs and the refugees he favored absorbing. While the former were merely residents who could not participate in parliamentary elections (only in municipal ones), the refugees would be full-fledged Israeli citizens, and as such play a significant role in the country's political and social life. Moreover, while the Jerusalem Arabs had been living under Israel's control for thirty-three years and were fully appreciative of the social and economic gains attending the association with Israel, the refugees whom Beilin agreed to absorb were part of the far more militant Palestinian Diaspora, which had lived under some of the Arab world's worst dictatorships, had never maintained direct contact with Israel, and were irrevocably committed to its destruction. None of this prevented the ambitious minister of justice from arguing later that the two parties had formulated "a real draft on the resolution of the refugee problem, as part of the framework agreement."[32]

In actuality the offer was a farce, not only because neither the Israeli public nor even Barak, for all his desperation to be reelected, was extremely unlikely to accept any agreement that recognized the Palestinian right of return, but also because Beilin's concessions were unacceptable to the Palestinians. They were of course amenable to his recognition of this "right" but not to its proposed implementation, underscoring their unwavering position that "the Palestinian refugees should have the right of return to their homes in accordance with the interpretation of UN General Assembly Resolution 194."[33] Abu Ala, head of the Palestinian delegation at Taba, commented, "No progress was made on the right of return of the Palestinian refugees. Any bridging of the gap on this issue seems to be impossible because our red line is based on acceptance of this right while the Israeli stand is based on no return."[34]

In spite of this somber judgment, the Palestinians came away from Taba with a real sense of achievement. Though no agreement had been reached, they had managed to extract additional and substantial concessions from Israel, which, they hoped, would serve as a starting point in the negotiations with the Israeli government that would be established after the elections. They believed these now included:

• The establishment of a fully contiguous Palestinian state in the entire Gaza Strip and in 97 percent of the West Bank. Together with the Israeli territory to be ceded in compensation of the above 3 percent, the nascent Palestinian state will be larger than the combined territory of the pre-1967 West Bank and Gaza.[35]

• Palestinian sovereignty over Arab East Jerusalem, including most of the Old City.

• Israeli agreement to discuss Palestinian property claims in West Jerusalem, which had been an integral part of Israel since 1948.[36]

• Near agreement with Israel on acceptance of Clinton's ideas regarding Palestinian sovereignty over al-Haram al-Sharif, without relinquishing their criticisms of other aspects of the U.S. plan on the holy sites.

• Israeli acceptance of the right of return. Though this did not extend at the time to other members of the Israeli delegation beyond Beilin who were unaware of his groundbreaking concessions, his non-paper had become an integral part of the Palestinian-Israeli negotiating record that was likely to be raised in any future talks.

Whatever the Palestinian gains, they were about to be eclipsed. The outbreak of Arafat's terrorist war, shortly after the Palestinians had been offered the most far-reaching political concessions since the 1948 war, shook the Israeli public to the core. Even the small minority of Israelis who thought that Barak could have made a more generous offer to the Palestinians in Camp David did not anticipate violence but rather a counteroffer that would keep the negotiations going. Arafat's decision to respond with war, and at a level of violence unmatched in scope and intensity since the Arab attempt to abort the creation of a Jewish state in 1948, destroyed Israelis' trust in the Palestinian sincerity about peace. Israel remained eager for an agreement that would end once and for all its hundred-year war with the Palestinians, and it was prepared to make far-reaching concessions to this end yet was unwilling to give in to violence (while expecting naively its concessions to be fully reciprocated). By the time Barak went to Taba, most Israelis believed he no longer had a mandate for concessions. When it was revealed that in this latest round of talks Arafat had turned down an Israeli offer to cede virtually the entire West Bank and the Gaza Strip to the nascent Palestinian state together with Israeli territory, Barak's fate was sealed. On February 6, 2001, he suffered the worst electoral defeat in Israel's history. Ariel Sharon, the Palestinian nemesis, became Israel's new prime minister.

13

The Turning of the Tide

The heroic martyrdom operation [of the man] who turned his body
into a bomb [is] the model of manhood and sacrifice for the sake of
Allah and the homeland.
> —Yasser Arafat to the family of the Tel Aviv disco
> suicide bomber, June 2001

Ariel Sharon's sweeping electoral victory could not have been a more unwelcome development for Arafat. Aside from his relentless opposition to
the Oslo process, or for that matter to any deal with the PLO, which he
considered an unreconstructed terrorist organization, Sharon was in many
ways the Arab nemesis, the epitome of their military and strategic impotence. Perhaps Israel's most illustrious general, he had participated in the
1948 War of Independence as a platoon commander and was seriously
wounded in the battle of Latrun, one of the war's bloodiest encounters.
He then went on to develop the IDF's paratrooper units, commanding
them in a string of retaliatory actions during the early 1950s and leading
them to battle in the 1956 Sinai War. Eleven years later, in the Six-Day
War of June 1967, his forces broke the backbone of the Egyptian army in
Sinai in a brilliant gambit that would be studied and admired in military
academies throughout the world. He repeated this performance in the Yom
Kippur War of October 1973, when his division daringly crossed the Suez
Canal and, in a flanking maneuver, encircled the Egyptian Third Army
and forced President Anwar Sadat to plead for a cease-fire.

The Palestinians' own experiences with Sharon have been mixed. As
OC Southern Command in the early 1970s, he had crushed the PLO's
attempt to transform the Gaza Strip into a springboard for terrorist attacks against Israel. Yet in September 1970, when King Hussein expelled

Palestinian guerrillas from his kingdom in a particularly bloody encounter, Sharon disputed the Israeli policy of supporting the Jordanian monarch. Instead, he advocated the substitution of a Palestinian state for that of Jordan in the hope that this would satisfy the Palestinians, and leave Judea and Samaria (or the West Bank, as it came to be known since its annexation to Jordan in 1950) in Israeli hands. In the summer of 1982, as minister of defense, Sharon drove the PLO out of Lebanon, where it had been based after its expulsion from Jordan, in an attempt to eliminate the organization as a military and political factor and pave the way for a possible settlement between Israel and the residents of the West Bank and Gaza.

Now that he was confronted yet again with his archenemy, Arafat instinctively resorted to a mixture of appeasement and bluster. In a televised address to the Palestinian Legislative Council on March 10, 2001, he called for the resumption of the negotiations at the point where they had been stopped but only if their outcome was predestined to "attain [Palestinian] national rights, safeguard their holy Christian and Islamic sites, and secure their rights to return, self-determination, and the establishment of an independent state with holy Jerusalem as its capital."[1]

Since it was clear that Sharon would not concede these demands, especially the Palestinian "right of return," having just been swept into power on a tidal wave of public resentment of Palestinian rejectionism, Arafat saw little choice but to escalate the fighting, in order to break the prime minister's resolve or, better yet, bring about his political demise, as he had done to his three ill-fated predecessors—Peres, Netanyahu, and Barak—during the past five years. "Escalate terror inside Israel to a point where no Israeli feels free or safe," Ziad Abu Ziad, a senior cabinet member and one of the foremost Palestinian moderates, described the new Palestinian strategy.

> Make them fear going to the malls or coffee shops, taking buses or trying to live normal lives. Bring the war onto the doorstep of Israeli society that, until now, as a whole, has hardly felt the effects of this intifada at all.[2]

This is indeed what happened. Sharon's nascent electoral victory disappeared from Israeli headlines when a powerful car bomb exploded in an ultra-Orthodox neighborhood in Jerusalem, injuring four people. A week later, on February 15, eight people were murdered and twenty-five injured when a bus driven by a Palestinian terrorist plowed into a group of passengers waiting at a bus stop near Holon, south of Tel Aviv. By the time Sharon held his first cabinet meeting on March 13, four more Israelis had been killed in two additional suicide bombings.

To everyone's surprise, the new prime minister reacted with restraint, a manner that was least expected of him. Mindful of the divisiveness caused by his 1982 Lebanon war, Sharon took great pains to unite the nation behind his policies, going so far as to entrust the key ministries of defense and foreign affairs to the rival Labor Party. While the merits of this move were obvious—a war on terror led by Defense Minister Binyamin Ben-Eliezer and defended by Nobel Peace Prize laureate Foreign Minister Peres would be far more amenable to both domestic and international audiences—it also reflected a conscious decision by Sharon to narrow his military maneuverability for the sake of national unity as his Labor partners were unlikely to accept the kind of response that a purely right-wing government would have adopted.

Since Sharon believed that Arafat's war was as much anathema for many Palestinians as for their Israeli counterparts, he sought to ease the suffering of the civilian population while at the same time intensifying the military, political, and economic pressures on their belligerent leadership. In its first meeting on March 14, the security cabinet, comprising about half of the government's members, decided to lift a number of economic sanctions against the Palestinians but refrained from transferring money owed the Palestinian Authority. "Unfortunately, PA elements and forces under its control are intensively engaged in terror, violence, and incitement." A special statement from the Prime Minister's Office promised that the government would immediately allow raw materials, such as cement and other building material, into the PA areas and would also permit fishing off Gaza. It took measures to let merchandize into PA territory and allow the marketing of products from it, as well as free travel between the West Bank and the Gaza Strip in accordance with security requirements. At the same time, the IDF began reducing the number of tanks deployed in the West Bank, eased the cordon around Ramallah, and removed the closure on Qalqilya, Tulkarm, Bethlehem, and Hebron. A few days later, Defense Minister Ben-Eliezer approved a number of additional measures to stimulate the Palestinian economy, such as the issuance of permits for five hundred Palestinian businessmen to enter Israel for commercial purposes and the limited opening of border crossings with Jordan and Egypt. As late as May 21, 2001, in response to the publication of the report by the international fact-finding committee headed by former U.S. senator George Mitchell, Sharon announced a unilateral cease-fire, ordering IDF forces to open fire only when their lives were endangered.[3]

When dealing with Arafat, restraint proved counterproductive. On March 7, less than a week before the inauguration of the Sharon government, Arafat had secretly instructed his security chiefs to suspend shooting attacks on civilian Israeli vehicles. Several factors combined to produce this rather unusual step. Hamas, which Arafat had welcomed into his war from its start, seemed to be gaining too much prestige to the liking of the *rais*. Then there were the bitter recriminations of the Beit Jalla and Bethlehem residents about the transformation of their towns into battle zones following their use by Tanzim for attacks against Jerusalem's Gilo neighborhood. Arafat also feared an unpredictable response by the incoming prime minister in the event of an excessive terrorist attack, but having concluded that Sharon would follow a policy of restraint he ordered his forces to escalate the fighting.

On March 18, for the first time since the beginning of the war, and just after Sharon had announced the resumption of security cooperation with the Palestinians, members of Force 17, Arafat's praetorian guard, fired mortar shells from the Gaza Strip into the neighboring kibbutz of Nahal Oz, within Israel's pre-1967 territory. Force 17 was also implicated in the running of a large terrorist ring, uncovered by the Israeli security services in mid-March as it was about to stage a spectacular bombing in Jerusalem. In his evidence to the Knesset's Foreign Affairs and Defense Committee, the Israeli chief of staff, Lieutenant General Shaul Mofaz, revealed that over 60 percent of Israel's fatalities up to that point had been caused by the PA's security forces and Tanzim, with Force 17 spearheading this murderous spree and Hamas and the Islamic Jihad given free rein, if not tacit support, by the PA.

Though describing the Nahal Oz attack as unacceptable, Ben-Eliezer insisted that Israel would not fall for this transparent ploy to escalate the conflict. Sharon, upon being asked by an American interviewer whether he shared Mofaz's definition of the PA as a "terrorist entity," paused for a moment before replying evasively, "One must look at the facts. And the facts are that most terrorist attacks are executed by people who have been armed by the PA, with some of the shooting attacks on Israeli civilians carried out by the closest people to Arafat, belonging to his personal guard unit known as Force 17."[4]

The recent escalation only served to reinforce Sharon's sense of purpose. Unlike the hyperactive and overambitious Barak, Sharon had no illusions about his ability to resolve the hundred-year war between Arabs and Jews in the course of a single summit, believing instead in patient perseverance that would eventually convince the inherently hostile Arab world of its inability to destroy Israel and drive it to accept the reality of Jewish statehood. In his view, it was the left-wing's obsession with quick fixes and shortcuts, born of war weariness and a loss of purpose, that had led to the creation of a terrorist entity on Israel's borders. Now that this experiment had resulted in the worst terror onslaught in Israel's history, it had to be discarded in favor of a far slower and more cautious progression toward peace, through a string of long-term interim agreements that would create a connection between Palestinian compliance with written obligations and their advance toward statehood.

As an initial step, Arafat had to make a clear and concerted effort to quell both incitements to violence and the violence itself. As long as hostilities continued, there would be no further negotiations, only a relentless fight against Palestinian terrorism in which Israel would take the necessary action to protect its citizens, which would undoubtedly include deep incursions into PA-held territories. "There is no reason to see 'A' areas, in which the Palestinians have full authority, as sacrosanct," argued Major General (res.) Meir Dagan, Sharon's adviser on counterterrorism who would later become head of Mossad, Israel's celebrated intelligence agency. "I see no reason why Israel, which sent forces to rescue hostages in Entebbe, shouldn't send forces across the lines into Area A." He added, "I am not suggesting we should reconquer these territories. But we should go in and out to deal with terrorists. Under Barak, we gave the A areas immunity, and they turned into terrorist safe havens."[5]

On March 23, Sharon revealed that he had passed messages on to Arafat that unless he reined in the terror activities of Force 17, Israel would take matters into its own hands. Five days later, after three suicide bombings had killed two Israelis and wounded dozens, and a ten-month-old baby girl was murdered by a Palestinian sniper while in her mother's arms, Israel launched an air strike against Force 17 headquarters in Gaza and

Ramallah. On April 12, in response to a mortar attack on Israeli settlements in the Gaza Strip, the IDF carried out its first ground incursion into "Area A" since the beginning of the war, entering the Khan Yunis refugee camp and destroying a number of buildings that had been used by the Palestinians to launch mortar attacks and shoot at nearby Israeli communities and army posts. Five days later, a much larger operation was launched following yet another mortar attack on the small Israeli town of Sderot, some four kilometers from the northern tip of the Gaza Strip. Tanks, bulldozers, and infantry rolled into Gaza at several points, cutting the strip into thirds, in a raid that, according to its commander, would continue "for days, weeks, or even months." The soldiers were ultimately withdrawn within hours, under intense U.S. pressure.

While the Palestinians were delighted with Israel's apparent buckling to American pressure, they took notice that the new U.S. administration, which took office in January 2001 under President George W. Bush, was not only far less indulgent of Arafat than its predecessor, but also adopted a diametrically opposed approach to the Middle East problem. Rather than make a sustained effort to engineer a final-status agreement, the new administration viewed Clinton's deep engagement in the conflict as a grave error, maintaining that it was up to the Israelis and the Palestinians to demonstrate the seriousness of their interest in peace, with external parties acting as facilitators rather than catalysts of this process. After his first meeting with Sharon, on March 20, President Bush said he would not "try to force peace . . . we will facilitate peace, and we will work with those responsible for peace."[6]

In his first visit to the West Bank on February 25, prior to the formation of the Sharon government, Secretary of State Colin Powell told Arafat that he must immediately significantly reduce the level of violence, after which time the administration would move to shore up the Palestinian Authority, and only by Stage Three would it be possible to start talking about resuming negotiations with Israel. As for Arafat's invitation to Washington (the *rais* had been President Clinton's most frequent foreign visitor), this could happen only after he had reined in violence or, at the very least, addressed his own people—in Arabic—and instructed them to end hostilities.[7]

In his testimony to the House International Relations Subcommittee on the Middle East and South Asia, Edward Walker, assistant secretary of state for Near East Affairs, praised the measures taken by Sharon to ease the economic hardships of Palestinians while criticizing the Palestinian leader for encouraging violence:

> We've seen absolutely no response from Arafat to our urgings to him to now bring the violence to a stop. He has made no statements that would indicate that he even wants to see it stopped. In fact he has called for the continuation of the intifada. He has not given any orders secret or otherwise to his forces which would bring some measure of control over the situation.

Conceding that the Palestinian leader had planned his war well before Sharon's visit to Temple Mount in late September 2000, Walker believed that Arafat was in complete control of the situation. "His forces are prepared to do what he wants them to do. So we're perplexed."[8]

Walker's confusion was unwarranted, for Arafat's dictate was clear. Having launched his terrorist war with the clear aim of imposing his "peace" conditions on Israel, it was understood that the Oslo process had outlived its usefulness, having allowed the PLO to entrench itself in the territories but not to establish an independent Palestinian state in the West Bank and Gaza without ending its historic conflict with Israel. A new and critical stage in the PLO's struggle had begun, in which Israel would be coerced through sustained military and political pressure to concede this demand, as well as to allow millions of implacably hostile Palestinian refugees to swamp its territory in what would inexorably lead to its destruction. Succumbing to Palestinian pressure, Barak had come to the verge of surrender in the Taba summit. Now Sharon would have to move the extra mile in this direction, or vacate his place to an Israeli leader who would do so. Until then, the war would go on.

As for the U.S. administration, Arafat reasoned that if it wished to delude itself that it could keep a safe distance from the conflict and ignore "the most important person in the Middle East equation," as he had styled himself, then the conflict would steadily be escalated until it drew America's attention. This pointed message was conveyed as early as Powell's February 2001 West Bank visit, when shortly after his departure squads of Force 17 operatives, which had guarded him during the visit, shot and wounded Jewish settlers in a number of incidents just north of Ramallah.

Earlier, with split-second synchronization, a huge anti-American demonstration, in which effigies of the secretary of state were burned, had marched through the city center a few minutes after Powell had passed by, managing to make a point without interfering with the convoy.

In the following months Arafat further antagonized the administration both by doing nothing to rein in Palestinian violence (in April and May 2001 there were more than 1,200 terrorist attacks, including seven suicide bombings) and by consistently misleading U.S. officials about his actions and intentions. For example, he promised President Bush over the phone, as well as Middle East envoy William Burns during a visit in late May, that he would send his key security people to a meeting with Israeli security chiefs. Although subsequent meetings have convened, Palestinian officers failed to show up to that initial session.[9]

On Friday night June 1, a suicide bomber blew himself up outside a Tel Aviv disco while standing among a large group of teenagers waiting to enter the place, killing twenty-one people and wounding 120. Confronted with an American ultimatum to sever all contacts with the PLO unless Arafat issued an immediate call for a cease-fire, a European Union (EU) threat to suspend economic aid to the PA, and the specter of an Israeli invasion that could topple his regime, a visibly exasperated Arafat, standing beside the German foreign minister Joschka Fischer, who had heard the bomb blast from his Tel Aviv hotel, solemnly pledged "to do all that is needed to achieve an immediate, unconditional, real, and effective cease-fire."

The appeal achieved its immediate objective. Shocked by the latest carnage, the Israeli cabinet decided to change its approach to Arafat and the PA, which were "engaged in terrorism, encouraging terrorism, and inciting to hatred and violence." (Precisely a week before the bombing the PA-appointed mufti of Jerusalem, Ikrima Sabri, called in his Friday sermon, broadcast on the PA's television, for further suicide bombings against Israel.) Having considered a string of far-reaching retaliatory measures, including the possible expulsion of Arafat from the territories, the government ordered the IDF to launch a massive strike against the Authority, only to hold back following Arafat's cease-fire call and the administration's decision to send George Tenet, the CIA chief, to the region to try to stabilize the situation. Later that week, despite sporadic incidents in the West Bank and Gaza, Israel began to relax the blockade it had imposed around the territories after the atrocity. "Restraint is also an element of strength," Sharon explained.[10]

It is unlikely the prime minister believed his own words, knowing how difficult it was to extract the cease-fire call from Arafat. For two full hours the Palestinian leader haggled with Fischer, who came to his Ramallah headquarters understanding the need for such an appeal. Speaking in Arabic and raising his voice at his distinguished guest, Arafat claimed that he had been fighting terrorism for months and that a public cease-fire call would be interpreted as an admission of inaction on his part. It was only upon realizing that the EU, which had been unquestioningly indulging him for years, was adamant on a cease-fire call that he finally agreed. Like a hostage reading a prepared statement with his captors standing at his shoulder, Arafat recited the agreed-upon text of the cease-fire call, indicating clearly that it had been forced upon him against his will.[11]

On June 24, three weeks after the atrocity, a German TV network aired an item on the Tel Aviv bomber. In one segment of the report, the bomber's sister was shown flipping through a scrapbook that included pictures, news clippings, and letters regarding her brother's homicidal attack. The camera then focused on a letter from Arafat, sent in his name by the Palestinian embassy in Jordan, in which he praised the murderer's heroism. "With hearts that believe in Allah's will and predetermination, we have received the news about the martyrdom of the martyr," Arafat had his embassy write to the family. "The heroic martyrdom operation [of the man] who turned his body into a bomb [is] the model of manhood and sacrifice for the sake of Allah and the homeland . . . [signed] Yasser Arafat."[12]

This message was not lost on the Palestinians. Hamas and Islamic Jihad, integral parts of Arafat's terror coalition from the outbreak of hostilities, dismissed the cease-fire call out of hand as did PA officials and commanders in Arafat's own Fatah organization, vowing not to lay down their weapons despite their leader's public call to do so. While terrorist attacks in June 2001 dropped to their lowest level since the beginning of the war—"only" 368 incidents—in July they regained their past momentum, and in August they leaped to 1,073 attacks (including four suicide bombings)—making it the war's second most violent month to that time.[13] The most horrendous of these took place on August 9 at the Sbarro pizzeria in down-town Jerusalem, where fifteen people were murdered and 130 injured. As the bomber stepped into the eatery during lunchtime, the place was buzz-ing with families, enjoying a day out during the summer vacation. The heartbreaking shouts of wounded children realizing that they had lost limbs in the explosion traumatized the nation yet again, rallying the pub-lic behind a massive strike against the PA.

Israel again responded with restraint. By this time the June discotheque bombing had seemingly been all but forgotten, and international pressure on Arafat had withered away. Both the Mitchell report and the blueprint put forward by George Tenet following his Middle East visit sought to return Israelis and Palestinians to the negotiating table by refraining from identifying the aggressor and urging both sides to show "restraint." Walk-ing the tightrope between the need to clamp down on Palestinian terror-ism and the risk of international censure for the use of "disproportionate force," the Israeli government opted for a surgical military strike against Palestinian police headquarters in Rammalah coupled with a political body blow—the closure of Orient House, the de facto Palestinian Foreign Ministry. Until then, successive Israeli governments had turned a blind eye to Arafat's regular use of the site for such activities as intelligence gathering, diplomatic meetings, and political sessions, in flagrant violation of his commitment under the Oslo accords to forgo any governmental activities outside the areas under his control. In closing down the Pales-tinian flagship in East Jerusalem, Sharon sent a thinly veiled message of his determination to keep the city united under Israel's sovereignty, some-thing that his ill-fated predecessor had given up in Camp David, and, more concretely, of the potential closure of further Palestinian institutions should Arafat fail to rein in terror.[14]

This tough political message failed to improve the situation. Terror attacks continued unabated, and on September 9 a suicide bomber blew himself up in a busy railway station in the northern town of Nahariya, kill-ing three people and wounding ninety. Meanwhile, those in the Palestin-ian leadership who, rightly or wrongly, questioned the prudence of the continuation of the carnage, such as Abu Mazen and Jibril Rajoub, were kept at arm's length from the corridors of power. "The Jews," Arafat kept on telling his entourage, "will yet make the fatal mistake; all that is re-quired is patience. A bomb that misses its target and hits a concentration of people, or some other operational hitch. Something will happen to turn the tables," he reassured them, "and what now looks like an unprofitable investment will yet be converted into a successful gambit."[15]

The September 11 terror attack on the United States, and President Bush's proclaimed war on terror, drove Arafat into feigned solidarity with the American people, lest he end up on the administration's enemies' list. "We completely condemn this very dangerous attack," he said, weeping as he spoke to foreign reporters, "and I convey my condolences to the American people, to the American president, and to the American administration, not only in my name but on behalf of the Palestinian people." He even gave blood to be sent to the United States in full view of television crews from around the world.[16]

Arafat had good reason to be worried. Aside from the PLO's long terrorist track record, including its deep involvement in a vicious war of terror by the time of the September 11 atrocity, for years the Palestinian Authority had been systematically indoctrinating its subjects with hatred for the United States. At the same time that it assiduously lobbied the administration for political backing and economic support, the PA was castigating the United States in the vilest possible language, with its appointed mufti of Jerusalem pleading to Allah "to destroy America as it is controlled by Zionist Jews."[17]

When the Clinton administration in November 1997 threatened Saddam Hussein with punitive action if he continued to obstruct UN attempts to trace and destroy Iraq's remaining weapons of mass destruction, huge demonstrations in support of Iraq were held in Palestinian towns, with Arafat sending his public "blessings to the brotherly Iraqi people and its leadership." Hafez Barghouthi, editor of the PA's largest newspaper, *al-Hayat al-Jadida,* claimed that "History will not remember the United States, but it will remember Iraq, the cradle of civilization, and Palestine, the cradle of religions."[18] In a macabre coincidence, on the very day that Osama bin Laden's terrorists steered three hijacked airplanes into the World Trade Center and the Pentagon, an article in *al-Hayat al-Jadida* lauded suicide bombers as "the salt of the earth, the engines of history . . . the most honorable people among us," heaping special praise on "the Lebanese suicide bombers who taught the U.S.

marines a tough lesson."[19] (In September 1982, following the Sabra and Shatila massacre, the United States sent a marine force to Beirut to protect the Palestinians, but withdrew it shortly afterward following a suicide bombing of their barracks which killed 241 marines.)

In the wake of the September 11 atrocity, mass celebrations were held in Palestinian towns and cities. The incidents were far from isolated and sparsely attended as reported later by Palestinian apologists. Thousands of people took to the streets, chanting Allah Akbar (God is Great), distributing candies to passersby, and shooting guns in the air to express their delight. To keep these disturbing scenes from world attention, PA security forces confiscated filmed footage and intimidated foreign journalists, news agencies, and television networks. In Gaza, Palestinian policemen detained cameramen who had filmed a Hamas demonstration in which Palestinians carried pictures of Osama bin Laden. In Nablus, foreign photojournalists were reportedly forced to remain confined in their hotels, guarded by armed Palestinians—both in uniform and in plain clothes—while crowds celebrated in the streets. A freelance photographer on assignment for Associated Press Television News, who had somehow managed to film the festivities, was summoned to the Nablus security office and warned that the material must not be aired. This was backed by death threats from Tanzim operatives. Ahmad Abdel Rahman, Arafat's cabinet secretary, threatened Associated Press producers that the PA "cannot guarantee the life" of the cameraman if the footage was broadcast.

In a terse protest to the Palestinian Authority, the Foreign Press Association, representing hundreds of mainstream journalists in Israel, expressed deep concern over

> [t]he harassment of journalists by the Palestinian Authority as police forces and armed gunmen tried to prevent photo and video coverage of Tuesday's rally in Nablus where hundreds of Palestinians celebrated the terror attacks in N.Y. and Washington. We strongly condemn the direct threats made against local videographers by local militia members and the attitude of Palestinian officials who made no effort to counter the threats, control the situation, or to guarantee the safety of the journalists and the freedom of the press.

Information Minister Yasser Abd Rabbo denied any harassment of journalists, and Hanan Ashrawi, the PA's most eloquent spokesperson, worked hard to convince the international media that no mass celebrations had taken place. Arafat dismissed these celebrations as involving "less than ten children in east Jerusalem."[20]

On September 19, bowing to intense American pressure, Arafat announced a forty-eight-hour cease-fire to pave the way for a meeting with Foreign Minister Peres. Sharon reciprocated by ordering the IDF to pull back from Area A, and to stop all offensive operations against the Palestinians, including targeted killing of key terrorists. The meeting with Peres took place on September 26, but like similar occasions in the past there were no concrete results. A day before making his announcement, Arafat told leaders from the various Palestinian factions that this was a move born out of dire necessity. Unless the PA accepted a cease-fire, it might become the target of a massive Israeli assault in the wake of an American attack on Afghanistan.

Despite Arafat's cease-fire pledge, clashes between Israeli and Palestinian forces continued in the Gaza Strip, with the steep rise in terrorist attacks in October 2001 making it the fourth most violent month in the then thirteen-month-long war. The three-week lull in bombings inside Israel following September 11 came to an abrupt end on October 1, when a car bomb exploded in a Jerusalem neighborhood, wounding a number of people. This was followed later that month by two more suicide bombings, and two more in November.

In the last of these attacks, on November 29, a suicide bomber blew himself up on a bus en route from Nazareth to Tel Aviv, killing three people and wounding nine. This was by no means a high tally as compared to previous similar atrocities, yet its importance by far exceeded its actual carnage. It was the first suicide bombing by Arafat's own Fatah organization, which eagerly claimed responsibility, and it was executed in cooperation with Islamic Jihad.[21] At a time when Arafat was feigning a commitment to a cease-fire, the forces under his direct command were actively colluding with some of the most extreme terrorist groups in carrying out attacks.

Yet worse was to come. Just before midnight on December 1, two suicide bombers detonated powerful explosive devices in Jerusalem's main pedestrian mall, bustling with late-night revelers on their Saturday night outing. Eleven people were killed and about 180 injured. Less than twelve hours later, as the names of the Jerusalem victims were being released, another fifteen people were murdered and forty injured in a suicide attack on a Haifa bus. In between these atrocities, an Israeli civilian was shot dead in the Gaza Strip. Later the same day, a soldier and border policeman were shot and seriously wounded in two separate attacks.

Visiting the site of the Jerusalem attack the following day, U.S. special envoy to the Middle East General (ret.) Anthony Zinni could hardly conceal his shock and disgust. "This is the deepest evil that one can imagine, to attack young people and children, to attack rescue and emergency vehicles that are trying to come in," he said. "This is the lowest form of inhumanity that can be imagined, and I think that it is important that we do not let it deter us from our goal for peace."

Sharon, who learned of the attacks while on an official visit to Washington, had more pressing needs in mind than an eventual return to the negotiating table. When told by President Bush during their one-hour meeting at the White House of Bush's demand that Arafat arrest the perpetrators of the latest attacks and take concrete and serious action against Hamas and Islamic Jihad, the prime minister expressed skepticism. How could Arafat be expected to act against the militant Islamic groups at a time when his own Fatah organization had just carried out a joint suicide bombing with Islamic Jihad, and when Tanzim fighters in Beit Jalla and Bethlehem, temporarily holding their fire so as to avoid embarrassing Arafat, were allowing Islamic Jihad and Hamas terrorists to shoot at Jerusalem's Gilo neighborhood for payments of hundreds of shekels? What was required was not additional concessions, but an intensification of the war on terror. Since Arafat had done nothing to prevent terrorism, Israel had no choice but to fight it alone.

The recent atrocities, together with Arafat's abstention from arresting PLO terrorists who on October 17 murdered the Israeli minister of tourism, Rehavam Ze'evi (along with Arafat's bizarre claim that it was the Israeli government that had actually assassinated its own minister), confirmed Sharon's perception of Arafat as a bloodthirsty terrorist with no respect for human lives, impervious to his own people's needs and aspirations, and absolutely committed to Israel's destruction regardless of his pretences for peace.

"A war has been forced on us. A war of terror," Sharon said at a media conference upon his return to Israel. "Just as the United States is conducting its war against international terror, so too will we. With all the strength, determination, and resources we have used until today, and with resources at our disposal." He continued, "Arafat is responsible for everything that happens here." "Arafat is the greatest obstacle to peace and stability in the Middle East. We have seen this in the past, we are seeing it in the present, and will, unfortunately, probably continue to see this in the future. But," he added, "Arafat will not fool this government. This time Arafat will not succeed in fooling us."[22]

In an emergency meeting, the Sharon government declared Tanzim and Force 17 terrorist organizations, and the Palestinian Authority as "an entity that supports terrorism [that] must be dealt with accordingly." Shortly afterward Israeli airplanes and helicopters destroyed Arafat's headquarters in Jenin and, far more important, his three personal helicopters—two Mi-17s received as a gift from Russia and a German-made Bolkov 205 donated by Saddam Hussein (Arafat also had two older Mi-8s donated by Egypt, but they were believed not to be airworthy). In addition, Israel plowed up the Gaza airport runway and prevented Arafat from leaving Ramallah to attend an Arab summit in Qatar, insisting that he stay put and tackle the extremists.

While having no direct impact on the war on terror, the helicopters were one of the most potent emblems of Arafat's prowess and maneuverability. Their destruction not only dealt a painful blow to his status and prestige and effectively confined him to his Ramallah headquarters but also indicated Israel's growing readiness to encroach on the Authority and its head in the event of further deterioration. Palestinian spokesmen quickly accused Israel of trying to destroy the PA through attacks on Palestinian symbols and institutions, warning that the alternative would be far worse.[23]

This claim was only partially correct. While there is little doubt that Sharon would have been happy to see Arafat and the PA branded as "supporters of terrorism" on a par with Afghanistan's Taliban regime, which had just been toppled for harboring and supporting Osama bin Laden and his al Qaeda terror network, the prime minister's hands were tied both domestically and internationally. With Foreign Minister Peres loath to concede the collapse of the Oslo accords by trying to rehabilitate Arafat's image and remake him into the peace partner he had supposedly been, and the other Labor ministers desperate to prove their relevance by opposing Sharon's decisions at every turn (one of them criticized the destruction of Arafat's helicopters as "irresponsible"), the idea of destroying the PA was a nonstarter for the government. At a meeting with Labor's political committee on November 28, two days before the Jerusalem and Haifa massacres, Peres argued that terrorism is simply "the way a person expresses his aspirations through weapons," and must therefore be met with "carrots—and creative listening to the other side."[24]

On the international level, there was widespread reluctance, especially among EU members and the Muslim nations, to acknowledge the analogy between America's war on terror (which many opposed in the first place) and Israel's antiterror struggle. Even within the U.S. administration there were two contending schools of thought on the issue. The first, represented by Vice President Dick Cheney, Secretary of Defense Donald Rumsfeld, and National Security Adviser Condoleezza Rice, viewed terror as an absolute evil that had to be relentlessly resisted, and was therefore sympathetic to Israel's attempts to defeat the Palestinian terrorist assault. The other, articulated by Secretary Powell, warned of the dire consequences to regional stability if the United States did not at least attempt to resolve the Israeli-Palestinian conflict before forging ahead with its own war on terror.

President Bush, favorably disposed to Sharon's predicament, with whom he had established a close and warm relationship, was not impervious to Powell's attempts at persuasion. While expressing his deep sympathy for Israel, especially in the aftermath of the worst atrocities, and pressuring Arafat to rein in Palestinian terror, Bush demanded that Israel show restraint and attempt to negotiate a cease-fire with the PA rather than defeat it by force of arms as the United States was doing in Afghanistan. Whenever the IDF went into Palestinian cities, most notably after Ze'evi's assassination, the administration joined and often led international pressure on Israel to withdraw its forces.

As Israeli forces took up posts on the north and south approaches to Ramallah and moved into controlling heights southwest of Nablus to

block suicide bombers from slipping out, the Palestinian media intensified their propaganda, broadcasting songs of heroism and martial music
and urging the masses to "martyrdom." Within the span of one week
(December 5–12), four suicide bombers blew themselves up in Israeli
cities, albeit with no fatalities. Then on December 12 came another joint
terrorist attack, this time between Fatah and Hamas, on a bus making
its way from Bnei Brak, near Tel Aviv, to the town of Emmanuel in
Samaria. Having exploded two powerful roadside bombs alongside the
bus, a number of terrorists attacked the passengers and passing cars with
antitank grenades and light-arms fire, murdering ten people (another
one died later of his wounds) and injuring about thirty. One of the terrorists charged at the bus and passing vehicles firing his M-16 rifle, killing and wounding people at point-blank range.

The Israeli government responded by severing all contacts with the
PA and declared Arafat "irrelevant." The U.S. administration, while clari-
fying that it had no intention of following the Israeli example, did not
fail to signal its growing exasperation with Arafat. Asked what would
happen if the Palestinian leader failed yet again to rein in terror, Powell
opined, "The consequence for him is that he will slowly lose authority
within the region." At a closed meeting with European officials the secretary of state was far less diplomatic, reportedly telling his peers that
"If Arafat was to commit suicide, then we won't stand in his way." Recognizing the intensity of American frustration, and fearing for Arafat's
position, the Europeans appealed to Arafat to intensify his efforts to fight
Palestinian terror.[25]

Finding himself cornered yet again, Arafat reverted to another public
cease-fire call. In a televised address to his people on December 16, on
the eve of Id al-Fitr, the holiday ending the holy month of Ramdan, he
urged them to unite behind the Palestinian Authority in its struggle
against Israel's "barbaric war." Accusing Sharon of using attacks against
Israelis as a pretext to destroy the PA and to reoccupy Palestinian areas,
he announced his determination to clamp down on terrorism, "particularly the suicide bombings, which we have already condemned," vowing
to "punish anyone who provides the occupation with a pretext to act
against our people."[26]

This was undoubtedly the furthest Arafat had gone up to that point in asking for restraint by his people, and many in the international community were impressed. The Europeans praised this apparent moderation, while the U.S. administration instructed Zinni, who had returned to the United States after the Jerusalem and Haifa atrocities, to head back to the Middle East. Yet a closer inspection of the speech reveals that Arafat failed to call for the termination of hostilities, or even the indefinite ending of suicide bombings, and only for their *tactical suspension*. And he adopted this tactical measure not because he disapproved of the morality of what Amnesty International would later condemn as a crime against humanity, but because, at this particular juncture, suicide bombings were counterproductive to his own position.

Not surprisingly, the message was fully understood and decoded by its target audience. Hamas and Islamic Jihad spokesmen quickly announced on the ubiquitous *al-Jazeera* satellite television network that they would continue suicide bombings of Israelis, while a Fatah official told Israel Radio that Arafat's speech did not prohibit continued terrorism against Israelis in the West Bank and Gaza or attacks against Israeli soldiers.

Under pressure from Zinni, Arafat ordered his security forces to start closing down Hamas and Islamic Jihad institutions in the West Bank and Gaza, and even detained a number of his own policemen implicated in terrorist activities. Yet, as on numerous past occasions, this turned out to be a sham. An unnamed Palestinian security official acknowledged, "We had to do something to demonstrate to the Americans that we are serious about fighting terrorism."[27]

On December 15, a day before his Id al-Fitr address, Arafat convened a group of Palestinian intellectuals in the Casablanca Hotel in Ramallah where he detailed a long-term strategy for the destruction of the state of Israel. Two days after his televised address, he made a fiery speech in Ramallah in which he pledged to continue the struggle for the liberation of Palestinian lands and expressed his readiness to sacrifice seventy martyrs for one dead Israeli. The following month, on January 27, 2002, immediately after issuing an on-camera condemnation of this day's homicide bombing in Jerusalem, in which an elderly Israeli was murdered and more than 150 were injured, Arafat went back to his office and celebrated with his close confidants, effusively praising the "operation" carried out by a female member of his Fatah faction of the PLO, and urging more of the same.[28]

Arafat's next move was to actively lay the groundwork for the next, and far bloodier, round of fighting. Since its establishment in the spring of 1994, the PA had been systematically smuggling in large quantities of weapons in flagrant violation of its commitments under the Oslo accords. These efforts intensified after the outbreak of hostilities, leading to a number of bungled attempts in early 2001 to smuggle weapons by sea. In May, while on an official visit to Moscow, Arafat instructed two top aides—Fouad Shubaki, the PLO's chief financial officer, and Fathi Razem, deputy commander of the Palestinian naval police—to meet secretly with Iranian government officials in the Russian capital with a view to acquiring Iranian weapons, in return for access to Palestinian intelligence on Israeli military positions and defenses.

Relations between the PLO and Iran had sunk to an historic low following the signing of the Oslo accords, but a visit by Arafat to Tehran in March 1997 led to an Iranian-Palestinian rapprochement and the gradual resurrection of bilateral cooperation. Now that the Authority was offering them yet deeper collaboration, the Iranians reciprocated. The Moscow rendezvous was followed by a string of additional clandestine meetings, and in late 2001 a PA-owned vessel, *Karine A*, was loaded with some fifty tons of weapons, ammunitions, and explosives at the Iranian port at Kish island, before setting off for Gaza via the Suez Canal.

Unknown to the Palestinians and the Iranians, the operation had been closely monitored from the start by the Israelis, who in early January 2002 intercepted the ship in the Red Sea, detained its crew, and confiscated its cargo. This included sixty-two Katyusha rockets capable of hitting almost any city in Israel, hundreds of mortars and grenades, antitank and antipersonnel mines, and two tons of explosives, including one ton of C-4, nearly three times more powerful than the homemade explosives used by homicide bombers.

In absolute terms, these weapons, though prohibited by the Oslo accords, were a far cry from the IDF's formidable arsenal. Yet since Arafat's war was never an ordinary military encounter between two armed forces but rather a terror assault on an unprotected civilian population, the smuggled weapons would have produced a quantum leap in firepower that could have changed the conflict's strategic calculus.

As demonstrated by the Nazi rocket attacks on Britain, Iraq's missile offensive against Iranian cities during the Iran-Iraq War (1980–88), and the sustained PLO and Hizbullah rocket assaults on Israeli towns and villages in the Galilee during the 1980s and the '90s, a relatively small number of surface-to-surface missiles or even far less sophisticated rockets can easily terrorize large population areas. Palestinian Katyusha attacks on Tel Aviv or for that matter a "mega" atrocity claiming hundreds or thousands of civilian lives and perpetrated with the new powerful explosives would have triggered the kind of extreme Israeli response that Arafat had been desiring all along, with the attendant possible deployment of international forces in the territories, more active Arab intervention in the conflict, or, at the very least, heavy pressure on Israel to stop fighting and withdraw its forces.

Now that this scenario failed to materialize, and with Israel parading the captured weapons in front of the international media, PA officials went out of their way to disclaim any connection with the captured ship, dismissing the allegations as an Israeli ploy to discredit Arafat so as to justify increased attacks on the Palestinians. "This is a factory of lies," claimed Minister of Information Abd Rabbo. "Israel is like any colonial power. When they get in trouble, they try to blame outsiders. There has not been a single Iranian here since the fourteenth century."

Arafat went a step further. "I will tell you who was behind the *Karine A* affair," he knowingly whispered to Terje Larsen, the Oslo architect turned UN envoy to the Middle East who came to his Ramallah headquarters to plead for a reduction in hostilities. "It was Israel's Mossad. And do you know who organized the homicide bombing in Jerusalem's pedestrian mall?" he continued, to Larsen's growing disbelief. "It was Mofaz. Yes, yes, General Mofaz is very dangerous. He is against peace and is the representative of the settlers and the extreme right in the Israeli army."[29]

The specific atrocity attributed by Arafat to the Israeli chief of staff was the murder of three Israelis and the wounding of another eighty-three in a suicide bombing on Jerusalem's King George's Street on March 21, 2002. During that month, Israel experienced the worst ever suicide-bombing assault in its history, not to mention hundreds of other terrorist attacks, with bombers blowing themselves up among innocent civilians every other day. In March alone, 126 Israelis were murdered, nearly half the death toll for the entire preceding seventeen months of the war.[30]

One of these attacks, which claimed the lives of eleven Israelis, occurred at the Moment Café, a popular hangout for left-leaning Jerusalemites. The bomber managed to avoid detection by mingling with a group of Peace Now activists arriving at the venue, unperturbed by the political views of those he was about to butcher. An even more horrific attack took place at the Park Hotel in the coastal city of Netanya, when a suicide bomber killed twenty-nine people and injured another 140 while they were in the midst of the Passover holiday Seder with 250 guests.

Half of the March homicide bombings were carried out by the PLO, mostly by Tanzim's al-Aqsa Brigade, a militant unit established after the outbreak of hostilities. The Israeli response was immediate. In early March the IDF entered a number of West Bank refugee camps, which it had hitherto shunned, killing scores of terrorists and capturing hundreds. As this failed to stem the tidal wave of terror, on March 29, two days after the Seder massacre, Israel launched its biggest military operation since the 1982 Lebanon war with the specific aim of smashing the extensive terrorist infrastructure established in the West Bank since the PA's takeover six years earlier.

Code-named Operation Defensive Shield, the Israeli offensive began with an incursion into Ramallah and the surrounding of Arafat's presidential compound, followed by entry into Tulkarm, Qalqilya, Bethlehem, Jenin, and Nablus. By April 3, six of the largest cities in the West Bank, and their surrounding towns, villages, and refugee camps, had been occupied by the Israeli military, which also detained thousands of suspected terrorists, destroyed scores of bomb laboratories, and seized large quantities of weapons and explosives, including suicide-bomber belts. On April 21, Israel officially announced the operation's end.

A particularly ferocious battle took place in the refugee camp in the town of Jenin. In an attempt to minimize civilian casualties, before the start of the fighting the IDF urged the local population, using loudspeakers broadcasting in Arabic, to evacuate the camp. Approximately 11,000 did so. The Israelis then decided to engage their infantry soldiers in hand-to-hand, door-to-door combat in the camp's narrow alleys, rather than use their aircraft and artillery to bomb the terrorists into submission. This proved to be a public relations catastrophe, as the Palestinians immediately claimed the massacre of some two thousand civilians by the Israeli forces, though this number was quickly pared down to five hundred.

The international media jumped on the hoax with alacrity, and the UN quickly appointed an international fact-finding team to visit the area. As the Israeli government refused to cooperate with what it considered a deeply prejudiced move, the team made its investigations without entering the area, and on May 7, 2002, presented its report to UN Secretary-General Kofi Annan. They found no evidence whatsoever of the alleged massacre and asserted that even the reduced numer of victims claimed by a "Palestinian official" (i.e., Saeb Erekat) "has not been substantiated in the light of the evidence that has emerged." Instead, and on the basis of the Jenin hospital records, the report placed the Palestinian death toll at fifty-two, compared with Israel's twenty-three dead, but refrained from saying how many of them were civilians, noting instead the various assessments.

> Israeli officials informed United Nations personnel that they believed that, of the 52 dead, 38 were armed men and 14 were civilians. The Palestinian Authority has acknowledged that combatants were among the dead, and has named some of them, but has placed no precise estimates on the breakdown. Human rights organizations put the civilian toll closer to 20— Human Rights Watch documented 22 civilians among the 52 dead, while Physicians for Human Rights noted that "children under the age of 15 years, women and men over the age of 50 years accounted for nearly 38 per cent of all reported fatalities."[31]

Jenin again served Arafat by diverting world public opinion from the pervasive terrorist infrastructure uncovered in the territories under his control. In Arafat's own Ramallah presidential compound (or the Muqata'a, as it is known in Arabic), the soldiers found scores of weapons and explosives, including forty-three RPG antitank rocket launchers prohibited by the Oslo accords, four pipe bombs, an unspecified number of empty suicide-bomber belts, substances for the preparation of chemical weapons, as well as hundreds of thousands of counterfeit Israeli bills in denominations of 50, 100, and 200 shekels, printing plates for counterfeiting millions more, and $100,000 in counterfeit U.S. bills.[32] Arafat was also found to be sheltering in his compound the masterminds of the Ze'evi assassination, whom he had promised to arrest months earlier and whose whereabouts he had feigned ignorance. Caught red-handed, Arafat presided over a summary trial, sentenced the culprits to various periods of imprisonment, and had them transferred to a jail in Jericho where they were to be detained, together with Fouad Shubaki of the *Karine A* affair, under Anglo-American supervision.

The most damning and virtually incontrovertible evidence of Arafat's, the Palestinian Authority's, and its security forces' deep involvement in terrorist activities was provided by the hundreds of thousands of documents seized by the Israelis in the Muqata'a and other PA headquarters throughout the West Bank. Though no "smoking gun" linking Arafat with specific terrorist attacks has been found, the Israelis have unearthed massive evidence of his personal remuneration of numerous terrorists, of close cooperation between the al-Aqsa Brigade, Fatah's main terrorist arm, and the militant Islamic groups, and of the PA's leniency toward, if not complicity with, Hamas and Islamic Jihad terrorists.

The Palestinians quickly dismissed the documents as an Israeli fabrication. The international media were amenable to this claim, as were many European governments who were loath to concede that a substantial part of the money they had given the Palestinians had been used to finance terror attacks rather than to help impoverished Palestinians. Yet once the authenticity of the documents was universally recognized, the PA conveyed an official demand, through European institutions, to have the documents returned to them on the grounds that it could not function without them. Germany sent its own experts from the Federal Intelligence Service (BND) to conduct an investigation, and in mid-April 2002 the BND filed its first report, which verified the documents' authenticity and agreed with the Israeli conclusions. Its second report, filed two weeks later, reaffirmed the conclusions of its precursor and asserted that "Arafat evidently doesn't distinguish between the structure of the Palestinian Authority and his Fatah Movement" and therefore: "At no point could it be realistically assumed that EU-funds were . . . 100% accounted for." Following these reports, the BND quietly suspended the antiterror training it had been covertly giving to the PA for several years.[33]

Having never shared his predecessor's warmth toward the Palestinian leader, President Bush by the end of 2001 had apparently come to view

Arafat as the fundamental block to peace in the region.[34] After the *Karine A* Iranian affair the president was furious over Arafat's unabashed denial, in a personal letter, of any prior knowledge of the bungled operation. In a phone conversation with Egyptian president Hosni Mubarak, Bush voiced his extreme disappointment over the Palestinian-Iranian arms deal "because I was led to believe [Arafat] was willing to join us in the fight on terror. I took him at his word." (As late as June 23, 2002, Arafat still denied that the PA had anything to do with the *Karine A* smuggling attempt, arguing that the weapons were destined for Lebanon's Hizbullah organization.)

Vice President Cheney echoed this sentiment in public. "We don't believe him," he said, brushing aside Arafat's feigned innocence. "Based on the intelligence we've seen, the people that were involved were so close to him it's hard to believe that he wasn't." Cheney added:

> The really disturbing part of this, of course, is that there are a lot of places he could go in the Arab world if he were looking for support and sustenance or for help in moving the peace process forward. Clearly, he hasn't done that. What he's done is gone to a terrorist organization, Hizbullah, and a state that supports and promotes terrorism, that's dedicated to ending the peace process, Iran, and done business with them.[35]

Bush was quietly sympathetic to Israel's harsh response to the March 2002 terror offensive, and it was only on April 4, about a week after the start of Operation Defensive Shield, that he publicly urged Israel to "halt incursions into Palestinian areas [and to] begin the withdrawal from the cities it has occupied." Yet this call, which he repeated with a greater sense of urgency a couple of days later, was merely a means to deflect international criticism of his administration's alleged aloofness vis-à-vis the Middle East crisis, as was the dispatching of Secretary of State Powell to the region to try to negotiate a cease-fire. Having lost all trust in Arafat, Bush was skeptical about the success of Powell's mission. "You're going to have to spend some political capital," he told him. "You have plenty. I need you to do it."[36]

No sooner had Powell returned empty-handed from the Middle East than harsh voices began to emanate from Washington. In his meetings with U.S. officials during Operation Defensive Shield, former prime minister Netanyahu was repeatedly asked why Israel had failed to ex-

ploit the operation in order to get rid of Arafat. On May 5, during a visit
by Sharon to Washington in which he tried to convince his hosts to sever
all ties with Arafat and start cultivating a new generation of Palestinian
leaders, National Security Adviser Condoleezza Rice publicly called for
the reform of the PA. "We are not going to try to choose the leadership
for the Palestinian people. Chairman Arafat is there . . . but he does have
responsibilities that he has not been meeting and we are going to press
him," she told the *Fox News Sunday* program.

> We are going to call on Arab allies, the Europeans, and others to press him
> and we are going to be very clear that the Palestinian leadership that is
> there now, the authority, is not the kind of leadership that can lead to
> the kind of Palestinian state that we need. It has got to reform.

The Palestinian leadership must be "democratic, transparent, and non-
corrupt," Rice concluded. "[This is] what we ask of every government
in the world. And we are going to start demanding [that] of the Palestinian leadership."[37]

Though the U.S. State Department had sought to promote a cease-
fire by pressuring Israel rather than the Palestinian Authority, President
Bush was increasingly won over to the idea of Palestinian reform. Already
during Sharon's May visit Bush voiced support for reforms in the PA,
though he did not yet call for Arafat's replacement, as suggested by the
Israeli prime minister. "Mr. Arafat has let the Palestinian people down.
He hasn't led," he said, adding that "there's a high level of disappointment" with the Palestinian leader. "He has disappointed me. He must
lead. He must show the world that he believes in peace."[38]

Bush's exasperation with Arafat was further reinforced by both a string
of suicide bombings (one of which resulted in sixteen people murdered
and fifty-five wounded in a crowded gaming club in Rishon Lezion,
southeast of Tel Aviv, and took place while Sharon was in Washington),
and fresh evidence from Israeli intelligence of Arafat's cultivation of
terrorism. The president was particularly appalled by the murder of seven
Israelis, on June 19, by a suicide bomber who blew himself up at a crowded
bus stop and hitchhiking post in Jerusalem as people were returning
home from work. The atrocity was quickly condemned by Arafat, but it
soon transpired that the bomber had belonged to Fatah's al-Aqsa Brigade, answerable directly to Arafat himself.[39]

"For too long, the citizens of the Middle East have lived in the midst of death and fear," Bush argued emphatically in a long-awaited speech on June 24, 2002. "And this casts a dark shadow over an entire region . . . For the sake of all humanity, things must change in the Middle East," he said, gradually coming to the main point of his speech:

> My vision is two states, living side by side, in peace and security. There is simply no way to achieve that peace until all parties fight terror . . .
> Peace requires a new and different Palestinian leadership, so that a Palestinian state can be born. I call on the Palestinian people to elect new leaders, leaders not compromised by terror.

"A Palestinian state will never be created by terror," Bush warned.

> It will be built through reform. And reform must be more than cosmetic change or a veiled attempt to preserve the status quo. True reform will require entirely new political and economic institutions based on democracy, market economics and action against terrorism.

Having outlined his demands of Palestinian society, the president quickly moved to underscore the substantial gains attending the envisaged regime change.

> If the Palestinian people actively pursue these goals, America and the world will actively support their efforts. If the Palestinian people meet these goals, they will be able to reach agreement with Israel and Egypt and Jordan on security and other arrangements for independence.
> And when the Palestinian people have new leaders, new institutions and new security arrangements with their neighbors, the United States of America will support the creation of a Palestinian state, whose borders and certain aspects of its sovereignty will be provisional until resolved as part of a final settlement in the Middle East . . .
> Today, the Palestinian people live in economic stagnation, made worse by official corruption. A Palestinian state will require a vibrant economy, where honest enterprise is encouraged by honest government.
> The United States, the international donor community and the World Bank stand ready to work with Palestinians on a major project of economic reform and development. The United States, the EU, the World Bank and the International Monetary Fund are willing to oversee reforms in Palestinian finances, encouraging transparency and independent au-

diting. And the United States, along with our partners in the developed world, will increase our humanitarian assistance to relieve Palestinian suffering.[40]

The significance of Bush's speech cannot be overstated. Here was the leader of the free world and of the only remaining superpower proposing the creation of a Palestinian state in short order, yet conditioning this development on the substitution of an entirely new Palestinian leadership for the existing regime.

Arafat immediately set about subverting the president's initiative. While implying his readiness to introduce certain reforms, especially in the finance and the judicial systems—two areas of considerable American concern—he emphasized that only the Palestinians were entitled to choose their own leadership and indicated his intention to hold new elections by early 2003, in which he would be a candidate.

This public show of confidence barely disguised Arafat's grave concern. Not only did Operation Defensive Shield result in the virtual decimation of the Palestinian Authority and its institutions, but the IDF had reestablished a lasting presence there, steadily and persistently eradicating the remaining terror manifestations in Palestinian territories. (Though suicide bombings continued after Operation Defensive Shield, their frequency has been substantially reduced, while the overall number of West Bank terrorist attacks has dropped to a fraction of its former levels.) This has led to a rapid deterioration in Arafat's standing among his Palestinian subjects. "We all remember the words of Palestinian officials who said that if Israel ever dared to reenter our areas, they would teach it an unforgettable lesson," said an embittered Fatah operative in Tulkarm. "Now we know that all these threats were worth nothing." A Bethlehem schoolteacher expressed his resentment of Arafat using a more colorful language. "Eight years ago," he said, "he came to Gaza and Jericho and said, 'I'll make it into Hong Kong.' Instead, he turned it into Somalia. He's like a pair of old shoes. It's time for him to be cast aside."[41]

In early July 2002, for the first time since the establishment of the Palestinian Authority eight years earlier, thousands of Gazans took to the streets to protest against the PA's failure to provide them with jobs or financial assistance against a background of rapidly burgeoning unemployment and poverty. Marching from the parliament building to Arafat's Gaza headquarters, they chanted angry slogans, including the refrain "Where are the millions?" routinely used by the Palestinian media to inflame spirits and bring the masses to the streets for violent demonstrations. Only now the demonstrators had other millions in mind, those donated to the Palestinians by the international community that had disappeared into the secret bank accounts of Arafat and his PLO and PA cronies.[42]

Even Arafat's close associates were not deterred from harsh criticism of his leadership style, or even from direct calls for his removal. "Wherever Arafat goes, lawlessness, corruption, and instability follow," lamented Abbas Zaki, a veteran Fatah leader and a longtime Arafat supporter, who returned to the West Bank in 1994 following the signing of the Oslo accords. "There should be honor in the battlefield. When you lose, you quit." Hussam Khader, a member of the Palestinian Legislative Council and an influential leader of Fatah in the Balata refugee camp near Nablus, concurred. "I don't think that Arafat cares about anything other than being in power," he argued. "When Arafat disappears, they will write about him as they wrote about Mao—they will write about his criminality and his catastrophes." Khader was doubtful as to whether this would happen in the foreseeable future. "Arafat will win this election in spite of the fact that everybody blames him for destroying Palestinian life and keeping thieves in his government," he said. "We are like the Bedouin. We follow our sheik. It is not easy to leave your traditional culture. We have to wait until God takes this sheik to him."[43]

In an article in the PA daily *al-Ayyam* on the first anniversary of the September 11 atrocity, the prominent Palestinian journalist Tawfiq Abu Bakr bitterly complained about the PA's policy. "Oslo's rationale is predicated on one basic principle, namely Israel's withdrawal from Palestinian land (a single inch of which the entire Arab world has failed to liberate by force of arms) in return for our ensuring of security in the territory transferred to us and the prevention of armed operations from it," he wrote. "Had we strictly implemented this commitment, Benjamin Netanyahu would have not come to power and the final-status talks would have been concluded as scheduled in May 1999."[44]

The most senior critic of Arafat within the cabinet was Nabil Amr, the Palestinian Authority minister of parliamentary affairs who for years had loyally and ably defended Arafat's most extreme actions. He resigned his post in early May 2002 after the rejection of his demand for major reforms. "Everybody feels that an earthquake has taken place in Palestinian society. So the changes must be equal in size to what happened," Amr told reporters in Ramallah, referring to Operation Defensive Shield. "I say the change must come from within the Palestinian Authority."[45]

In a public letter to Arafat, published in the Beirut newspaper *al-Hayat* in early September 2002, Amr did not spare the Palestinian leader. "In our internal conflict and in our negotiating struggle with Israel, we have abandoned one of our most important weapons—that of building institutions worthy of receiving support from the world and capable of winning the trust of the Palestinians," he wrote. "What did we do to the Legislative Council? What did we do to the judiciary? What did we do to the Finance Ministry? What did we do to the administration? What did we achieve in these spheres?"

Amr rejected the claim that the PA's many shortcomings were natural manifestations of the PLO's transformation from a revolutionary movement into a ruling authority. Instead, he argued that they were the combined outcome of the PLO's inability to transcend its "outside" mentality and connect with its new "inside" constituents, first and foremost its predatory approach to the momentous task of state building. "We treated our project with the mentality of sharing booty, not of shouldering a heavy responsibility," he lamented. "Not a single committee was formed to study the qualifications of those who were given big and small jobs. In forming our governments we paid no attention to professional and behavioral considerations. We returned to the tribe as the main point of reference."

Amr piled on his criticism. "Let us be frank with each other. There are other reasons, rather than conspiracy, that have led the entire world to either oppose or fail to help us. Having a just cause does not give us a carte blanche to do whatever we want. Does the justness of our cause justify this chaos in our house? You complain about this chaos more than others do, though you are accused of encouraging it as tactical ploy to confound the enemy."

The PA's disastrous conduct, in Amr's opinion, was not limited to the domestic sphere but was also manifested in a shortsighted and extremist foreign policy.

Didn't we jump with joy over the failure of Camp David? Didn't we throw mud at the picture of President Clinton who dared submit a proposal for a [Palestinian] state with some modifications? Didn't we do this? Were we sincere with ourselves? No, we were not. This is because after two years of bloodshed we now accept what we rejected, perhaps because we have realized that it is impossible to achieve.

How many times did we accept, reject, and then accept? Our timing in saying yes or no has never been good. How many times have we been asked to do something that was within our reach but failed to do so? Then, when this something became unfeasible, we begged the world to propose it to us yet again. Between our rejection and acceptance the world either distanced itself from us or set new conditions that we could not even think of.

Now that the Palestinian national cause has been severely eclipsed—"from the point when we stood on the threshold of a state during Bill Clinton's [proposals] and Camp David, to the point where Bethlehem is rewarded by the lifting of curfew"—there is no choice but to acknowledge past mistakes, however grave, and embark on a new and more promising road. To start with, there should be a "serious domestic dialogue" among all the Palestinian factions with a view to establishing a period of calm "for redressing the Palestinian wounds and attempting to create a climate that would help us renovate our cracking home and eroded alliances." Having done this, the PA should immediately carry out comprehensive reforms in all walks of life regardless of the security situation. "Mr. President," Amr concluded his letter emotionally,

> We have not yet done what we must do. Perhaps we have become accustomed to finding justifications for our failures. How easy it is for Sharon's tanks to carry all our sins over their sins! . . .
>
> Mr. President: We have committed a serious mistake against our people, authority, and the dream of the establishment of our state. However, we can be forgiven if we admit our mistake and get to work immediately. What this people deserve is for us to work hard with them and for them—not to place their destiny at the mercy of coincidental international winds or to mortgage their future until doomsday without opening a window of hope.[46]

Epilogue

[Yasser Arafat] has appealed not to his people's best instincts, but to their worst.

—Edward W. Said, 2001

Wherever Arafat goes, lawlessness, corruption, and instability follow.

—Abbas Zaki, a prominent PLO official, July 2002

To the nineteenth-century military strategist Carl von Clausewitz, war was the continuation of politics by other means. To Yasser Arafat, peace has been the continuation of war by other means. From the beginning of Arafat's political career in the early 1950s, violence has occupied a prominent position in his world. It has allowed him to overcome the deep dissonance between his private history and the public role he has always coveted, and it has proved an indispensable tool for personal advancement and gain. The more he resorted to violence, the more enamored with it he became, until violence was an inextricable part of his identity. Like the Roman emperor Nero, who purportedly reveled in the sight of his burning imperial capital, set aflame on his orders, Arafat feels most comfortable when wreaking havoc and death on a large scale. In 1970 he nearly brought about the destruction of Jordan, and in the process caused thousands of civilian deaths. Five years later, he helped trigger the horrendous Lebanese civil war, which raged on for more than a decade and claimed hundreds of thousands of innocent lives. In 1990–91 he supported the brutalization of Kuwait by Saddam Hussein's occupation, at an exorbitant cost to the Palestinians living in the emirate, with thousands murdered in revenge attacks and hundreds of thousands expelled after Kuwait's liberation.

Arafat has never evinced any remorse either for the consequences of his actions or for the untold suffering and destruction wrought on his own people and fellow Arabs. Instead, he has viewed these atrocities as natural, if not exemplary, revolutionary exploits on the road to Palestinian "liberation." As he gloated to fellow members of the Fatah leadership, when trying to convince them to endorse the Oslo accords, "Just as I ruled Lebanon from Fakhani, so I will rule the territories from Jericho."[1]

This is precisely what Arafat accomplished with the Oslo accords by achieving a firm foothold in the West Bank and Gaza. For all his rhetoric about Palestinian independence, Arafat has never been as interested in the actual attainment of statehood as in the violence attending its pursuit. As far back as 1978, he told Ceauşescu that the Palestinians lacked the tradition, unity, and discipline to become a formal state, and that a Palestinian state would be a failure from the first day.[2] The past decade has seen this bleak prognosis turn into a self-fulfilling prophecy. Rather than lay the groundwork for Palestinian statehood as envisaged by Oslo, Arafat created an extensive terrorist infrastructure and used it against his Israeli peace partner. At first he did it tacitly, discreetly giving green lights to terrorist organizations such as Hamas and Islamic Jihad, and then, later, he operated openly and directly.

In a replay of his Jordanian and Lebanese disasters, in September 2000 Arafat pitted Palestinians and Israelis in their bloodiest and most destructive confrontation since the 1948 war, inflicting great damage on Israel and virtually destroying the fragile fabric of civil society that had been developing in the territories during the decades prior to his arrival. "What's happening in our city reminds me of what happened in Beirut in the seventies," lamented a Christian hotel owner in Bethlehem. "Every twenty-year-old masked man carrying a rifle thinks that he is a general and can do whatever he likes."[3]

When the DOP was signed in September 1993, and despite the steep economic decline in the West Bank and Gaza during the six years of the intifada (1987–93), social and economic conditions in the territories were far better than in most neighboring Arab states. Within six months of Arafat's arrival in Gaza in July 1994, the standard of living in the Strip fell by 25 percent. By September 1997, nearly two years after the PA had extended its control over virtually the entire Palestinian population of the West Bank and Gaza, per capita income in the territories had dropped 35 percent from its pre–September 1993 level. Even so, at the time Arafat started his war of terror against Israel, Palestinian income per head was nearly double Syria's, more than four times Yemen's, and 10 percent higher than that of Jordan (one of the better-off Arab states). Only the oil-rich Gulf states and Lebanon were more affluent.[4] Three years later, this income had dropped to a fraction of its earlier levels, with numerous Palestinians reduced to poverty and despondency.

What makes Arafat's war all the more tragic is that its initiation was anathema to the vast majority of the West Bank and Gaza residents (the "inside," in the Palestinian parlance), not only because their economic situation from 1997 was steadily improving after four years of decline but also because they have always been better disposed to a two-state solution than the "outside," spearheaded by the PLO, which has adamantly rejected Israel's right to exist and has persistently sought its destruction.

There have of course been such "inside" militant groups as Hamas and Islamic Jihad, which have been no less committed to Israel's destruction than the PLO. Yet despite the significant increase in their power and influence during the intifada years, at the time of the DOP they still represented a small minority of Palestinian society. According to Palestinian commissioned public opinion polls taken in September 1993, 65 percent of residents in the territories supported the peace process, with 57 percent amenable to revising the Palestinian Covenant as promised by Arafat's letter to Rabin of the same month (among Gaza and Jericho residents, who were to be the first beneficiaries of the process, support ran even higher, at 70 and 75 percent, respectively). By January 1996, when Israel transferred responsibility for the West Bank's Palestinian population to the PA (control of the Gaza residents had already been surrendered in 1994), support for the peace process had risen to 80 percent, while endorsement of terrorist attacks had dropped dramatically to about 20 percent. Even after the tension of the Netanyahu era, support for the peace process remained as high as 60 percent.[5]

These findings become even more significant when one considers the fact that support for peace, and opposition to terrorism, was strongest among the less educated parts of Palestinian society—representing the vast majority of the population—whereas the greatest propensity for violence was exhibited by the best-educated strata. For example, some 82 percent of people with a low level of education supported the Interim Agreement of September 1995, and 80 percent opposed terror attacks against Israeli civilians, compared to 55 and 65 percent, respectively, among university graduates. Even on the thorniest issue of the Palestinian-Israeli dispute, and the one central to the PLO's persistent effort to destroy Israel, namely, the Palestinian right of return, residents of the territories have been far less dogmatic than their PLO and PA leaders. In a survey held in March 1999, two months before the lapse of the official deadline for the completion of the final-status negotiations, less than 15 percent of respondents viewed the refugee question as the most important problem facing the Palestinian people, compared to 46 percent who considered Jerusalem the foremost item on the Palestinian agenda and 31 percent who felt the settlements to be the key issue.

Unlike Diaspora Palestinians upholding the extremist dream of returning to their former dwellings at the cost of Israel's destruction, West Bank and Gaza residents have been far more concerned with issues that have affected their daily lives. While "outside" Palestinians have had no direct interaction with Israelis, or for that matter with any other democratic system, and have thus been susceptible to the vilest forms of indoctrination, twenty-seven years of Israeli rule have given "inside" Palestinians a far more realistic and less absolutist perspective. Contrary to sustained propaganda claims by the PLO and its Western apologists about the repressive nature of Israel's control of the territories, the vast majority of their Palestinian residents tend to view Israel as more democratic than the major Western nations, and infinitely more democratic than Arafat's PA.

Within less than a year from the establishment of the Palestinian Authority in Gaza, more than half of the area's residents claimed to have been happier under Israel's rule. In December 1996, only a couple of months after Israelis and Palestinians had been fighting each other in the so-called tunnel war, 78 percent of Palestinians in the West Bank and Gaza rated Israeli democracy as very good or good, compared to 68 percent for the United States, 62 for France, and 43 percent for the PA. Only 6.9 percent of Palestinians had a negative opinion of Israeli democracy. "I'll never forget that day during the Lebanon war," marveled a Ramallah resident, "when an Arab Knesset member got up and called [Prime Minister Menachem] Begin a murderer. Begin didn't do a thing. If you did that to Arafat, I don't think you'd make it home that night."[6]

The Oslo accords thus gave Arafat a unique opportunity to steer a willing populace in the direction of peace and statehood. With the territories overwhelmingly disposed to a settlement, the Israeli public fatigued by decades of fighting and yearning for normalcy, the radical Arab regimes at one of their lowest ebbs following the collapse of their communist backers, and the international community eager to extend generous political and financial support to the nascent Palestinian entity, there were no obvious obstacles to the attainment of a lasting Israeli-Palestinian peace. But then, instead of making the leap from a hardened terrorist to a state builder, Arafat refused to hang up his ubiquitous battle dress (not even for the signing of the various Oslo accords or the ceremony for the reception of the Nobel Prize for peace) and used "peace" as a strategic deception aimed at promoting the eternal goal of Israel's destruction. Rather than teach Palestinians the virtues of tolerance, coexistence, and respect for the Other, he indoctrinated them with a hatred of Jews and Israelis, unparalleled in scope and intensity since Nazi Germany. Reluctant to eradicate violence from Palestinian social and political life, through both education and a strict enforcement of law and order, including the disarming of the numerous militias operating in the territories under his control as required by the Oslo accords, Arafat chose to make it the defining characteristic of his rule.

The story doesn't end here, however. Aside from denying his people the fruits of peace, Arafat has also imposed an oppressive and corrupt regime in the worst tradition of Arab dictatorships. The PA cabinet is effectively a puppet show where Arafat pulls all the strings. (At one typical session, he spoke for four and a half hours, gave the rest of the ministers less than half an hour of speaking time among themselves, then ended the session without bringing up any proposals for decision.)[7] Municipal and civil services evolved into a corrupt system of patronage aimed at serving Arafat's interests and swamped with thousands of his loyalists, from the top positions to the lowest-paid jobs. Within half a year of his arrival in Gaza, 830 directors general were appointed to various government ministries and offices, one for every nineteen workers.[8] The judiciary was made fully subservient to Arafat's whims through the creation of institutionalized lawlessness, and the wholesale appointment of judges lacking legal training or judicial experience.

The media and numerous human rights groups, which, despite their vehement criticism of its policies, had enjoyed wide latitude under Israel, were brutally suppressed. The pro-Jordanian newspaper *al-Nahar* was forcefully driven out of business, while *al-Quds,* the highest-circulation daily in the territories, was cowed into toeing the official line. When in December 1995 one of its editors ran a trivial anecdote relating to Arafat on page eight rather than on the front page he was summoned to Jericho by Jibril Rajoub, head of the Preventive Security Service (PSS) in the West Bank, where he was interrogated and detained for nearly a week before being released. When he asked Rajoub why he had been summoned, he was told, "If you don't come, I'll cut you into pieces, stick you in the trunk of my car, and bring you to me that way."[9] Despite her public loyalty to Arafat, Hanan Ashrawi was ruthlessly blocked in her early attempts at championing human rights in the PA, with Arafat referring to her contemptuously as the *sharmuta,* the whore.[10]

Within a year of its establishment, the Palestinian Authority had become the largest police state in the world, with one policeman for every forty residents—four times as many as in Washington, D.C., the American city with the highest police to population ratio. In subsequent years, the Palestinian "police" would swell to a 45,000-strong force, twice the size allowed by the Oslo accords, backed by a dozen intelligence services, all of which answered directly to Arafat. These forces were designed to enforce law and order and to combat anti-Israel terrorism, which is why the Israeli government ignored their burgeoning size. In reality, they served instead as Arafat's oppressive arm and, during the war years, instrument of terror. Particularly effective in this regard has been the PSS, whose wide range of activities included the silencing, detention, and torturing of political opponents and critics of the regime, intimidation of the media and human rights groups, spying on university students, and keeping the population in constant awe. As Muhammad Dahlan, the PSS head in the Gaza Strip, candidly told a fellow Israeli negotiator shortly before taking office: "After our arrival [from Tunis], I will close the Strip for three or four weeks and prevent the departure of Palestinian laborers [for work in Israel]. While the population will celebrate I will be working. I will salute some, buy off some, and put a bullet in others' heads. This is how order will be established."[11]

One of the main tasks of the PSS was to protect the intricate web of economic and financial arrangements woven by Arafat. Because the most direct way of gaining loyalty is financial reward, Arafat had always gone to great lengths to keep PLO finances under his tight personal control. Once the PA was in place, he extended this practice to the territories by entrusting key economic posts to three of his "outside" lackeys: Muhammad Zuhdi Nashashibi, a senior PLO economic functionary who was made minister of finance; Abu Ala, chief negotiator at Oslo and director of Samed, the PLO's financial arm, who became minister of economics and trade; and Nabil Shaath, a longtime Arafat adviser and confidant, who was made minister of planning and international cooperation in charge of securing the billions of dollars in foreign aid that had been pledged to the PA.

In no time, the territories were rife with stories about personal enrichment by PA officials at the expense of ordinary Palestinians. Extensive protection and racketeering networks that would not shame the most hardened mafia organizations sprang up by the day, notably those run by Dahlan and Rajoub. Dahlan supplemented his salary by collecting more than one million shekels ($250,000) per month in protection money (from suppliers of oil and cigarettes and the like), kickbacks for issuing licenses, and border crossing fees, while Rajoub was reported to have extorted protection money from oil distributors, and to have received kickbacks from the Jericho casino until it closed after the outbreak of war.

Lower-ranking officials developed their own extortionist techniques, such as forcing landowners to sell them plots of land at marked-down prices, siphoning a percentage of land and property sales, or coercing ordinary citizens to pay protection money for securing basic and self-evident rights and services. The more affluent members of society were subjected to frequent arrests by the security services on false charges from which they were released for hefty ransoms. In one such case, a Tulkarm businessman paid $100,000 to have his brother released; in another, an influential businessman from Nablus was tortured to death by the local security services for having refused to pay protection money. The sight of his mutilated body was shocking even by the harsh standards of the Middle East, having been savagely beaten, with his right hand severely burnt and drilled deep inside. Even Hamas and Islamic

Jihad terrorists would often have to pay PSS officers thousands of dollars to be tipped off in advance of impending raids.[12]

In May 1997, the first-ever report by the PA's comptroller stated that $325 million, out of the 1996 budget of $800 million, had been "wasted" by Palestinian ministers and agencies or embezzled by officials. At first Arafat sought to ignore the entire affair, and only after the Israeli and foreign media brought the report to global attention did he order the Legislative Council to form a special committee to examine the charges. This recommended the dismissal of Arafat's entire cabinet, accusing all but four of its ministers of corruption and misuse of funds. Four ministers were singled out for particular criticism and possible criminal investigation for embezzlement, theft, and breach of trust: Shaath, Jamil Tarifi (civilian affairs), Yasser Abd Rabbo (information), and Ali Kawasmeh (transport). Tarifi had allegedly imported 4,300 cars under his name without paying customs duties. Kawasmeh was accused of taking personal payments from bus and taxi companies and companies that administer vehicle licensing tests. Abd Rabbo was found to have taken $7,000 to install central heating in his Ramallah home. Shaath was said to have used funds from his ministry for personal expenses, including $25,000 for his wedding. (A widower, Shaath remarried in 1996, throwing four lavish wedding receptions—two in Jerusalem, one in Nablus, and one in Gaza—to the disgust and fury of ordinary Palestinians.) None of these ministers was ever charged, nor did this practice stop. At the height of his terrorist war, Arafat continued to disburse lavish sums of money to senior PA officials for personal needs, including $50,000 for the wedding of the daughter of a cabinet minister, $100,000 for the construction of a home for a senior official, and the doubling of the living expenses of Shaath's son who was studying in France. This at a time when many Palestinians were reduced to poverty, and when people, whose homes had been destroyed in the fighting, were forced to wait for months for the paltry compensation promised by Arafat.[13]

This was only the tip of the iceberg. From the beginning of his personal rule in the territories, Arafat has created a two-tiered economy: the official side, which ostensibly runs the population's daily life and is burdened with debts and deficits, and its highly lucrative informal counterpart, whose revenues never reach the Palestinian population. The control of the economy has thus been handed to a group of Arafat cronies, a few members of the top political echelon, a small coalition of security men, and a number of mid-level professionals who have been with him since Beirut. They control all the deals, and "clip coupons" from them through scores of concessions, of which the most notorious are the monopoly rights for the production and sale of virtually all basic goods affecting the population's daily life, from wheat, petrol, and cement, to wood, gravel, cigarettes, and cars. This has not only allowed Arafat's cronies to make incredible profits at the expense of ordinary Palestinians by grossly inflating the price of basic commodities (annual revenues from the monopolies were estimated in 2000 at $300 million, none of which has been accounted for), but also has had a detrimental effect on the economy as a whole by preventing competition and subverting almost every potentially profitable aspect of daily Palestinian life.

The foremost monopoly owner has been the Palestine Commercial Services Company, ostensibly the economic arm of the Palestinian Authority but in reality a wholly unsupervised venture controlled by Arafat, run by his trusted economic adviser, Muhammad Rashid, a Kurd. The PCSC dominates most aspects of the economic activity in the PA territories. In addition, Rashid co-owns an oil monopoly, together with Arafat's adviser, Hassan Asfour, among other business interests. Shaath has a computer monopoly, while Abu Ala is co-owner of cigarettes, preserves, and dairy monopolies.

Though Arafat has by and large managed to keep out of the limelight as far as personal corruption is concerned, his wife co-owns pharmaceutical and apparel monopolies together with Rashid and Nabil Abu Rudaina, Arafat's communications adviser, and is a major shareholder in the al-Bahar (meaning "the sea" in Arabic) construction company in Gaza, whose tentacles reach so far afield that it has come to be known notoriously as al-Muhit ("the ocean"). According to the 1994 Paris economic agreement between Israel and the PA, Israel is supposed to transfer the tax receipts it collects on imported goods for the Palestinian territories directly to the PA. At Arafat's insistence, these sums were deposited in a secret account in a Tel Aviv bank, which can be accessed only by himself and by Rashid. Between 1994 and 2000, Israel transferred nearly eleven billion shekels (about $2.5 billion) to this account, of which only a small, unspecified part has reached its designated target audience.[14]

These excesses did not escape the notice of the Palestinian masses. In September 1996, less than a year after the PA had gained control of the West Bank and Gaza population, about half of all Palestinians believed in the existence of corruption in the PA's institutions and agencies. A year later this figure had risen to 65 percent of the population, reaching as high as 100 percent among the better-educated parts of society (ironically the same strata wherein Arafat's terrorist activities have their strongest support).[15]

As the economic situation in the PA territories substantially worsened, these mutterings of discontent culminated in occasional violent demonstrations against the regime, accompanied by the odd criticism of Arafat by his Arab donors. In the summer of 2002, for example, the Gulf states temporarily suspended their contributions to the PA following revelations that Arafat had used $5.1 million of this aid money to maintain the expensive lifestyle of his wife, who had been living in Paris for quite some time. Yet this was only a pittance compared to the $300 million that Rashid transferred at the height of the war from a Geneva-based bank account held on behaf of Arafat to an unknown destination.[16]

Nor was Arafat the only Palestinian leader siphoning donor money, given to help ordinary Palestinians survive the horrors of war, to a private account abroad. Prior to his death in the summer of 2001, Faisal Husseini had funneled $1.8 million into his personal accounts in Switzerland and Austria, while Abu Mazen had transferred some $70 million to accounts in Europe, using his brother, a wealthy businessman in the Gulf, as a conduit; so did Ghazi Jabali, head of the Palestinian police in Gaza, who in 2002 transferred his money to an Amman bank. Muhammad Rashid sought to profit from the war started by Arafat by investing in the Jordan Cement Company, in anticipation of a steep rise in the price of cement due to increased demand for building materials following Operation Defensive Shield in April 2002.[17]

President George W. Bush was right when in June 2002 he spoke about Arafat's betrayal of the Palestinian people. He might have also noted that this was the second grand betrayal of the Palestinians by their leadership in half a century. In 1947, as now, the Palestinians were offered a state of their own in part of Mandatory Palestine, only to turn down the offer and wage a war of annihilation against their Jewish neighbors. Then, as now, they were led by an extremist and shortsighted leadership, which subordinated the collective good to its self-serving interests, betraying their constituents at the most critical stage of the fighting.

It is indeed the tragedy of the Palestinians that the two leaders who determined their national development during the twentieth century—Hajj Amin Husseini, onetime mufti of Jerusalem, who led them from the early 1920s to the late 1940s, and Yasser Arafat, who has dominated Palestinian politics since the mid-1960s—were bigoted and megalomaniac extremists blinded by anti-Jewish hatred (the mufti spent most of World War II in Berlin rallying support for Hitler's war effort in the Muslim world) and profoundly obsessed with violence. Had the mufti chosen to lead his people to peace and reconciliation with their Jewish neighbors, as he had promised the British officials who appointed him to this high rank in the early 1920s, the Palestinians would have had their independent state over a substantial part of Mandatory Palestine in 1948 at the very latest, and thus would have been spared the traumatic experience of dispersion and exile. Had Arafat been genuinely interested in peace, a Palestinian state could have been established in the early 1980s as a corollary to the Egyptian-Israeli Camp David Accords of 1978, or by May 1999 as a part of the Oslo process.

That such a state has failed to materialize amounts to nothing short of a profound act of betrayal, not least since Arafat's terrorist war can hardly be considered a popular uprising or a struggle for national liberation, given that since the beginning of 1996, and following the completion of the redeployment from Hebron in January 1997, 99 percent of the Palestinian population of the West Bank and the Gaza Strip have not lived under Israeli occupation.

Nor is it a war for the establishment of a Palestinian state alongside Israel. Apart from Arafat's and the PLO leadership's reiteration that they have never abandoned their historic goal of substituting a Palestinian state for Israel, and the reassertion of this objective after the outbreak of hostilities, the incontrovertible fact is that during the Camp David summit of July 2000 the Palestinians, by their own account, were offered a fully contiguous independent state in ninety-two percent of the West Bank and the entire Gaza Strip, with East Jerusalem as its capital. Arafat was under no obligation to accept this offer, and was entitled to try to negotiate a better deal, but not to start a war of terror against his peace partner in its wake, both because Security Council Resolution 242 of November 1967, on which the Oslo process had been predicated, asked Israel to withdraw "from territories occupied in the recent conflict" rather than from all of the territories, and because the Oslo accords unequivocally and irrevocably exclude the use of violence from future Palestinian-Israeli relations.

Arafat's abysmal failure to live up to this fundamental obligation, together with his brutal political oppression and shameless economic exploitation of his Palestinian subjects, and their sacrifice in a devastating and wholly unnecessary war, further underscores President Bush's assertion that "peace requires a new and different Palestinian leadership" and that "a Palestinian state will never be created by terror. It will be built through reform."[18]

Given Arafat's violent experience during the past half century, anything short of the full and unqualified implementation of this vision would amount to yet another betrayal of the Palestinian people. Just as the creation of free and democratic societies in Germany and Japan after World War II necessitated, above and beyond the overthrow of the ruling parties, a comprehensive purge of the existing political elites and the reeducation of the entire populace, so the Palestinians deserve a profound structural reform that will sweep Arafat and his PA from power, free the "inside" from the stifling PLO grip, eradicate the endemic violence from Palestinian political and social life, and teach the virtues of peaceful coexistence with their Israeli neighbors. This is certain to be a difficult and protracted process, one requiring sustained international guidance and support. Yet if history tells us anything, it is that any other alternative is an assured recipe for disaster.

Notes

Introduction

1. Ion Pacepa, *Red Horizons. Inside the Romanian Secret Service—The Memoirs of Ceausescu's Spy Chief* (London: Coronet Books), 1989, pp. 23–29. Lieutenant General Pacepa was head of Romanian Intelligence and a personal adviser to President Nicolae Ceauşescu until his defection to the United States.
2. Ehud Ya'ari, "A Dangerous Cocktail," *Jerusalem Report*, October 31, 1996.
3. Arafat's interview with *al-Anwar* (Beirut), August 2, 1968.
4. Ibid.
5. *Al-Arabi* (Cairo), June 24, 2001.
6. *Jordan Television Network in Arabic*, September 13, 1993.
7. Ehud Ya'ari, "The Return of the PLO," *Jerusalem Report*, May 6, 2002.
8. Mamduh Nawfal, "Fi Taba Taarafa al-Tarafan ala Haqiqat Mawaqif Kul Minhuma," *Majalat al-Dirasat al-Filastiniya*, no. 48, Autumn 2001, p. 101.

1. The Man and His World

1. Article 5 of the Palestinian National Covenant, in Yehoshafat Harkabi, *The Palestinian Covenant and its Meaning* (London: Vallentine, Mitchell, 1979), p. 113.
2. Thus according to Arafat's birth certificate. Arafat himself claims August 4, 1929, as his date of birth. See John and Janet Wallach, *Arafat: In the Eyes of the Beholder* (London: Heinemann, 1990), pp. 28–29. Biographers of Arafat cannot even agree on his real name. According to the Israeli journalist Ehud Ya'ari, who was the first to reveal Arafat's true name, it is Abdel Rahman Abdel Rauf Arafat al-Qudwa al-Husseini. Thomas Kiernan maintains that it is Rahman Abdel Rauf Arafat al-Qudwa al-Husseini, while according to both Wallach and Wallach and Gowers and Walker it is Muhammad Abdel Rauf Arafat al-Qudwa al-Husseini. According to Alan Hart, it is Muhammad Yasser Arafat, and to Mamduh Nawfal, Arafat's longtime PLO associate, it is Muhammad Abdel Rauf Arafat al-Qudwa.
3. Wallach and Wallach, *Arafat*, p. 29.
4. "The Playboy Interview: Yasir Arafat," www.playboy.com/magazine/historic/Arafat/10.html.

5. Danny Rubinstein, *The Mystery of Arafat* (South Royalton, Vt.: Steerforth Press, 1995), p. 12.

6. Wallach and Wallach, *Arafat*, p. 28.

7. Rubinstein, *The Mystery of Arafat*, p. 13.

8. Andrew Gowers and Tony Walker, *Arafat: The Biography* (London: Virgin, 1994), pp. 62–63. According to biographer Said Aburish, Arafat was convicted for the murder of the Palestinian activist and sentenced to death, but his sentence was commuted by Salah Jadid, the strongman in Damascus and patron of the nascent Fatah organization. See Said Aburish, *Arafat: From Defender to Dictator* (London: Bloomsbury, 1998), pp. 63–64.

9. *Al-Sayad* (Beirut), January 23, 1969.

10. Aburish, *Arafat*, p. 19; Alan Hart, *Arafat: A Political Biography* (London: Sidgwick and Jackson, 1994), p. 46.

11. Hart, *Arafat*, p. 53.

12. A cousin of Hajj Amin Husseini, the leader of the Palestinian community at the time, Abdel Qader encountered great difficulties in recruiting volunteers to his militia, and was personally snubbed in numerous villages and towns he visited. Two months before his death, he was widely ridiculed in local coffeehouses as "Corporal Qader." See, for example, "Fortnightly Intelligence Newsletter No. 60, issued by HQ British Troops in Palestine for the period 2359 hrs 14 Jan–2359 hrs 28 Jan 1948," Public Record Office (PRO), WO 275/64, pp. 2–3; "Fortnightly Intelligence Newsletter No. 61, issued by HQ British Troops in Palestine for the period 2359 hrs 28 Jan–2359 hrs 11 Feb 1948," WO 275/64, pp. 1, 3.

13. Thomas Kiernan, *Yasir Arafat* (London: Abacus, 1976), p. 123.

14. Wallach and Wallach, *Arafat*, pp. 81–82.

15. Ibid.

16. Gowers and Walker, *Arafat*, p. 12. See also Rubinstein, *The Mystery of Arafat*, p. 38.

17. Wallach and Wallach, *Arafat*, p. 27.

18. Abu Iyad, *My Home, My Land: A Narrative of the Palestinian Struggle* (New York: Times Books, 1981), p. 38; Aburish, *Arafat*, pp. 26, 51–52; Gowers and Walker, *Arafat*, 1994, p. 69.

19. Aburish, *Arafat*, p. 143.

20. Gowers and Walker, *Arafat*, p. 60.

21. Pacepa, *Red Horizons*, p. 93; Connie Bruck, "The Wounds of Peace," *New Yorker*, October 14, 1996, p. 75.

22. Bruck, "The Wounds of Peace," p. 75.

23. Edward Said, *The Pen and the Sword: Conversations with David Barsamian* (Edinburgh: AK Press, 1994), pp. 136–37.

24. *Maariv* (Tel Aviv), December 23, 1993; Gowers and Walker, *Arafat*, p. 328.

25. See, for example, *al-Jazeera Television*, January 13, 2002; *Israel Television*, December 7–9, 2001.

26. Kiernan, *Yasir Arafat*, p. 45.

27. Aburish, *Arafat*, p. 27.

28. Hart, *Arafat*, p. 47.

29. See, for example, Wallach and Wallach, *Arafat*, pp. 12, 61; Rubinstein, *The Mystery of Arafat*, pp. 89–91.

30. Author's interviews; Wallach and Wallach, *Arafat*, p. 61.

31. Pacepa, *Red Horizons*, pp. 20, 36.

32. *Guardian*, November 15, 2001.

33. Arafat's *Playboy* interview.

34. Neil C. Livingstone and David Halevy, *Inside the PLO: Covert Units, Secret Funds, and the War Against Israel and the United States* (London: Robert Hale, 1990), pp. 91–93; Rubinstein, *The Mystery of Arafat*, p. 97.

35. Aburish, *Arafat*, p. 49.

36. *Jerusalem Post*, August 18, 19, 23, 2002.

37. Gowers and Walker, *Arafat*, p. 60.

38. Rubinstein, *The Myth of Arafat*, p. 110; Wallach and Wallach, *Arafat*, p. 256.

39. Kiernan, *Yasir Arafat*, pp. 137–138.

40. Pacepa, *Red Horizons*, p. 16.

41. Alan M. Dershowitz, *Why Terrorism Works* (New Haven and London: Yale University Press, 2002), p. 48; Livingstone and Halevy, *Inside the PLO*, pp. 276–82.

42. Ion Mihai Pacepa, "The Arafat I Knew," *Wall Street Journal*, January 10, 2002.

43. George Jonas, "Murder Plot Haunts Arafat; Veil of Secrecy Finally Lifted on Tapes Linking Him to Slaying of U.S. Diplomats," *Chicago Sun-Times*, January 29, 2002.

44. Livingstone and Halevy, *Inside the PLO*, p. 281. See also "James Welsh vs Yasser Arafat," *Ha'aretz*, December 14, 2001.

45. Robert Fisk, *Pity the Nation: Lebanon at War* (Oxford: Oxford University Press, 1992), pp. 86, 102; Yezid Sayigh, *Armed Struggle and the Search for State: The Palestinian National Movement, 1949–1993* (Washington D.C. and London: Institute for Palestine Studies and Clarendon Press, 1997), p. 401.

46. Aryeh Yodfat and Yuval Arnon-Ohana, *PLO Strategy and Tactics* (New York: St. Martin's Press, 1981), p. 47, fn 27.

47. Gowers and Walker, *Arafat*, pp. 98–99; Aburish, *Arafat*, pp. 104, 108; James Lunt, *Hussein of Jordan* (London: Fontana, 1990), pp. 186–87; Moshe Shemesh, *The Palestinian Entity 1959–1974: Arab Politics and the PLO* (London: Frank Cass, 1988), pp. 132–33.

48. Aburish, *Arafat*, p. 105; Gowers and Walker, *Arafat*, p. 95.

49. *Beirut Radio*, May 7, 1948.

50. David Gilmour, *Lebanon: the Fractured Country* (London: Sphere Books, 1987), pp. 90–92.

51. Author's interview.

52. Aburish, *Arafat*, p. 151.

53. Gowers and Walker, *Arafat*, pp. 186, 200.

54. Ibid., p. x.

55. Arafat's interview with *Ha'olam Ha'ze* (Tel Aviv), September 8, 1993.

56. Wallach and Wallach, *Arafat*, p. 257.

2. The Road to Oslo

1. Hagana Archives (Tel Aviv), 105/105a, p. 47; Trygve Lie, *In the Cause of Peace: Seven Years with the United Nations* (New York: Macmillan, 1954), p. 165.

2. See, for example, Moshe Sasson, "The Emigration of the Eretz Israel Arabs in the Period 1.12.47–1.6.48," June 30, 1948, Israel Defense Forces Archive (IDFA), Intelligence-Golani, pp. 2–3; estimate by Sir Rafael Cilento, director of the UN Disaster Relief Operation, October 1948, Hagana Archives (HA), 105/88; Yossef Weitz, Ezra Danin, and Elias Sasson, "Memorandum on the Settlement of the Arab Refugees," submitted to Prime Minister David Ben-Gurion in November 1948, HA 105/88; report by the Research Department of the British Foreign Office, FO 371/75437/51809.

3. Muhammad Nimr al-Khatib, *Min Athar al-Nakba*, (Damascus: al-Matba'ah al-Umumiyah), 1951, p. 287.

4. See, for example, HA 105/215, pp. 19, 25, 51, 101; HA 105/143, p. 174; American Consulate (Port Said) to Department of State, 29 April 1948, RG 84, 800—Refugees.

5. HA 105/114, p. 24; HA 105/215, pp. 19, 25, 51, 101; HA 105/143, p. 174; American Consulate (Port Said) to Department of State, April 29, 1948, RG 84, 800—Refugees.

6. Sir J. Troutbeck, "Summary of general impressions gathered during week-end visit to the Gaza district," June 16, 1949, FO 371/75342/E7816, p. 123.

7. John Laffin, *The PLO Connections* (London: Corgi Books, 1983), p. 127.

8. Sayigh, *Armed Struggle*, pp. 71–72, 86–87, 91; Ehud Yaari, *Strike Terror: The Story of Fatah* (New York: Sabra Books, 1970), pp. 52, 65, 171–72.

9. Ahmad Shuqeiri, *Min al-Qimma ila-l-Hazima* (Beirut, Dor al-Awda 1971), p. 50; Sayigh, *Armed Struggle*, p. 98.

10. Ya'ari, *Strike Terror*, p. 50.

11. Sayigh, *Armed Struggle*, p. 141.

12. Abu Iyad, *My Home*, p. 64.

13. Hart, *Arafat*, pp. 232–33; Shemesh, *The Palestinian Entity*, pp. 48–50, 59–62, 80–81, 87–92, 104; Gowers and Walker, *Arafat*, pp. 81–91; Aburish, *Arafat*, pp. 88–89.

14. *Al-Kitab al-Sanawi li-l-Qadiya al-Filastiniya 1968* (Beirut: Institute for Palestine Studies, 1969), p. 88.

15. For Arafat's *Der Spiegel* interview, see Zuhair Diab, ed., *International Documents on Palestine 1968* (*hereinafter IDOP*) (Beirut: Institute for Palestine Studies, 1971), p. 383; for the PNC's statement, see *IDOP 1969*, p. 589.

16. Edward Said, "My Right of Return," *Ha'aretz Magazine* (Tel Aviv), August 18, 2000 (interview with journalist Ari Shavit).

17. "The Palestine National Charter Adopted by the Fourth Palestine National Assembly, Cairo, July 18, 1968," *IDOP* 1968, Article 6, p. 393.

18. David Landes, "Palestine before the Zionists," *Commentary*, February 1976, p. 52.

19. Lutfi Abdel Azim, "Who Will Destroy Whom: the Jews or the Arabs?" *al-Ahram al-Iqtisadi*, September 27, 1982.

20. *IDOP 1968*, p. 393.

21. Aburish, *Arafat*, p. 100.

22. The most comprehensive sources of information on the socioeconomic development of the West Bank and the Gaza Strip between 1967 and 1993 are the annual yearbooks of Israel's Central Bureau of Statistics, *Statistical Abstracts of Israel*, and the annual reports of the Administrator of Activities in the Territories: *The Administered Territories—Data on Civilian Activity in Judea and Samaria, the Gaza Strip, and North Sinai* (the latter category was of course dropped following the return of this territory to Egypt). Other valuable sources include the regular reports of World Bank (e.g., "World Development Indicators," "West Bank and Gaza at a Glance"), as well as various UN reports: United Nations Statistics Division (e.g., "Indicators on Income and Economic Activity," "Indicators on Literacy"); World Health Organization (e.g., "The World Health Report"), etc.

See also: "West Bank and Gaza: An Evaluation of [World] Bank Assistance," March 7, 2002 (report no. 23820); Adam Roberts et al., *Academic Freedom Under Israeli Occupation* (London and Geneva: World University Service and International Commission of Jurists, 1984); David Bar-Ilan, "Hardened Times man didn't have the hard facts," *Jerusalem Post*, September 1, 1995; Keith Marsden, "The Viability of Palestine," *Wall Street Journal*, April 25, 2002; Patrick Clawson, "The Palestinians' lost Marshall Plans," *Jerusalem Post*, August 9, 2002.

23. Menahem Milson, "How Not to Occupy the West Bank," *Commentary*, April 1986.

24. Alain Gresh, *The PLO: The Struggle Within* (London: Zed, 1985), p. 105.

25. Shemesh, *The Palestinian Entity*, p. 289.

26. "Political Program for the Present Stage Drawn Up by the 12th PNC, Cairo, June 9, 1974," *Journal of Palestine Studies*, vol. 3, no. 4 (Summer 1974), p. 224.

27. *IDOP 1968*, p. 383.

28. The Palestine Arab Delegation, New York, "Justice Will Triumph," June 5, 1968, Irish National Archives, NA 200143/100.

29. Article 5 of the PNC's political program of June 9, 1974.

30. Dershowitz, *Why Terrorism Works*, p. 50; Ariel Merari and Shlomi Elad, *The International Dimension of Palestinian Terrorism* (Jerusalem and Boulder: Jerusalem Post and Westview Press, 1986), pp. 136–42.

31. Dershowitz, *Why Terrorism Works*, p. 50.

32. Said, *The Pen and the Sword,* p. 137.

33. Efraim Karsh, *The Soviet Union and Syria* (London and New York: Routledge, 1988), p. 92.

34. *Ukaz* (Saudi Arabia), November 22, 1988. For a fascinating glimpse into the infighting behind the Algiers declarations, see Mamduh Nawfal, *al-Bahth An al-Dawla* (Amman: al-Ahliya, 2001), especially chapter 5.

35. *Al-Anba* (Kuwait), December, 5 and 13, 1988. For other Palestinian statements in the same vein see, for example, interview by Khaled Hassan, head of the PNC's committee for external and parliamentary relations, with *al-Musawar* (Cairo), January 20, 1989; interview with Salim Zaanun (aka Abu Adib), the PNC's deputy chairman, with *al-Anba* (Kuwait), November 21, 1988; interview by Rafiq al-Natsha (Abu Shakir), a member of the PLO's central committee, with *al-Sharq al-Awsat* (London), December 9, 1988, and with *al-Jazira* (Saudi Arabia), January 1, 1989.

36. Pierre Salinger and Eric Laurent, *Secret Dossier: The Hidden Agenda behind the Gulf War* (London: Penguin, 1991), p. 160.

37. *Baghdad Voice of the PLO,* January 8, 1991; *Al-Ra'i* (Amman), January 2, 1991.

38. Salinger and Laurent, *Secret Dossier,* p. 156.

39. Tlas's interview with *Ukaz* (Saudi Arabia), February 24, 1991.

40. *New York Times,* March 16, 1991; "A New Beginning," *U.S. News and World Report,* September 13, 1993, p. 30.

41. Ami Ayalon, ed., *Middle East Contemporary Survey 1991* (MECS) (New York: Holmes and Meyer, 1993), pp. 209–25; *MECS 1992,* pp. 264–65; Hanan Ashrawi, *This Side of Peace: A Personal Account* (New York: Simon and Schuster, 1995), pp. 217–18; Allon Groth, *The PLO's Road to Peace: Processes of Decision-Making* (London: Royal United Services Institute for Defence Studies, 1995), p. 24; Aburish, *Arafat,* p. 244.

42. Bruck, "The Wounds of Peace," p. 70.

43. Most participants in the Oslo secret negotiations have written their accounts of the process. See: Mahmoud Abbas, *Through Secret Channels* (Reading: Garnet, 1995); Shimon Peres, *Battling for Peace* (London: Weidenfeld and Nicolson, 1995); Uri Savir, *The Process: 1100 Days that Changed the Middle East* (New York: Random House, 1998); Yossi Beilin, *Laga'at Bashalom* (Tel Aviv: Yediot Aharonot, 1997).

44. Pinhas Inbari, "Still Far Away from Substance," *Al Ha'mishmar* (Tel Aviv), October 4, 1993.

3. A Trojan Horse

1. *Jerusalem Post,* February 23, 1996; *Jerusalem Report,* March 21, 1996, p. 12.

2. *Palestinian Authority Television,* July 12, 2000.

3. See, for example, *Radio Monte Carlo in Arabic*, September 1, 3, 1993; *Middle East News Agency* (*MENA*, Cairo), September 3, 1993; *al-Hayat* (London), September 12, 1993; *ESC Television in Arabic* (Cairo), September 13, 1993; *ENTV Television in Arabic* (Algiers), September 14, 1993; *MBC Television* (London), September 13, 1993; *Cairo Radio*, September 11, 1993.

4. *Amman Jordan Television Network in Arabic*, September 13, 1993.

5. Uzi Mahanaimi, "Arafat: I Know There Is an Agreement between Israel and Damascus," *Ha'olam Ha'ze*, September 8, 1993, pp. 3–4.

6. *Jerusalem Post*, May 23, 1994.

7. *Jerusalem Post*, May 24, 1994; *Al-Hamishmar*, May 24, 1994.

8. *Jerusalem Post*, June 1, 1994.

9. Kiernan, *Yasir Arafat*, pp. 34–35, 46–47.

10. *Palestinian Authority Television*, August 21, 1995.

11. *Hatsav* (IDF media monitoring unit), August 23, 1995, 836/1082. For further allusions to Hudaibiya see, for example, *al-Quds*, May 10, 1998; *Orbit Ttelevision* (Cairo), April 18, 1998.

12. See, for example, Arafat's interview with *al-Hayat* (London), October 5, 2002.

13. Sakhr Habash, *al-Mujazafa al-Tarikhiya wa-Atwaq al-Salama al-Wataniya* (no publication place, 1998 edition; originally published in 1994), pp. 45–75, as brought in Lt. Col. Jonathan D. H., "Understanding the Breakdown of Israeli-Palestinian Negotiations," *Jerusalem Viewpoints*, 15 September–1 October 2002, p. 4.

14. *Al-Hayat al-Jadida*, November 25, 1999.

15. Othman Abu Gharbiya, *al-Tanzim bayna al-Nazariya wa-l-Tatbiq fi Tajribatina*, 1999, p. 475, as quoted in Lt. Col. Jonathan D. H., "Understanding . . . ," p. 9.

16. *Al-Ra'i* (Amman), November 12, 1992.

17. Quoted by the Israeli news agency *IMRA*, September 9, 1996.

18. *Al-Safir* (Beirut), March 21, 2001.

19. *Al-Arabi* (Cairo), June 24, 2001.

20. *Jerusalem Post*, July 17, 1994.

21. *Al-Ayyam* (Ramallah), February 17, 1996.

22. *Jerusalem Post*, February 13, 1996.

23. *Jerusalem Post*, October 3, 2002; *Ha'aretz*, October 7, 2002.

24. *Jerusalem Post*, August 10, 1994.

25. *Jerusalem Post*, August 10, 11, 12, 1994.

26. *Maariv*, September 11, 1995; *Voice of Palestine*, November 11, 1995.

27. Yossi Beilin, *Madrich Leyona Ptsua* (Tel Aviv: Yediot Aharonot, 2001), p. 122.

28. *Al-Ittihad* (Internet edition), June 24, 1996; *Ha'aretz*, July 13, 1997; *Israeli Television*, December 23, 1995.

29. *Al-Misri* (Cairo), October 11, 1949.

30. Lt. Col. Jonathan D. H. "Understanding . . . ," p. 6.

31. See, for example, Arafat's messages as broadcast on *Algiers Voice of Palestine*, September 3, 8, 1993; and his interview with *al-Hayat* (London), September 12, 1993.

32. *Al-Bairaq* (Beirut), September 21–22, 1993.

33. See, for example, Ziad Abu Amda, "The Oslo Peace Process," *al-Siyasa al-Filastiniya* (Nablus), September 1994; *al-Quds,* October 19, 1994; *al-Dustur* (Amman), October 30, 1993; panel discussion of Palestinian political activists, *Israel Television,* February 1, 1994.

34. *Ha'aretz,* September 9, 1993; Qaddoumi's interview with *MBC Television in Arabic* (London), September 1, 1993; Reuters (Cairo), July 1, 1994; *Voice of Palestine* (Jericho), July 2, 1994; *al-Nahar* (Jerusalem), July 2, 1994.

35. *Al-Dustur,* May 29, 1994.

36. "Address by Hanan Ashrawi to the World Conference Against Racism, Racial Discrimination, Xenophobia, and Related Intolerances," Durban, South Africa, August 28, 2001, www.caabu.org/press/articles/ashrawi-durban-speech.html.

37. "Message to the Israeli Arabs from the Liaison Committee, Palestinian Presidential Bureau, September 30, 2001" (one of the thousands of documents captured by Israel in Arafat's Ramallah compound during Operation Defensive Shield, April 2002; hereinafter "Arafat Documents").

38. Arafat's interviews with *Israel Television,* September 13, 1993, 1416 and 1645 hours.

39. *Al-Ayyam,* December 4, 2000.

40. *Palestinian Authority Television,* July 16, 2000.

4. A License to Hate

1. Harkabi, *The Palestinian Covenant,* pp. 12–13.

2. See articles 1, 2, 16, 19, 20, 21, 22, 23 of the covenant in ibid., pp. 113–18.

3. Arafat's interview with *Vienna Television,* December 19, 1988.

4. Harkabi, *The Palestinian Covenant,* p. 18.

5. Abbas, *Through Secret Channels,* pp. 107–108, 208–209; Savir, *The Process,* pp. 70, 71, 74, 77.

6. Letter from Chairman Arafat to Prime Minister Yitzhak Rabin (paragraph 3) accompanying the "Gaza-Jericho Agreement" (emphasis added).

7. Ze'ev Begin, "Yasser Arafat's Lackey," *Jerusalem Post,* October 28, 1993.

8. *Jerusalem Post,* July 8, 11, 15, 21, 22, 23, 26, 1993.

9. Ibid. August 22, 24, 1994; *Al Ha'mishmar,* August 8, 1994; *al-Hayat* (London), May 18, 1996.

10. *Maariv,* March 15, 16, 1995; *Jerusalem Post,* November 17, 1994; *Al Ha'mishmar,* August 16, 1994.

11. *Jerusalem Post,* March 17, 1995.

12. Article XXXI(9) of the Interim Agreement, in Geoffrey W. Watson, *The Oslo Accords: International Law and the Israeli-Palestinian Peace Agreement* (Oxford: Oxford University Press, 2000), p. 366.

13. *MENA*, January 23, 1996; *Jerusalem Post*, January 21, 1996.

14. *Voice of Palestine*, January 23, February 6, 1996; *al-Hayat al-Jadida* (Ramallah), January 25, 1996; *al-Quds*, January 26, 1996; *Jerusalem Post*, February 7, 8, 1996; *al-Ittihad* (Abu Dhabi), February 9, 1996.

15. *Israel Information Service in English*, May 5, 1996, accessed online.

16. *Voice of Palestine*, April 24, 1996; *Israel Information Service in English*, May 5, 1996; *Jerusalem Post*, May 8, 1996.

17. Yehoshua Porath, "Antisocial Text: The PLO Charter Scam," *New Republic*, July 8, 1996, p. 9; *Jerusalem Post*, May 1, 6, 1996; *al-Nahar*, May 16, 1996; *Voice of Israel*, April 25, 1996.

18. *Al-Nahar*, May 5, 1996.

19. Porath, "Antisocial Text," p. 9.

20. *Voice of Palestine*, April 26, 1996.

21. "The Voting Session of the Palestinian National Council on the Palestinian Charter, Gaza, April 24, 1996," Institute for Peace Education, from TV newsreel purchased from Palestinian TV news crew and later aired with permission on *Israel TV Channel One News* on May 20, 1996.

22. *Jerusalem Post*, May 6, 1996.

23. *Voice of Palestine*, April 22, 23, 1996; *al-Dustur* (Amman), April 22, 1996.

24. *Jerusalem Post*, May 6, 1996.

25. Ibid., May 22, 1996.

26. Yoel Singer, *Maariv*, June 19, 1998.

27. Watson, *The Oslo Accords*, pp. 375–76.

28. *Jerusalem Post*, January 26, 27, 1997.

29. Ibid., January 23, 1998.

30. Ibid.

31. Danny Naveh, *Sodot Memshala* (Tel Aviv: Yediot Aharonot, 1999), pp. 121, 126–27; "Wye River Momerandum (October 23, 1998)," Article C (2), in Watson, *The Oslo Accords*, p. 380.

32. *Jerusalem Post*, December 15, 1998.

33. *Al-Dustur*, August 13, 2000.

5. Hate Thy Neighbor

1. "Agreement on the Gaza Strip and the Jericho Area, May 4, 1994," Article XII (1), and "Israeli-Palestinian Interim Agreement on the West Bank and the Gaza Strip, September 28, 1995," Article XXII (1 and 2), and "The Wye River Memorandum, October 23, 1998," Article 3 (a and b), in Watson, *The Oslo Accords*, pp. 334, 363, 379.

2. *Radio Monte Carlo in Arabic,* September 1, 1993.

3. *Maariv,* October 28, 1993; *Jerusalem Post,* November 6, 1993; *Algiers Voice of Palestine,* September 18, 1993; Mahmoud Abbas's interview with *al-Sharq al-Awsat* (London), September 17, 1993.

4. *Maariv,* November 3, 1993.

5. *Al-Nahar,* April 1, 1995; *al-Sharq al-Awsat,* May 13, 1995.

6. *Jerusalem Report,* May 29, 1997, p. 12, and June 12, 1997, p. 10.

7. Warren Christopher, *Chances of a Lifetime: A Memoir* (New York: Scribner, 2001), p. 204.

8. Ehud Ya'ari, "No Hope in Shame," *Jerusalem Report,* May 10, 1994, p. 28.

9. *Voice of Palestine,* July 7, 1994; *Agence Presse France,* July 2, 1994.

10. *Radio Monte Carlo in Arabic,* July 1, 1994; *al-Nahar,* July 3, 1994. The Koranic quote is from the 28th Sura, "The Story," verse 4. See, *The Koran,* translated and with an introduction by Arthur J. Abberry (Oxford: Oxford University Press, 1982), p. 392.

11. *BBC 2, Newsnight,* September 14, 1993; *Paris TV-5 Television Network,* September 19, 1993; *Cairo Radio,* July 1, 1994; *Hatzav,* 23/8/95/ 836/1082 & 20/8/ 95/844/1833.

12. *Al-Hayat al-Jadida,* September 26, 2000, December 25, 1997; *al-Jazeera Television,* January 13, 2002; Reuters, November 11, 1999.

13. *Al-Hayat al-Jadida,* November 30, 1997, December 21, 1997, July 2, 1998, November 7, 1998.

14. *Al-Hayat al-Jadida,* December 17, 1998.

15. Goetz Nordbruch, *Narrating Palestinian Nationalism: A study of the New Palestinian Textbooks* (Washington, D.C.: MEMRI, 2000), pp. 14–15, 22–26.

16. *Palestinian Authority Television,* December 1, 1997. See also, Raphael Israeli, "Education, Identity, State Building and the Peace Process," *Policy Paper 58,* Ariel Center for Policy Research, 1999, p. 16.

17. *Ha'aretz,* July 6, 1997.

18. Benny Morris, "Camp David and After: An Exchange: An Interview with Ehud Barak," *New York Review of Books,* June 13, 2001.

19. Mahmoud Abbas, *al-Wajh al-Akhar: al-Alaqat al-Sirriya bayna al-Naziya wa-l-Sihyuniya* (Amman: Dar Ibn Rushd, 1984).

20. *Al-Hayat al-Jadida,* July 2, 1998.

21. *Al-Hayat al-Jadida,* December 9, 1997 (emphasis added).

22. *Al-Hayat al-Jadida,* January 1, 1998.

23. *Voice of Palestine,* May 23, 1997.

24. *Palestinian Authority Television,* August 6, 1998.

25. See, for example, *al-Hayat al-Jadida,* July 14, 16, 17, 2000; *New York Times,* August 3, 2000.

26. Bernard Lewis, *The Jews of Islam* (Princeton: Princeton University Press, 1984), pp. 165–66.

27. See, for example, Kiernan, *Yasir Arafat*, chapter 4.

28. *Algeirs Voice of Palestine*, September 3, 1993; *al-Dustur*, September 20, 1993; *Maariv*, February 19, 1995.

29. *Voice of Palestine*, October 24, 1997.

30. Khaled Abu Toameh, "Sermons of Fire," *Jerusalem Report*, March 23, 1995, pp. 20–21.

31. See, for example, *Jerusalem Post*, November 28, 1994; *Maariv*, May 2, 1995.

32. *Kul al-Arab* (Nazareth), August 18, 2000; *al-Hayat al-Jadida*, October 15, 2000.

33. *Palestinian Authority Television*, MEMRI, Special Dispatch Series, No. 226, June 6, 2001.

6. Terror Until Victory

1. Bruck, "The Wounds of Peace," p. 74.

2. See Article 7 of the phased strategy.

3. Sayigh, *Armed Struggle*, p. 624.

4. Arafat interview with *Vienna Television*, December 19, 1988.

5. Abu Iyad interview with *al-Fiqr al-Dimuqrati* (Nicosia), vol. 7, Summer 1989. See also Abu Iyad's interviews with *al-Yamama* (Saudi Arabia), November 16, 1988; *al-Madina*, November 24, 1988; *al-Qabas* (Kuwait), December 16, 1988; *Kuwaiti News Agency* (KUNA), December 29, 1988; *al-Anba* (Kuwait), January 3, 1989. See also *Radio Monte Carlo in Arabic*, November 12, 1988; *al-Siyyasa* (Kuwait), November 24, 1988.

6. Yigal Carmon, "The Story Behind the Handshake," in Neal Kozodoy, ed., *The Mideast Peace Process: An Autopsy* (San Francisco: Encounter Books, 2002), pp. 13–14.

7. Watson, *The Oslo Accords*, pp. 315–316.

8. See Articles 8, 9, 18 in the Gaza and Jericho Agreement and Articles 12–16 in the Interim Agreement, ibid., pp. 333–34, 336, 356–59.

9. Bruck, "The Wounds of Peace," p. 70.

10. Savir, *The Process*, pp. 20, 38, 42, 44; Abbas, *Through Secret Channels*, p. 108.

11. Bruck, "The Wounds of Peace," p. 76.

12. *Al Ha'mishmar*, October 4, 1993.

13. Arafat's interviews with *al-Musawwar* (Cairo), September 10, 1993; *Paris TV-5 Television Network*, September 19, 1993.

14. *Maariv*, September 23, 1993.

15. *Jordan Television Network in Arabic*, September 24, 1993; *Al Ha'mishmar*, September 19, 26, 1993.

16. Hakam Balawi interview with *Ha'artez*, September 14, 1993.

17. *New York Times*, October 5, 1993.

18. *Jerusalem Post* and *Maariv*, November 14, 1994.

19. *Maariv*, 18 November, 1994.

20. *Al-Dustur*, September 24, 1998.

21. Bruck, "The Wounds of Peace," p. 76; Naveh, *Sodot Memshala*, p. 139.

22. "The PLO's and the Palestinian Authority's Compliance with their Obligations to Prevent Terrorism during the Authority's First Two Years," Jerusalem, Peace Watch, 1996, pp. 17–20.

23. *Time*, June 20, 1994, p. 34.

24. Savir, *The Process*, p. 147.

25. See, for example, "Protocol of meetings between Fatah and Hamas representatives in Khartum, January 1993," *al-Safir* (Beirut), February 2, 1993.

26. *Jerusalem Report*, April 4, 1996, p. 6.

27. For the essence of the agreement see *al-Quds*, December 22, 1995. See also Yigal Carmon, "So Now We All Know," *Jerusalem Post*, January 5, 1996.

28. *Maariv*, December 14, 1993. See also *al-Sharq al-Awsat* (London), September 27, 1993.

29. Ze'ev Binyamin Begin, *Sipur Atsuv* (Tel Aviv: Yediot Aharonot, 2000), p. 81.

30. *Economist*, September 3, 1994; *Jerusalem Post*, August 21, 1994; *al-Quds*, August 18, 1994.

31. Savir, *The Process*, pp. 154, 166–67.

32. *Ha'aretz*, October 5, 1994.

33. *Maariv*, January 19, 24, and 27 (Saturday magazine), 1995, February 7, 1995; *Jerusalem Post*, February 7, 1995.

34. *Ha'aretz*, January 25, 1995.

35. Ibid., p. 167.

36. *Jerusalem Post*, May 18, 1994; *Time*, May 30, 1994, p. 32.

37. *Ha'aretz*, November 22, 1994.

38. *Maariv*, May 22, 1995.

39. *Jerusalem Post*, August 3, 1995; Jonathan Torop, "Arafat and the Uses of Terror," *Commentary*, May 1997, p. 32.

40. *Maariv*, November 24, 1993.

41. *AFP*, May 1, 1995.

42. Torop, "Arafat and the Uses of Terror," p. 32.

43. *Jerusalem Post*, March 15, 1996.

44. Ibid.

45. Uri Dromi, "Waiting for Arafat to go away," *International Herald Tribune*, July 19, 2002; *Jerusalem Post*, January 26, 1996. See also "Hamas Military Leader Met Arafat before Homicide Bombings," *al-Sharq al-Awsat*, April 1, 1996.

46. Savir, *The Process*, pp. 295–96.

47. *Jerusalem Post*, January 5, 2003.

48. *Jerusalem Post*, January 7 and February 9, 1996; *Ha'aretz*, January 7, 1996.

49. *Economist*, March 9, 1996, p. 47; Human Rights Watch/Middle East, "Palestinian Self-Rule Areas: Human Rights Under the Palestinian Authority," September 1997.

50. *Al-Ayyam*, March 11, 1996.

7. Eyeless in Gaza

1. Yair Hirschfeld, *Oslo: Nusha Leshalom* (Tel Aviv: Am Oved and Rabin Center, 2000), p. 153.

2. Yossi Beilin's interview with Ari Shavit, *Ha'aretz Weekly Magazine*, March 7, 1997.

3. Bruck, "The Wounds of Peace," p. 76.

4. Ibid., p. 65.

5. Letter to the editor, *Jerusalem Post*, May 21, 1996.

6. Bruck, "The Wounds of Peace," p. 66.

7. David Bar-Ilan, "Amos Oz's Blood Libel Compounded by Falsehood," *Jerusalem Post*, April 14, 1995.

8. "Meeting at General Meir Amit's Home, 27.11.1966," Israel State Archives, Hetz 4091/19.

9. *Yediot Aharonot*, September 2, 1994.

10. Beilin's interview with *Al Ha'mishmar*, September 29, 1993, and with *Ha'aretz Weekly Magazine*, March 7, 1997; Shimon Peres, "Oslo Cannot be Erased," *Maariv*, September 25, 2001.

11. Ronen Bergman, *Veharashut Netuna* (Tel Aviv: Yediot Aharonot, 2002), p. 36.

12. Beilin's interview with *Al Ha'mishmar*, May 19, 1994; *Maariv Weekly Magazine*, September 15, 1995.

13. *Al Ha'mishmar*, May 24, 1994.

14. *Maariv*, November 14, 1993, and August 23, 1995; *Ha'aretz*, July 25, 1995.

15. Efaim Inbar, *Rabin and Israel's National Security* (Baltimore and London: Johns Hopkins University Press, 1999), pp. 138–41.

16. Mamduh Nawfal, *Qisat Ittifaq Uslu: al-Riwaya al-Haqiqiya al-Kamila* (Amman: al-Ahliya, 1995), pp. 61–63.

17. Efraim Sneh, *Nivut Beshetach Mesukan* (Tel Aviv: Yediot Aharonot, 2002), pp. 22–23.

18. Yossi Beilin, *Lagaat Bashalom* (Tel Aviv: Yediot Aharonot, 1997), p. 153.

19. Nawfal, *Qisat Ittifaq Uslu*, pp. 65–67.

20. Christopher, *Chances of a Lifetime*, pp. 202, 204; Shimon Peres's interview with Dan Shilon, *Maariv*, November 6, 2000; David Remnick, "Letter from Jerusalem: The Dreamer," *New Yorker* (Internet edition); *Jerusalem Post*, November 21, 1993.

21. *Maariv*, October 20, 1993.

22. Mohamed Heikal, *Secret Channels: The Inside Story of Arab-Israeli Peace Ne-gotiations* (London: HarperCollins, 1996), p. 473.

23. Ha'aretz, November 16, 1993; *Jerusalem Post*, May 27, 1994.

24. *Maariv*, February 7, 1994.

25. *Yediot Aharonot*, September 15, 1993.

26. Brook, "The Wounds of Peace," p. 72.

27. "From Here to Eternity?" *U.S. News and World Report*, September 20, 1993, p. 62.

28. Dov Goldstein in *Ha'olam Ha'ze*, October 13, 1993; *Al Ha'mishmar*, November 16, 1993; Ze'ev Begin, "Yasser Arafat's Lackey," *Jerusalem Post*, October 28, 1993.

29. Ze'ev Begin, "Revealing Mistakes," *Jerusalem Post*, December 26, 1993.

30. Begin, *Sipur Atsuv*, p. 77; *Jerusalem Post*, April 18, 19 and May 27, 1994.

31. *Al Ha'mishmar*, August 11, 16, and September 1, 1994; *Jerusalem Post*, October 14, 1994 .

32. Ehud Ya'ari, "Slow Down on the Oslo Track," *Jerusalem Report*, December 29, 1994, p. 29; *Jerusalem Post*, January 27, 1995; *Maariv*, November 1, 1995.

33. *Jerusalem Post*, October 20, 1994; *Ha'aretz*, January 20, 1995.

34. *Ha'aretz*, January 24, 29, 1995; *Maariv*, January 24, 27, 1995; *Jerusalem Post*, March 5, 1995.

35. *Maariv*, January 19, 23, and March 14, 1995; "Can Peace Survive?" *Time*, February 6, 1995, p. 21.

36. *Ha'aretz*, May 10, 2002.

37. *Ha'aretz*, April 17, 1995.

38. *Maariv Weekly Magazine*, April 13, 1995; *Maariv*, April 16 and June 7, 1995; *Jerusalem Post*, April 14, 1995.

39. *Maariv*, August 14, 1995.

40. *Maariv*, August 23 and September 13, 1995.

41. *Maariv*, October 1, 1995; *Jerusalem Post*, October 6, 1995.

42. *Ha'aretz*, August 2, 2002.

8. The Tunnel War

1. Netanyahu interview with *Channel 4 News* (London), September 5, 1993.

2. Benjamin Netanyahu, *Makom Tahat Hashemesh* (Tel Aviv: Yediot Aharonot, 1995), pp. 14–15.

3. Netanyahu interview with *Maariv Weekly Magazine*, September 13, 1996.

4. *Al-Ahram* (Cairo), July 4, 1996.

5. Abu Ala interview with *al-Ittihad* (Internet edition), June 24, 1996.

6. *ARD Television Network* (Munich), May 31, 1996; *al-Ayyam*, June 3, 1996.

7. *Voice of Palestine,* June 11, 13, 1996; *Voice of Israel,* June 13, 1996; *Yediot Aharonot,* June 16, 1996; *MENA,* June 28, 1996.

8. *Voice of Israel,* June 13, July 4, 1996; *Israel Television Channel 1,* June 18, 1996; *Jerusalem Post,* June 14, 1996.

9. *Al-Hayat al-Jadida,* July 28, 1996.

10. *Voice of Palestine,* August 30, 1996; *Jerusalem Post,* September 1, 1996.

11. *Al-Hayat* (Cairo), September 1, 1996; *Palestinian Authority Television,* September 1, 1996.

12. Brook, "The Wounds of Peace," p. 87; *Maariv,* September 2, 1996.

13. *Voice of Israel,* August 30 and September 4, 1996; *Yediot Aharonot,* September 5, 1996.

14. *Al-Hadath* (Amman), September 9, 1996.

15. *Voice of Palestine,* September 24, 1996.

16. Andrea Levin, "The Media's Tunnel Vision," *Middle East Quarterly,* December 1996, pp. 3, 5–6.

17. *Palestinian Authority Television,* September 24, 1996.

18. *Voice of Palestine,* September 24, 1996.

19. *Voice of Israel,* September 24, 1996; "Reconstruction of the Events of Late September 1996 in the West Bank and the Gaza Strip," Ramallah, al-Haq, West Bank Affiliate, 1996, p. 2.

20. Ehud Ya'ari, "Take Arafat at his Violent Word," *Jerusalem Report,* November 28, 1996; Graham Usher in *Middle East International,* October 4, 1996; *Voice of Palestine,* September 25, 1996, 1350 gmt; *Radio Monte Carlo in Arabic,* September 25, 1996, 1500 gmt; *Voice of Israel,* September 25, 1996, 1400 gmt; *Voice of Palestine,* September 28, 1996.

21. For an excellent discussion of this issue see Levin, "The Media's Tunnel Vision."

22. *Voice of Palestine,* August 3, 5, 1996; *AFP,* August 3, 4, 1996.

23. *Israel TV Channel 1,* September 25, 1996; *Economist,* October 5, 1996, p. 46.

24. *Voice of Palestine,* October 10, 1996.

25. Ya'ari, "Take Arafat at his Violent Word."

26. Nearly 60 percent of the West Bank's 1.4 million residents live in Area A, and another 40 percent reside in Area B. Only a few dozen thousands Palestinians, or 2 percent of the West Bank's population, live in Area C.

27. Watson, *The Oslo Accords,* p. 106.

28. Bruck, "The Wounds of Peace," p. 78.

29. Text of the documents brought in Naveh, *Sodot Memshala,* pp. 218–24.

30. Peter Hirschberg, "Can Arafat Switch Off Terror?" *Jerusalem Report,* April 17, 1997, pp. 12–14; *Yediot Aharonot,* March 23, 1997; *al-Hayat al-Jadida,* March 27, 1997; *al-Sharq al-Awsat* (London), March 25, 1997; *Ha'aretz,* March 25 and April 10, 1997; *Israel Television Channel 1,* March 23, 1997.

31. *Ha'aretz,* July 18 and September 8, 24, and November 11, 16, 1997.

32. *Al-Alim*, August 30, 1997, p. 18; "A Poorer Peace," *Newsweek*, September 1, 1997, p. 28; *Jerusalem Post*, August 21, 1997; *Financial Times*, August 29, 1997; *Ha'aretz*, September 2, 7, 1997.

33. *Yediot Aharonot*, July 13, 1997; *AFP*, July 19, 1997; *Israel Television Channel 1*, March 23, 1997; *Maariv Weekly Magazine*, August 8, 1997.

34. *Al-Hayat al-Jadida*, August 6, 1997; *al-Ittihad* (Abu Dhabi), May 18, 1997.

9. Showdown in Camp David

1. *Palestinian Authority Television*, July 16, 2000.

2. *Al-Ayyam*, November 16, 1998. The first to have made the threat of a unilateral proclamation of a Palestinian state was Faisal Husseini, in an interview with *Palestinian Authority Television* on September 1, 1996.

3. Ze'ev Begin, *Sippur Atsuv*, p. 122.

4. *Maariv*, February 15, 1996.

5. For the text of the agreement see Watson, *The Oslo Accords*, pp. 385–89.

6. Raviv Druker, *Harakiri: Ehud Barak—Hakishalon* (Tel Aviv: Yediot Aharonot, 2002), p. 237.

7. Akram Haniya, "The Camp David Papers," *al-Ayyam*, July 29 and August 6, 2000.

8. Deborah Sontag, "Quest for Mideast Peace: How and Why It Failed," *New York Times*, July 26, 2001.

9. Haniya, "The Camp David Papers," July 29, 2000.

10. Druker, *Harakiri*, p. 262. Druker's book provides a fascinating insight, drawn from numerous firsthand interviews with Barak's friends, aides, political partners, and foes, among others, into the prime minister's personality and mind-set.

11. Ben Caspit, "How the 1993 Oslo Peace Hopes had Turned into War and Desperation by 2001," *Maariv*, Holiday Magazine, September 17, 2001.

12. Ben Caspit, "Clinton's and Barak's Big Plan," *Maariv*, Friday Magazine, July 14, 2000.

13. *Al-Hayat al-Jadida*, August 19, 2000.

14. Haniya, "The Camp David Papers," August 6, 8, and 10, 2000.

15. Haniya, "The Camp David Papers," August 6, 2000; *al-Hayat al-Jadida*, August 10, 2000.

16. Sontag, "Quest for Mideast Peace."

17. Bergman, *Veharashut Netuna*, p. 329.

18. Sontag, "Quest for Mideast Peace."

19. Ben Caspit, "Scores of Mistakes," *Maariv*, Friday Magazine, August 25, 2000.

20. Hussein Agha and Robert Malley, "Camp David: The Tragedy of Errors," *New York Review of Books*, August 9, 2001. A similar revisionist account has been

provided by the Israeli journalist Amnon Kapeliouk: "Camp David dialogues," *Le Monde diplomatique*, September 2000 (Internet edition).

21. Joel Greenberg, "Arafat's Allies Say He Stands Taller at Home for Firmness at Talks," *New York Times*, July 26, 2000.

22. *Jerusalem Post*, August 6, 2000.

23. Hasaan Asfour's interview with *al-Sharq al-Awsat* (London), August 1, 2000.

24. *Palestinian Authority Television*, July 28, 2000; *al-Hayat al-Jadida*, July 28, 2000.

25. *Al-Ra'i*, no. 33, July 15–August 2000, p. 9; *al-Hayat*, November 23/24, 2000.

26. *Al-Quds*, August 18, 2000.

27. *Al-Musawwar* (Cairo), August 18, 2000. Other Palestinian officials gave similar accounts of the Camp David talks. According to Shaath, the Israelis offered the Palestinians an equivalent of 1 percent of the West Bank's territory on the border with Gaza in return for the annexation of 9 percent of the West Bank, only to be rejected by the Palestinian delegation. Tayyib Abdel Rahim, the presidency's secretary-general, reported that Israel agreed to withdraw from 92 percent of the West Bank during the Camp David summit. See, *al-Quds*, August 30, 2000.

28. Agha and Malley, "Camp David."

29. See, for example, Shaath's comments to *al-Quds*, July 5, 2000; Abu Mazen's interview with *al-Hayat al-Jadida*, August 19, 2000; Abu Ala's interview with *al-Ayyam*, August 12, 2000; Saeb Erekat's interview with *al-Hayyat al-Jadida*, August 11, 2000; Hanan Ashrawi's interview with *Jerusalem Post Radio*, July 26, 2000; Yasser Abd Rabbo's interview with *Radio Monte Carlo in Arabic*, September 20, 2000; Dahlan's interview with *al-Ayyam*, August 19, 2000; Asfour's interview with *al-Sharq al-Awsat*, July 7, 2000.

30. *Al-Ayyam*, August 8, 2000.

31. *Al-Ayyam*, September 16, 2000.

32. See, for example, *Maariv*, August 3, 2000.

33. *Al-Ayyam*, July 30, 2000; *al-Hayat al-Jadida*, August 12, 2000; Dennis Ross, "Letter to the Editors" *New York Review of Books*, August 9, 2001; *Ha'aretz*, July 27, 2000; *Maariv*, July 28, 2000.

34. *Jerusalem Post*, September 8, 2000.

10. Countdown to War

1. Agha and Malley, "Camp David."

2. *Jerusalem Post*, July 26, 30, 2000; *New York Times*, July 26, 2000.

3. *Jerusalem Post*, July 27, 2000; *al-Hayat al-Jadida*, August 3, 11, 2000.

4. *Al-Ayyam*, July 26, 2000.

5. *Al-Hayat al-Jadida,* August 25, 2000. For international reactions to a unilateral proclamation of state see also: *al-Quds,* August 13, 2000; *MENA,* August 12, September 2, 2000; *AFP,* August 16, 2000; *Jordan Times,* August 17, 2000; *al-Ayyam,* August 11, 15, and September 24, 2000.

6. *Voice of Palestine,* September 9, 2000.

7. *Al-Ayyam,* September 9, 2000; *al-Quds,* September 11, 2000.

8. *Al-Hayat al-Jadida,* June 26, 2000.

9. *Al-Hayat al-Jadida,* June 20, 2000.

10. *Al-Hayat al-Jadida,* July 10, 2000.

11. *Al-Ayyam,* June 15, 2000.

12. *Al-Ayyam,* July 2, 2000.

13. *Al-Sharq al-Awsat,* July 21, 2000; *Maariv,* July 21, 2000; Khaled Abu Toameh, "City of Rage," *New Republic Online,* post date July 27, 2000.

14. Muhammad Dahlan interview, *al-Ayyam,* July 28, 2000.

15. *Jerusalem Post,* August 6, 2000; *al-Hayat al-Jadida,* August 16, 2000.

16. *Jerusalem Post,* August 10, 2000.

17. Nabil Shaath interview, *Le Monde,* August 27, 2000.

18. *Al-Ayyam,* July 24, 2000.

19. *Al-Hayat* (Beirut), July 14, 2000; *Maariv,* July 21, 2000.

20. *Al-Sharq al-Awsat,* July 19, 2000; *Maariv,* July 21, 28, 2000; *Yediot Aharonot,* July 23, 2000.

21. *Maariv,* July 28 and 31 2000; *Ha'tzoefe,* September 3, 24, 2000.

22. *Al-Hayat al-Jadida,* August 11, 2000.

23. Khaled Abu Toameh, "Uniform Culture," *Jerusalem Report,* July 31, 2000; Ron Ben Yishai, "Army Intelligence: Arafat Will Not Reach An Agreement Without Another Confrontation," *Yediot Aharonot,* July 21, 2000; Roni Shaked, "Ten Vessels, A Few Squadrons, and 45,000 Soldiers," *Yediot Aharonot,* July 28, 2000; *Ha'aretz,* January 6, 1997, and July 7, 1998; Khaled Abu Toameh, "No Farewell to Arms," *Jerusalem Report,* April 16, 1998, pp. 26–29.

24. *New York Times,* August 3, 2000; *Ha'tzofe,* July 16, 2000.

25. *Al-Hayat al-Jadida,* May 24, 2000.

26. *Palestinian Authority Television,* July 6, 2000; *al-Hayat al-Jadida,* August 3, 2000; Roni Shaked in *Yediot Aharonot,* May 19 and 26, 2000.

27. *Yediot Aharonot,* May 26, 2000.

28. *Maariv,* July 14, 2000; Druker, *Harakiri,* pp. 136–37, 201; Gilead Sher, *Bemerhak Negi'a* (Tel Aviv: Yediot Aharonot, 2001), pp. 139–40.

29. Druker, *Harakiri,* pp. 304–305.

30. *Maariv,* September 7 and 10, 2000; Sher, *Bemerhak Negi'a,* p. 266.

31. Letter from Dennis Ross, head of the U.S. peace team, to the editors, *New York Review of Books,* September 20, 2001.

32. For Palestinian fears of the American bridging paper see, for example, *al-Quds,* September 23, 24, 2000.

33. *Al-Quds,* August 11, 2000.

34. For the full text of Arafat's speech see, "al-Quds: Miftah al-Salam," *Mulhaq al-Rai,* no. 34, September 2000, pp. 4–5. See also *al-Ra'i,* no. 34, September 15–October 2000, pp. 12–13.

35. *Al-Quds,* September 20, 2000.

36. Yasser Abd Rabbo interview, *Le Monde,* September 26, 2000.

37. *Al-Sabah,* September 11, 2000. See also *al-Hayat al-Jadida,* September 21, 2000.

11. Why War?

1. Ehud Barak interview, *Jerusalem Post* and *Maariv,* September 29, 2000. See also *Jerusalem Post,* September 26, 2000; *Maariv,* September 26, 27, 2000; Sontag, "Quest for Mideast Peace."

2. *Voice of Palestine,* October 1, 2000; *Palestinian Satellite Channel TV* (Gaza), October 21, 2000.

3. *MENA,* September 28, 2000.

4. David Remnick, "Rage and Reason," *New Yorker,* May 6, 2002 (Internet edition).

5. *Jerusalem Post,* October 4, 2002; *Maariv,* October 6, 2000; Sher, *Bemerhak Negi'a,* p. 287.

6. *Al-Ayyam,* September 27, 2000.

7. *Jerusalem Post* and *Maariv,* September 29, 2000; *Economist,* October 7, 2000, p. 61.

8. *Al-Musawwar* (Cairo), November 10, 2000.

9. Ehud Ya'ari, "Buying Time," *Jerusalem Report,* August 28, 2000, p. 28; Lee Hockstader, "Some Arabs Prefer an Israeli-Run Jerusalem," *Washington Post,* July 25, 2000; John F. Burns, "Hero's Welcome for Arafat, from Those Who Showed Up," *New York Times,* July 27, 2000.

10. *Voice of Israel,* September 29, 2000.

11. Lee Hockstader, "Street Army Spearheads Arab Riots," *Washington Post,* October 7–9, 2000.

12. Ehud Ya'ari, "Super-Intifada," *Jerusalem Report,* October 23, 2000, p. 19; Khaled Abu Toameh, "Militia King," *Jerusalem Report,* November 6, 2000, p. 23.

13. For the Nakba 2000 confrontation see, for example, *Yediot Aharonot,* May 14, 15, 16, 18, 19, 21, 2000.

14. *Voice of Palestine,* September 30, 2002; *Maariv,* October 2, 2000; *Yediot Aharonot,* October 4, 2000.

15. Hockstader, "Street Army."

16. Roni Shaked, "The Orders Came from the Rais's Office," *Yediot Aharonot,* Friday Magazine, October 13, 2000.

17. Barghouthi's interview with *La Republica* (Rome), as quoted in *Yediot Aharonot,* October 16, 2000.

18. *Al-Jazeera* (Doha), October 1, 2000.

19. Barghouthi interview, *al-Musawwar*, November 10, 2000; *Yediot Aharonont*, October 11, 2000.

20. *Al-Ayyam*, December 6, 2002.

21. *Al-Hayat al-Jadida*, September 20, 2000.

22. *Al-Hayat al-Jadida*, November 7 and December 7, 2000.

23. "Points of View on the Development of the Intifida and Its Goals," *Majalat al-Dirasat al-Filastiniya*, no. 47 (Summer 2001), pp. 44–45.

24. *Akhbar al-Khalil* (Hebron), no. 4, March 4, 2000.

25. *Al-Musawwar* (Cario), November 10, 2000.

26. *Al-Hayat* (London), September 29, 2001.

27. *Wafa* (the official Palestinian news agency), May 15, 2001.

28. *Palestinian Authority Television*, October 2, 2000.

29. *Palestinian Authority Television*, July 23, 2000.

30. *Palestinian Authority Television*, July 26, 2000.

31. *Palestinian Authority Television*, July 25 and August 28, 2000.

32. *Al-Hayat al-Jadida*, July 22, 2000.

33. *Al-Shuhada*, no. 28, July 28, 2000.

34. *Al-Hayat al-Jadida*, January 30, 2001 (emphasis added).

12. Violence Pays

1. Fouad Ajami, "The Great Circle of Enmity," *U.S. News and World Report*, October 23, 2000.

2. *Economist*, October 14, 2000, p. 57.

3. The clip can be obtained from Palestine Media Watch (PMW), 4 King George, Jerusalem, Israel.

4. *MENA*, September 30, 2000.

5. *Maariv*, October 5, 2002.

6. *Jerusalem Post*, October 10, 2000.

7 Sharm el-Sheikh Fact-Finding Committee, "Final Report," presented to U.S. President George W. Bush on April 30, 2001 (accessed on the website of the U.S. Department of State, International Information Programs).

8. Evelyn Gordon, "A World Gone Mad," *Jerusalem Post*, October 10, 2000.

9. *Maariv and Jerusalem Post*, October 2, 2000.

10. *Jerusalem Report*, November 6, 2000, p. 22.

11. *Israel Channel 2 TV*, October 18, 2000.

12. Morris, "Camp David and After."

13. *Economist*, October 14, 2000, p. 55.

14. Ari Shavit, "The Day Peace Died" (interview with Shlomo Ben-Ami), *Ha'aretz*, Friday Magazine, September 14, 2001.

15. Druker, *Harakiri*, p. 233.

16. Shavit, "The Day Peace Died"; Druker, *Harakiri*, pp. 374–75.

17. *Jerusalem Post*, December 29, 2000; Dennis Ross on *Fox News*, April 21, 2002.

18. Shavit, "The Day Peace Died."

19. Ross on *Fox News*; Sontag, "Quest for Mideast Peace."

20. *Al-Ayyam*, January 19, 2001.

21. *Al-Ayyam*, January 3, 2001.

22. Ross on *Fox News*.

23. "Special Document file: The Taba Negotiations (January 2001,)" *Journal of Palestine Studies*, vol. XXXI, no. 3 (Spring 2002), p. 79.

24. "EU Description of the Outcome of Permanent Status Talks in Taba," *Ha'aretz English Edition*, February 14, 2001. This report was prepared by Miguel Moratinos, EU Special Representative to the Middle East, who was the only outsider present at Taba. Though not attending the meetings, Moratinos interviewed the negotiators after each session and prepared the document on the basis of these reports.

25. "EU Description"; Shavit, "The Day Peace Died."

26. *Maariv*, November 26, 1993.

27. Beilin, *Madrich Leyona Ptsu'a*, p. 84.

28. "Private Response to Palestinian Refugee Paper of January 22, 2001," Articles 1, 6, 7, *Le Monde diplomatique*, September 4, 2001. See also "EU Description," Article 3.

29. "EU Description," Article 3.2.

30. "Private Response," Article 5.

31. *Al-Ayyam*, January 26, 2001; Druker, *Harakiri*, p. 398.

32. See, for example, Beilin's interview with Ari Shavit, *Ha'aretz Weekly Magazine*, June 15, 2001.

33. "EU Description"; Beilin, "What Really Happened in Taba," *Ha'aretz*, July 15, 2002.

34. *Al-Ayyam*, January 28, 2001.

35. Mamduh Nawfal, "Fi Taba Taarafa al-Tarafan ala Haqiqat Mawaqif Kul Minhuma," *Majalat al-Dirasat al-Filastiniya*, no. 48, Autumn 2001, p. 101. According to Saeb Erekat, already before Taba the Israelis had presented the Palestinians with "a map that included territorial contiguity in the West Bank." *Al-Ayyam*, January 31, 2001.

36. "EU Description."

13. The Turning of the Tide

1. *Voice of Israel*, March 8, 2001; *al-Ra'i*, no. 38 (February–March 2001), p. 9.

2. Hirsh Goodman, "A Recipe for Palestinian Disaster," *Jerusalem Report*, June 18, 2001, p. 6.

3. *Jerusalem Post*, March 15, 18, 2001; *Maariv*, March 13, 2001; *New York Times*, May 23, 2001.

4. *Maariv*, March 9, 12, 15, and 21, 2001; *Jerusalem Post*, March 19, 2001.

5. Eric Schechter, "Sharon's Security Blueprint," *Jerusalem Report*, March 12, 2001, pp. 14–15.

6. *Jerusalem Post*, March 21, 2001.

7. Ehud Ya'ari, "Wait and Fire," *Jerusalem Report*, March 26, 2001, p. 21; Leslie Susser, "Where's Uncle Sam?" *Jerusalem Report*, July 2, 2001, p. 14; *Maariv*, March 15, 2001.

8. *Jerusalem Post*, March 30, 2001.

9. Ya'ari, "Wait and Fire"; Susser, "Where's Uncle Sam?" p. 15.

10. *Economist*, June 9, 2001, p. 54; *Maariv*, June 4, 2001.

11. *Maariv*, June 8, 2001.

12. MEMRI, "Special Dispatch—PA," July 8, 2001.

13. "Monthly Analysis of All Terrorist Incidents since September 2000," *www.idf.il;* "Suicide and Other Bombing Attacks in Israel Since the Declaration of Principles (September 1993), www.mfa/gov.il.

14. *Maariv*, August 12, 2001; *Jerusalem Post*, August 12, 14, 2001.

15. Ehud Ya'ari, "Unhappy Anniversary," *Jerusalem Report*, September 24, 2001, p. 26.

16. *Jerusalem Post*, September 12, 14, 2001.

17. *Voice of Palestine*, July 11, 1997.

18. *Al-Hayat al-Jadida*, November 15, 1997.

19. *Al-Hayat al-Jadida*, September 11, 2001.

20. *Jerusalem Post*, September 12, 13, 14, 17, 2001.

21. GIA Report, February 4, 2002, captured by the IDF during Operation Defensive Shield.

22. *Jerusalem Post*, December 3, 4, 7, 2001.

23. *Jerusalem Post*, December 4, 2001; Leslie Susser, "No Half Measures?" *Jerusalem Report*, December 31, 2001.

24. *Jerusalem Post*, December 18, 2001.

25. *Jerusalem Post*, December 13, 14, 18, 19, 2001.

26. For the full text of Arafat's speech see *al-Ra'i*, no. 46 (December 2001), pp. 12–14.

27. Khaled Abu Toameh, "Still Juggling," *Jerusalem Report*, January 14, 2002, p. 27.

28. *Jerusalem Post*, December 18, 19, 2001; Leslie Susser, "Anyone But Arafat," *Jerusalem Report*, February 25, 2002, p.12; *al-Hayat* (London), December 13, 2001.

29. Douglas Frantz and James Risen, "A Secret Iran-Arafat Connection Is Seen Fueling the Mideast Fire," *New York Times*, March 24, 2002; Ehud Ya'ari, "Arafat Is Arafat," *Jerusalem Report*, January 28, 2002, p. 31; Mamduh Nawfal, "Sharon Succeeded in Captivating Zinni with the Karine A," *al-Ayyam*, January 20, 2002; Daniel Ben-Simon, "Killing the Messenger," *Ha'aretz*, April 25, 2002.

30. "Cover Story: Will It work This Time?" *Jerusalem Report*, April 22, 2002, p. 12.

31. "Report of the Secretary-General prepared pursuant to General Assembly resolution ES-10/10," www.un.org/english/index.html, paragraph 47.

32. Mark Steyn, "Say Goodbye, Yasser Arafat," *Spectator*, April 6, 2002 (internet edition); "Report: Palestinian Produced Bio-Chemical Weapons," *Jerusalem Post*, April 26, 2002.

33. The IDF has posted dozens of these documents on its web site: www.idf.il. See also: *Jerusalem Post*, April 2, 2002; Ronen Bergman, "Documents Seized in Arafat's Compound," *Yediot Aharonot*, Weekend Magazine, July 11, 2002; Thomas Kleine-Brockhoff and Bruno Schirra, "Arafat Bombs, Europe Pays," translated from *Die Zeit*, 24/2002, June 7, 2002 (Internet edition); Thomas Kleine-Brockhoff, "With Unyielding Faith," translated from *Die Zeit*, 34/2002, August 15, 2002 (Internet edition).

34. Bob Woodward, *Bush At War* (New York: Simon & Schuster, 2002), p. 297.

35. *Jerusalem Post*, January 28, 29, and February 15, March 12, 24, 2002; Frantz and Risen, "A Secret Iran-Arafat Connection"; Akiva Eldar's interview with Arafat, *Ha'aretz*, June 23, 2002.

36. Woodward, *Bush At War*, pp. 323–324.

37. *Jerusalem Post*, April 19, May 6, 2002.

38. *Jerusalem Post*, May 7, 10, 2002.

39. Ze'ev Schiff, "Saudi Arabia and Egypt Pressured, Arafat Refused," *Ha'aretz*, May 26, 2002.

40. www.ABCNews.Com, June 24, 2002.

41. Khaled Abu Toameh and Isabel Kershner, "The Cost of Defeat," *Jerusalem Report*, May 6, 2002, p. 26; *Jerusalem Post*, July 8, 2002.

42. *Ha'aretz*, July 1, 2002; *Jerusalem Post*, July 3, 2002.

43. *Jerusalem Post*, July 8, 2002.

44. *Al-Ayyam*, September 11, 2002.

45. *Al-Ayyam*, May 5, 2002.

46. *Al-Hayat* (Beirut), September 2, 2002.

Epilogue

1. Pinhas Inbari, "Still Far Away from Substance," *Al Ha'mishmar*, October 4, 1993.

2. Pacepa, *Red Horizons*, p. 28

3. Khaled Abu Toameh and Isabel Kershner, "From Beirut to Bethlehem," *Jerusalem Report*, August 13, 2001, p. 29.

4. "A Poorer Peace," *Newsweek*, September 1, 1997, p. 29; Keith Marsden, "The Viability of Palestine," *Wall Street Journal*, April 25, 2002; Patrick Clawson, "The Palestinians' Lost Marshall plans," *Jerusalem Post*, August 9, 2002.

5. Khalil Shikaki, "Palestinian Public Opinion about the Peace Process, 1993–1999," Washington, D.C., Center for Policy Analysis on Palestine, 1999; "New Beginning," *U.S. News and World Report*, September 13, 1993, p. 27.

6. "Results of Public Opinion Poll, No. 19: The West Bank and the Gaza Strip, August/September 1995," Nablus, Center for Palestine Research and Studies (CPRS), p. 10; "Results of Public Opinion Poll, No. 20: The West Bank and the Gaza Strip, 13–15 October 1995," CPRS, p. 5; "Results of Public opinion Poll, No. 25," 26–28 December 1996, CPRS, p. 14; "Public Opinion Poll No. 31—Part I On Palestinian Attitudes towards Politics," Jerusalem Media and Communications Center (JMCC), March 1999, p. 3; Maariv, March 14, 1995; Peter Hirschberg, "The Dark Side of Arafat's Regime," *Jerusalem Report*, August 21, 1997, p. 25.

7. Daniel Polisar, "Yasser Arafat and the Myth of Legitimacy," *Azure*, no. 13 (Summer 2002), p. 40.

8. *Al-Hayat al-Jadida*, February 27, 1995.

9. Polisar, "Yasser Arafat," pp. 53–54. See also, "Ensuring Compliant Media," *Al-Ahram Weekly*, June 8–14, 2000.

10. Aburish, *Arafat*, p. 314.

11. *Yediot Aharonot Weekend Magazine*, January 24, 1995.

12. Bergman, *Veharashut Netuna*, pp. 157-161; Aburish, *Arafat*, p. 306; Rachel Ehrenfeld, "Where Does the Money Go? A Study of the Palestinian Authority," New York, American Center for Democracy, 2002, p. 10.

13. *AFP*, May 24 and July 30, 1997; Khaled Abu Toameh, "Money Down the Drain?" *Jerusalem Report*, January 8, 1998, p. 26; Bergman, *Vehardshut Netuna*, p. 156.

14. Ehud Ya'ari, "The Independent State of Arafat," *Jerusalem Report*, September 5, 1996, pp. 22–23; Bergman, *Veharashut Netuna*, pp. 113–41; Ehrenfeld, "Where Does the Money Go?" pp. 7–10; Aburish, *Arafat*, p. 306.

15. "The Peace Process, Performance of the Palestinian Authority, Performance of the Legislative Council 26 September–17 October 1996," CPRS, p. 5; "Performance of the PNA, the Peace Process, the Status of Democracy in Palestine, and Corruption," Results of Poll No. 29, 18–20 September 1997, CPRS, p. 4. "Performance of the Palestinian Authority, "Performance of the Legislative Council 26 September–17 October 1996," CPRS, p. 5. "Performance of the Palestinian Authority, Performance of the Legislative Council 26 September–17 October 1996," CPRS, p. 5.

16. *Al-Watan* (Kuwait), June 7, 2002; Ben Caspit, "How a Foreign Official of Israeli Intelligence, Yossi Ginosar Managed a Secret Account for Arafat," *Maariv*, December 5, 2002.

17. Bergman, *Veharashut Netuna*, pp. 162–63; Ehrenfeld, "Where Does the Money Go?" p. 9; *Yediot Aharonot*, July 14, 2002.

18. The text of President Bush's speech can be found on ABC News.Com, June 24, 2002.

Select Bibliography

Abbas, Mahmoud, *Through Secret Channels*, Reading, Garnet, 1995.

———, *Ba'da Thalath Sanawat ala Oslo: Abu Mazin Yatadhakaru wa-Yatahadathu ala-l-Wad' al-Rahin*, Ramallah, 1996.

———, *Al-Qadiya, Afaq Jadida*, Beirut, Dar al-Quds, 1979.

———, *Al-Wajh al-Akhar: al-Alaqat al-Sirriya bayna al-Naziya wa-l-Sihyuniya*, Amman, Dar Ibn Rushd, 1984.

———, *Miat Am al-Sihyuniya: Shahadat al-Qarn*, Amman, Markaz Jenin li-l-Dirasat al-Istratijiya, 1997.

Abdel Sattar, Qassem, *al-Mawqif al-Filastini al-Rasmi Tujaha Filastin, 1919–1994*, Nablus, Markaz al-Buhuth al-Ilmaiya, 1994.

Abu Bakr, Tawfiq, *al-Ra'is Yasser Arafat fi Id Miladihi al-Sab'in. Talthun amman fi-l-Qimma 4 Ab 1929–4 Ab 1999*, Jenin, Markaz Jennin li-l-Dirasat al-Istratijiya, 1999.

Abu Iyad, *My Home, My Land: A Narrative of the Palestinian Struggle*, New York, Times Books, 1981.

Aburish, Said, *Arafat: From Defender to Dictator*, London, Bloomsbury, 1998.

Alexander, Yonah & Sinai, Joshua, *Terrorism: The PLO Connection*, New York, Crane Russak, 1989.

Asfour, Hassan, "Ru'ya Li'itifaq I'lan al-Mabadi,' *Majalat al-Dirasat al-Filastiniya*, No. 17, Autumn 1993, pp. 19–26.

Ashrawi, Hanan, *This Side of Peace: A Personal Account*, New York, Simon & Schuster, 1995.

Astal, Kamal D., "Tabiat al-Sira al-Arabi-al-Sihiyuni wa-Manahijatuhu al-Mustaqbaliya," *al-Siyasa al-Filastiniya*, No. 25, Winter 2000, pp. 6–23.

Barazi, Tammam, *Kayfa Dakhala Arafat al-Bayt al-Abyad*, Beirut, al-Maktaba al-Thaqafiya, 1997.

Beilin, Yossi, *Laga'at Bashalom*, Tel Aviv, Yediot Aharonot, 1997.

———, *Madrich Leyona Ptsu'a*, Tel Aviv, Yediot Aharonot, 2001.

Becker, Jillian, *The PLO: The Rise and Fall of the Palestine Liberation Organization*, New York, St. Martin's Press, 1984.

Bruck, Connie "The Wounds of Peace," *New Yorker*, October 14, 1996.

Cobban, Helena, *The Palestine Liberation Organization: People, Power, and Politics*, Cambridge, Cambridge University Press, 1984.

Darwish, Mahmoud (panel moderator), *Palestinian Leaders Discuss the New Challenges for the Resistance*, Beirut, Palestine Liberation Organization Research Center, 1974.

Dershowitz, Alan M. *Why Terrorism Works*, New Haven & London, Yale University Press, 2002.

Ferber, Elizabeth, *Yasir Arafat: A Life of War and Peace*, Brookfield, Conn., Millbrook Press, 1995.

Gowers, Andrew and Walker, Tony, *Arafat: The Biography*, London, Virgin, 1994.

Gresh, Alain, *The PLO: The Struggle from Within*, London, Zed Books, 1983.

Groth, Allon, *The PLO's Road to Peace: Processes of Decision-Making*, London, Royal United Services Institute for Defence Studies, 1995.

Hadi, Karam, *al-Rasa'il al-Sirriya al-Mutabadala bayna Yasser Arafat wa-Ishaq Rabin*, Limasol, Dar-Aqqad, 1994.

Hamid, Rashid, ed., *Muqarrarat al-Majlis al-Watani al-Filastini 1964–1974*, Beirut, Munazamat al-Tahrir al-Filastiniya, Markaz al-Abhath, 1975.

Harkabi, Yehoshafat, *The Palestinian Covenant and Its Meaning*, London, Vallentine, Mitchell, 1979.

Hart, Alan, *Arafat: A Political Biography*, London, Sidgwick & Jackson, 1994.

Hassan, Khaled, *Grasping the Nettle of Peace*, London, Saqi Books, 1992.

Heikal, Mohamed, *Secret Channels: The Inside Story of Arab-Israeli Peace Negotiations*, London, HarperCollins, 1996.

Hirschfeld, Yair, *Oslo: Nusha Leshalom*, Tel Aviv, Am Oved & Rabin Center, 2000.

Institute for Palestine Studies, *International Documents on Palestine, 1968–1981*, Beirut, 1969–1982.

Israeli, Raphael, ed. *PLO in Lebanon: Selected Documents*, New York, St. Martin's Press, 1983.

Kadi, Leila S., ed., *Basic Political Documents of the Armed Palestinian Resistance Movement*, Beirut, Palestine Liberation Organization Research Center, 1969.

———, *Arab Summit Conferences and the Palestine Problem*, Beirut, Palestine Research Center, 1966.

Kazziha, Walid, *Revolutionary Transformation in the Arab World: Habash and His Comrades from Nationalism to Marxism*, London, Charles Knight, 1975.

Khatib, Muhammad Nimr, *Min Athar al-Nakba*, Damascus, al-Matba'ah al-Umumiyah, 1951.

Kiernan, Thomas, *Yasir Arafat*, London, Abacus, 1976.

Korn, David A., *Assassination in Khartum*, Bloomington, Indiana University Press, 1993.

Laffin, John, *The PLO Connections*, London, Corgi Books, 1983.

Livingstone, Neil C. and Halevy, David, *Inside the PLO: Covert Units, Secret Funds, and the War Against Israel and the United States*, London, Robert Hale, 1990.

Lunt, James, *Hussein of Jordan*, London, Fontana, 1990.

Makovsky, David, *Making Peace with the PLO*, Boulder, Westview, 1996.

Markaz, Jenin li-l-Dirasat al-Istratijiya, *Tatawur al-Fiqr al-Siyasi al-Filastini al-Muasir 1968–1999*, Jenin, 2000.

Merari, Ariel and Elad, Shlomi, *The International Dimension of Palestinian Terrorism*, Jerusalem and Boulder, Jerusalem Post & Westview Press, 1986.

Miller, Aaron David, *The PLO and the Politics of Survival*, New York, Praeger, 1993.

Nasser Jamal, R., *The Palestine Liberation Organization: From Armed Struggle to the Declaration of Independence*, New York, Praeger, 1991.

Nawfal, Mamduh, *Qisat Ittifaq Uslu: al-Riwaya al-Haqiqiya al-Kamila*, Amman, al-Ahliya, 1995.

———, *Al-Inqilab: Asrar Mufawadat al-Masar al-Filastini-al-Israili "Madrid-Washinton,"* Amman, Dar al-Shuruq, 1996.

———, *al-Bahth An al-Dawla*, Amman, al-Ahliya, 2001.

———, "al-Amal al-Askari fi-l-Istratijiya al-Filastiniya," *Majalat al-Dirasat al-Filastiniya*, No. 30, Spring 1997, pp. 79–91.

———, "Fi Taba Taarafa al-Tarafan ala Haqiqat Mawaqif Kul Minhuma," *Majalat al-Dirasat al-Filastiniya*, No. 48, Autumn 2001, pp. 99–104.

———, et. al., "Wujhat Nathar fi Tatawurat al-Intifada wa-Ahdafuha," *Majalat al-Dirasat al-Filastiniya*, No. 47, Summer 2001, pp. 42–71.

Peres, Shimon, *Battling for Peace*, London, Weidenfeld and Nicolson, 1995.

Rubinstein, Danny, *The Mystery of Arafat*, South Royalton, Vermont, Steerforth Press, 1995.

Sahliyeh, Emile F., *The PLO After the Lebanon War*, Boulder, Westview, 1986.

Savir, Uri, *The Process: 1100 Days that Changed the Middle East*, New York, Random House, 1998.

Sayigh, Yezid, *Armed Struggle and the Search for State: The Palestinian National Movement, 1949–1993*, Washington D.C. and London, Institute for Palestine Studies & Clarendon Press, 1997.

Shafiq, Munir, al-Qadiya al-Filastiniya bayna 'al-Hal al-Askari' wa 'al-Hal al-Siyasi,' *Majalat al-Dirasat al-Filastiniya*, No. 30, Spring 1997, pp. 92–113.

Shemesh, Moshe, *The Palestinian Entity 1959–1974: Arab Politics and the PLO*, London, Frank Cass, 1988.

Sher, Gilead, *Bemerhaq Negi'a*, Tel Aviv, Yediot Aharonot, 2001.

Shuqeiri, Ahmad, *Mina-l-Qima Ila-l-Hazima*, Beirut, Dar al-Awda, 1971.

———, *Ala Triq al-Hazima Ma'a al-Muluk wa-l-Ru'asa*, Beirut, 1972.

Tuma, Imil, *Munathamat al-Tahrir al-Filastiniya*, Nazareth, Dar al-Ittihad, 1986.

Wallach, John and Janet, *Arafat: In the Eyes of the Beholder*, London, Heinemann, 1990.

Yaari, Ehud, *Strike Terror: The Story of Fatah*, New York, Sabra Books, 1970.

Index